Mometrix
TEST PREPARATION

DSST®

Introduction to World Religions Exam Secrets Study Guide

DEAR FUTURE EXAM SUCCESS STORY

First of all, **THANK YOU** for purchasing Mometrix study materials!

Second, congratulations! You are one of the few determined test-takers who are committed to doing whatever it takes to excel on your exam. **You have come to the right place.** We developed these study materials with one goal in mind: to deliver you the information you need in a format that's concise and easy to use.

In addition to optimizing your guide for the content of the test, we've outlined our recommended steps for breaking down the preparation process into small, attainable goals so you can make sure you stay on track.

We've also analyzed the entire test-taking process, identifying the most common pitfalls and showing how you can overcome them and be ready for any curveball the test throws you.

Standardized testing is one of the biggest obstacles on your road to success, which only increases the importance of doing well in the high-pressure, high-stakes environment of test day. Your results on this test could have a significant impact on your future, and this guide provides the information and practical advice to help you achieve your full potential on test day.

Your success is our success

We would love to hear from you! If you would like to share the story of your exam success or if you have any questions or comments in regard to our products, please contact us at **800-673-8175** or **support@mometrix.com**.

Thanks again for your business and we wish you continued success!

Sincerely,
The Mometrix Test Preparation Team

Need more help? Check out our flashcards at:
http://MometrixFlashcards.com/DSST

Written and edited by the Mometrix Exam Secrets Test Prep Team
Printed in the United States of America

TABLE OF CONTENTS

Introduction

Thank you for purchasing this resource! You have made the choice to prepare yourself for a test that could have a huge impact on your future, and this guide is designed to help you be fully ready for test day. Obviously, it's important to have a solid understanding of the test material, but you also need to be prepared for the unique environment and stressors of the test, so that you can perform to the best of your abilities.

For this purpose, the first section that appears in this guide is the **Secret Keys**. We've devoted countless hours to meticulously researching what works and what doesn't, and we've boiled down our findings to the five most impactful steps you can take to improve your performance on the test. We start at the beginning with study planning and move through the preparation process, all the way to the testing strategies that will help you get the most out of what you know when you're finally sitting in front of the test.

We recommend that you start preparing for your test as far in advance as possible. However, if you've bought this guide as a last-minute study resource and only have a few days before your test, we recommend that you skip over the first two Secret Keys since they address a long-term study plan.

If you struggle with **test anxiety**, we strongly encourage you to check out our recommendations for how you can overcome it. Test anxiety is a formidable foe, but it can be beaten, and we want to make sure you have the tools you need to defeat it.

Secret Key #1 – Plan Big, Study Small

There's a lot riding on your performance. If you want to ace this test, you're going to need to keep your skills sharp and the material fresh in your mind. You need a plan that lets you review everything you need to know while still fitting in your schedule. We'll break this strategy down into three categories.

Information Organization

Start with the information you already have: the official test outline. From this, you can make a complete list of all the concepts you need to cover before the test. Organize these concepts into groups that can be studied together, and create a list of any related vocabulary you need to learn so you can brush up on any difficult terms. You'll want to keep this vocabulary list handy once you actually start studying since you may need to add to it along the way.

Time Management

Once you have your set of study concepts, decide how to spread them out over the time you have left before the test. Break your study plan into small, clear goals so you have a manageable task for each day and know exactly what you're doing. Then just focus on one small step at a time. When you manage your time this way, you don't need to spend hours at a time studying. Studying a small block of content for a short period each day helps you retain information better and avoid stressing over how much you have left to do. You can relax knowing that you have a plan to cover everything in time. In order for this strategy to be effective though, you have to start studying early and stick to your schedule. Avoid the exhaustion and futility that comes from last-minute cramming!

Study Environment

The environment you study in has a big impact on your learning. Studying in a coffee shop, while probably more enjoyable, is not likely to be as fruitful as studying in a quiet room. It's important to keep distractions to a minimum. You're only planning to study for a short block of time, so make the most of it. Don't pause to check your phone or get up to find a snack. It's also important to **avoid multitasking**. Research has consistently shown that multitasking will make your studying dramatically less effective. Your study area should also be comfortable and well-lit so you don't have the distraction of straining your eyes or sitting on an uncomfortable chair.

The time of day you study is also important. You want to be rested and alert. Don't wait until just before bedtime. Study when you'll be most likely to comprehend and remember. Even better, if you know what time of day your test will be, set that time aside for study. That way your brain will be used to working on that subject at that specific time and you'll have a better chance of recalling information.

Finally, it can be helpful to team up with others who are studying for the same test. Your actual studying should be done in as isolated an environment as possible, but the work of organizing the information and setting up the study plan can be divided up. In between study sessions, you can discuss with your teammates the concepts that you're all studying and quiz each other on the details. Just be sure that your teammates are as serious about the test as you are. If you find that your study time is being replaced with social time, you might need to find a new team.

Secret Key #2 – Make Your Studying Count

You're devoting a lot of time and effort to preparing for this test, so you want to be absolutely certain it will pay off. This means doing more than just reading the content and hoping you can remember it on test day. It's important to make every minute of study count. There are two main areas you can focus on to make your studying count.

Retention

It doesn't matter how much time you study if you can't remember the material. You need to make sure you are retaining the concepts. To check your retention of the information you're learning, try recalling it at later times with minimal prompting. Try carrying around flashcards and glance at one or two from time to time or ask a friend who's also studying for the test to quiz you.

To enhance your retention, look for ways to put the information into practice so that you can apply it rather than simply recalling it. If you're using the information in practical ways, it will be much easier to remember. Similarly, it helps to solidify a concept in your mind if you're not only reading it to yourself but also explaining it to someone else. Ask a friend to let you teach them about a concept you're a little shaky on (or speak aloud to an imaginary audience if necessary). As you try to summarize, define, give examples, and answer your friend's questions, you'll understand the concepts better and they will stay with you longer. Finally, step back for a big picture view and ask yourself how each piece of information fits with the whole subject. When you link the different concepts together and see them working together as a whole, it's easier to remember the individual components.

Finally, practice showing your work on any multi-step problems, even if you're just studying. Writing out each step you take to solve a problem will help solidify the process in your mind, and you'll be more likely to remember it during the test.

Modality

Modality simply refers to the means or method by which you study. Choosing a study modality that fits your own individual learning style is crucial. No two people learn best in exactly the same way, so it's important to know your strengths and use them to your advantage.

For example, if you learn best by visualization, focus on visualizing a concept in your mind and draw an image or a diagram. Try color-coding your notes, illustrating them, or creating symbols that will trigger your mind to recall a learned concept. If you learn best by hearing or discussing information, find a study partner who learns the same way or read aloud to yourself. Think about how to put the information in your own words. Imagine that you are giving a lecture on the topic and record yourself so you can listen to it later.

For any learning style, flashcards can be helpful. Organize the information so you can take advantage of spare moments to review. Underline key words or phrases. Use different colors for different categories. Mnemonic devices (such as creating a short list in which every item starts with the same letter) can also help with retention. Find what works best for you and use it to store the information in your mind most effectively and easily.

Secret Key #3 – Practice the Right Way

Your success on test day depends not only on how many hours you put into preparing, but also on whether you prepared the right way. It's good to check along the way to see if your studying is paying off. One of the most effective ways to do this is by taking practice tests to evaluate your progress. Practice tests are useful because they show exactly where you need to improve. Every time you take a practice test, pay special attention to these three groups of questions:

- The questions you got wrong
- The questions you had to guess on, even if you guessed right
- The questions you found difficult or slow to work through

This will show you exactly what your weak areas are, and where you need to devote more study time. Ask yourself why each of these questions gave you trouble. Was it because you didn't understand the material? Was it because you didn't remember the vocabulary? Do you need more repetitions on this type of question to build speed and confidence? Dig into those questions and figure out how you can strengthen your weak areas as you go back to review the material.

Additionally, many practice tests have a section explaining the answer choices. It can be tempting to read the explanation and think that you now have a good understanding of the concept. However, an explanation likely only covers part of the question's broader context. Even if the explanation makes perfect sense, **go back and investigate** every concept related to the question until you're positive you have a thorough understanding.

As you go along, keep in mind that the practice test is just that: practice. Memorizing these questions and answers will not be very helpful on the actual test because it is unlikely to have any of the same exact questions. If you only know the right answers to the sample questions, you won't be prepared for the real thing. **Study the concepts** until you understand them fully, and then you'll be able to answer any question that shows up on the test.

It's important to wait on the practice tests until you're ready. If you take a test on your first day of study, you may be overwhelmed by the amount of material covered and how much you need to learn. Work up to it gradually.

On test day, you'll need to be prepared for answering questions, managing your time, and using the test-taking strategies you've learned. It's a lot to balance, like a mental marathon that will have a big impact on your future. Like training for a marathon, you'll need to start slowly and work your way up. When test day arrives, you'll be ready.

Start with the strategies you've read in the first two Secret Keys—plan your course and study in the way that works best for you. If you have time, consider using multiple study resources to get different approaches to the same concepts. It can be helpful to see difficult concepts from more than one angle. Then find a good source for practice tests. Many times, the test website will suggest potential study resources or provide sample tests.

Practice Test Strategy

If you're able to find at least three practice tests, we recommend this strategy:

UNTIMED AND OPEN-BOOK PRACTICE

Take the first test with no time constraints and with your notes and study guide handy. Take your time and focus on applying the strategies you've learned.

TIMED AND OPEN-BOOK PRACTICE

Take the second practice test open-book as well, but set a timer and practice pacing yourself to finish in time.

TIMED AND CLOSED-BOOK PRACTICE

Take any other practice tests as if it were test day. Set a timer and put away your study materials. Sit at a table or desk in a quiet room, imagine yourself at the testing center, and answer questions as quickly and accurately as possible.

Keep repeating timed and closed-book tests on a regular basis until you run out of practice tests or it's time for the actual test. Your mind will be ready for the schedule and stress of test day, and you'll be able to focus on recalling the material you've learned.

Secret Key #4 – Pace Yourself

Once you're fully prepared for the material on the test, your biggest challenge on test day will be managing your time. Just knowing that the clock is ticking can make you panic even if you have plenty of time left. Work on pacing yourself so you can build confidence against the time constraints of the exam. Pacing is a difficult skill to master, especially in a high-pressure environment, so **practice is vital**.

Set time expectations for your pace based on how much time is available. For example, if a section has 60 questions and the time limit is 30 minutes, you know you have to average 30 seconds or less per question in order to answer them all. Although 30 seconds is the hard limit, set 25 seconds per question as your goal, so you reserve extra time to spend on harder questions. When you budget extra time for the harder questions, you no longer have any reason to stress when those questions take longer to answer.

Don't let this time expectation distract you from working through the test at a calm, steady pace, but keep it in mind so you don't spend too much time on any one question. Recognize that taking extra time on one question you don't understand may keep you from answering two that you do understand later in the test. If your time limit for a question is up and you're still not sure of the answer, mark it and move on, and come back to it later if the time and the test format allow. If the testing format doesn't allow you to return to earlier questions, just make an educated guess; then put it out of your mind and move on.

On the easier questions, be careful not to rush. It may seem wise to hurry through them so you have more time for the challenging ones, but it's not worth missing one if you know the concept and just didn't take the time to read the question fully. Work efficiently but make sure you understand the question and have looked at all of the answer choices, since more than one may seem right at first.

Even if you're paying attention to the time, you may find yourself a little behind at some point. You should speed up to get back on track, but do so wisely. Don't panic; just take a few seconds less on each question until you're caught up. Don't guess without thinking, but do look through the answer choices and eliminate any you know are wrong. If you can get down to two choices, it is often worthwhile to guess from those. Once you've chosen an answer, move on and don't dwell on any that you skipped or had to hurry through. If a question was taking too long, chances are it was one of the harder ones, so you weren't as likely to get it right anyway.

On the other hand, if you find yourself getting ahead of schedule, it may be beneficial to slow down a little. The more quickly you work, the more likely you are to make a careless mistake that will affect your score. You've budgeted time for each question, so don't be afraid to spend that time. Practice an efficient but careful pace to get the most out of the time you have.

Secret Key #5 – Have a Plan for Guessing

When you're taking the test, you may find yourself stuck on a question. Some of the answer choices seem better than others, but you don't see the one answer choice that is obviously correct. What do you do?

The scenario described above is very common, yet most test takers have not effectively prepared for it. Developing and practicing a plan for guessing may be one of the single most effective uses of your time as you get ready for the exam.

In developing your plan for guessing, there are three questions to address:

- When should you start the guessing process?
- How should you narrow down the choices?
- Which answer should you choose?

When to Start the Guessing Process

Unless your plan for guessing is to select C every time (which, despite its merits, is not what we recommend), you need to leave yourself enough time to apply your answer elimination strategies. Since you have a limited amount of time for each question, that means that if you're going to give yourself the best shot at guessing correctly, you have to decide quickly whether or not you will guess.

Of course, the best-case scenario is that you don't have to guess at all, so first, see if you can answer the question based on your knowledge of the subject and basic reasoning skills. Focus on the key words in the question and try to jog your memory of related topics. Give yourself a chance to bring the knowledge to mind, but once you realize that you don't have (or you can't access) the knowledge you need to answer the question, it's time to start the guessing process.

It's almost always better to start the guessing process too early than too late. It only takes a few seconds to remember something and answer the question from knowledge. Carefully eliminating wrong answer choices takes longer. Plus, going through the process of eliminating answer choices can actually help jog your memory.

Summary: Start the guessing process as soon as you decide that you can't answer the question based on your knowledge.

How to Narrow Down the Choices

The next chapter in this book (**Test-Taking Strategies**) includes a wide range of strategies for how to approach questions and how to look for answer choices to eliminate. You will definitely want to read those carefully, practice them, and figure out which ones work best for you. Here though, we're going to address a mindset rather than a particular strategy.

Your odds of guessing an answer correctly depend on how many options you are choosing from.

Number of options left	5	4	3	2	1
Odds of guessing correctly	20%	25%	33%	50%	100%

You can see from this chart just how valuable it is to be able to eliminate incorrect answers and make an educated guess, but there are two things that many test takers do that cause them to miss out on the benefits of guessing:

- Accidentally eliminating the correct answer
- Selecting an answer based on an impression

We'll look at the first one here, and the second one in the next section.

To avoid accidentally eliminating the correct answer, we recommend a thought exercise called **the $5 challenge**. In this challenge, you only eliminate an answer choice from contention if you are willing to bet $5 on it being wrong. Why $5? Five dollars is a small but not insignificant amount of money. It's an amount you could afford to lose but wouldn't want to throw away. And while losing $5 once might not hurt too much, doing it twenty times will set you back $100. In the same way, each small decision you make—eliminating a choice here, guessing on a question there—won't by itself impact your score very much, but when you put them all together, they can make a big difference. By holding each answer choice elimination decision to a higher standard, you can reduce the risk of accidentally eliminating the correct answer.

The $5 challenge can also be applied in a positive sense: If you are willing to bet $5 that an answer choice *is* correct, go ahead and mark it as correct.

Summary: Only eliminate an answer choice if you are willing to bet $5 that it is wrong.

Which Answer to Choose

You're taking the test. You've run into a hard question and decided you'll have to guess. You've eliminated all the answer choices you're willing to bet $5 on. Now you have to pick an answer. Why do we even need to talk about this? Why can't you just pick whichever one you feel like when the time comes?

The answer to these questions is that if you don't come into the test with a plan, you'll rely on your impression to select an answer choice, and if you do that, you risk falling into a trap. The test writers know that everyone who takes their test will be guessing on some of the questions, so they intentionally write wrong answer choices to seem plausible. You still have to pick an answer though, and if the wrong answer choices are designed to look right, how can you ever be sure that you're not falling for their trap? The best solution we've found to this dilemma is to take the decision out of your hands entirely. Here is the process we recommend:

Once you've eliminated any choices that you are confident (willing to bet $5) are wrong, select the first remaining choice as your answer.

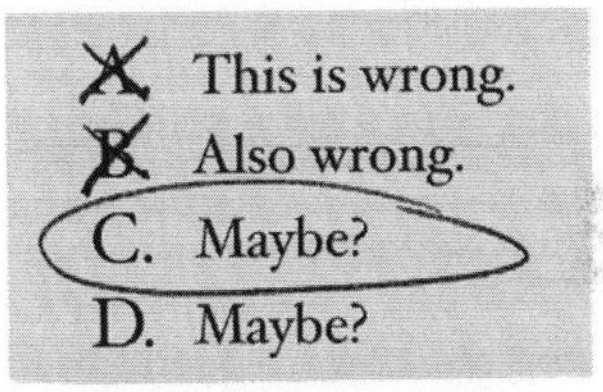

Whether you choose to select the first remaining choice, the second, or the last, the important thing is that you use some preselected standard. Using this approach guarantees that you will not be enticed into selecting an answer choice that looks right, because you are not basing your decision on how the answer choices look.

This is not meant to make you question your knowledge. Instead, it is to help you recognize the difference between your knowledge and your impressions. There's a huge difference between thinking an answer is right because of what you know, and thinking an answer is right because it looks or sounds like it should be right.

Summary: To ensure that your selection is appropriately random, make a predetermined selection from among all answer choices you have not eliminated.

Test-Taking Strategies

This section contains a list of test-taking strategies that you may find helpful as you work through the test. By taking what you know and applying logical thought, you can maximize your chances of answering any question correctly!

It is very important to realize that every question is different and every person is different: no single strategy will work on every question, and no single strategy will work for every person. That's why we've included all of them here, so you can try them out and determine which ones work best for different types of questions and which ones work best for you.

Question Strategies

✓ Read Carefully

Read the question and the answer choices carefully. Don't miss the question because you misread the terms. You have plenty of time to read each question thoroughly and make sure you understand what is being asked. Yet a happy medium must be attained, so don't waste too much time. You must read carefully and efficiently.

✓ Contextual Clues

Look for contextual clues. If the question includes a word you are not familiar with, look at the immediate context for some indication of what the word might mean. Contextual clues can often give you all the information you need to decipher the meaning of an unfamiliar word. Even if you can't determine the meaning, you may be able to narrow down the possibilities enough to make a solid guess at the answer to the question.

✓ Prefixes

If you're having trouble with a word in the question or answer choices, try dissecting it. Take advantage of every clue that the word might include. Prefixes can be a huge help. Usually, they allow you to determine a basic meaning. *Pre-* means before, *post-* means after, *pro-* is positive, *de-* is negative. From prefixes, you can get an idea of the general meaning of the word and try to put it into context.

✓ Hedge Words

Watch out for critical hedge words, such as *likely, may, can, often, almost, mostly, usually, generally, rarely*, and *sometimes*. Question writers insert these hedge phrases to cover every possibility. Often an answer choice will be wrong simply because it leaves no room for exception. Be on guard for answer choices that have definitive words such as *exactly* and *always*.

✓ Switchback Words

Stay alert for *switchbacks*. These are the words and phrases frequently used to alert you to shifts in thought. The most common switchback words are *but, although*, and *however*. Others include *nevertheless, on the other hand, even though, while, in spite of, despite*, and *regardless of*. Switchback words are important to catch because they can change the direction of the question or an answer choice.

✅ FACE VALUE

When in doubt, use common sense. Accept the situation in the problem at face value. Don't read too much into it. These problems will not require you to make wild assumptions. If you have to go beyond creativity and warp time or space in order to have an answer choice fit the question, then you should move on and consider the other answer choices. These are normal problems rooted in reality. The applicable relationship or explanation may not be readily apparent, but it is there for you to figure out. Use your common sense to interpret anything that isn't clear.

Answer Choice Strategies

✅ ANSWER SELECTION

The most thorough way to pick an answer choice is to identify and eliminate wrong answers until only one is left, then confirm it is the correct answer. Sometimes an answer choice may immediately seem right, but be careful. The test writers will usually put more than one reasonable answer choice on each question, so take a second to read all of them and make sure that the other choices are not equally obvious. As long as you have time left, it is better to read every answer choice than to pick the first one that looks right without checking the others.

✅ ANSWER CHOICE FAMILIES

An answer choice family consists of two (in rare cases, three) answer choices that are very similar in construction and cannot all be true at the same time. If you see two answer choices that are direct opposites or parallels, one of them is usually the correct answer. For instance, if one answer choice says that quantity *x* increases and another either says that quantity *x* decreases (opposite) or says that quantity *y* increases (parallel), then those answer choices would fall into the same family. An answer choice that doesn't match the construction of the answer choice family is more likely to be incorrect. Most questions will not have answer choice families, but when they do appear, you should be prepared to recognize them.

✅ ELIMINATE ANSWERS

Eliminate answer choices as soon as you realize they are wrong, but make sure you consider all possibilities. If you are eliminating answer choices and realize that the last one you are left with is also wrong, don't panic. Start over and consider each choice again. There may be something you missed the first time that you will realize on the second pass.

✅ AVOID FACT TRAPS

Don't be distracted by an answer choice that is factually true but doesn't answer the question. You are looking for the choice that answers the question. Stay focused on what the question is asking for so you don't accidentally pick an answer that is true but incorrect. Always go back to the question and make sure the answer choice you've selected actually answers the question and is not merely a true statement.

✅ EXTREME STATEMENTS

In general, you should avoid answers that put forth extreme actions as standard practice or proclaim controversial ideas as established fact. An answer choice that states the "process should be used in certain situations, if…" is much more likely to be correct than one that states the "process should be discontinued completely." The first is a calm rational statement and doesn't even make a definitive, uncompromising stance, using a hedge word *if* to provide wiggle room, whereas the second choice is far more extreme.

☑ Benchmark

As you read through the answer choices and you come across one that seems to answer the question well, mentally select that answer choice. This is not your final answer, but it's the one that will help you evaluate the other answer choices. The one that you selected is your benchmark or standard for judging each of the other answer choices. Every other answer choice must be compared to your benchmark. That choice is correct until proven otherwise by another answer choice beating it. If you find a better answer, then that one becomes your new benchmark. Once you've decided that no other choice answers the question as well as your benchmark, you have your final answer.

☑ Predict the Answer

Before you even start looking at the answer choices, it is often best to try to predict the answer. When you come up with the answer on your own, it is easier to avoid distractions and traps because you will know exactly what to look for. The right answer choice is unlikely to be word-for-word what you came up with, but it should be a close match. Even if you are confident that you have the right answer, you should still take the time to read each option before moving on.

General Strategies

☑ Tough Questions

If you are stumped on a problem or it appears too hard or too difficult, don't waste time. Move on! Remember though, if you can quickly check for obviously incorrect answer choices, your chances of guessing correctly are greatly improved. Before you completely give up, at least try to knock out a couple of possible answers. Eliminate what you can and then guess at the remaining answer choices before moving on.

☑ Check Your Work

Since you will probably not know every term listed and the answer to every question, it is important that you get credit for the ones that you do know. Don't miss any questions through careless mistakes. If at all possible, try to take a second to look back over your answer selection and make sure you've selected the correct answer choice and haven't made a costly careless mistake (such as marking an answer choice that you didn't mean to mark). This quick double check should more than pay for itself in caught mistakes for the time it costs.

☑ Pace Yourself

It's easy to be overwhelmed when you're looking at a page full of questions; your mind is confused and full of random thoughts, and the clock is ticking down faster than you would like. Calm down and maintain the pace that you have set for yourself. Especially as you get down to the last few minutes of the test, don't let the small numbers on the clock make you panic. As long as you are on track by monitoring your pace, you are guaranteed to have time for each question.

☑ Don't Rush

It is very easy to make errors when you are in a hurry. Maintaining a fast pace in answering questions is pointless if it makes you miss questions that you would have gotten right otherwise. Test writers like to include distracting information and wrong answers that seem right. Taking a little extra time to avoid careless mistakes can make all the difference in your test score. Find a pace that allows you to be confident in the answers that you select.

✅ KEEP MOVING

Panicking will not help you pass the test, so do your best to stay calm and keep moving. Taking deep breaths and going through the answer elimination steps you practiced can help to break through a stress barrier and keep your pace.

Final Notes

The combination of a solid foundation of content knowledge and the confidence that comes from practicing your plan for applying that knowledge is the key to maximizing your performance on test day. As your foundation of content knowledge is built up and strengthened, you'll find that the strategies included in this chapter become more and more effective in helping you quickly sift through the distractions and traps of the test to isolate the correct answer.

Now that you're preparing to move forward into the test content chapters of this book, be sure to keep your goal in mind. As you read, think about how you will be able to apply this information on the test. If you've already seen sample questions for the test and you have an idea of the question format and style, try to come up with questions of your own that you can answer based on what you're reading. This will give you valuable practice applying your knowledge in the same ways you can expect to on test day.

Good luck and good studying!

Definitions and Origins of Religion

RELIGION

Religion is an organized attempt to connect human beings with the "sacred," that which is unknowable and mysterious in the universe. Religion seeks to order the unknowable world in a way that makes it more accessible to people. It is defined by William Young as "human transformation in response to perceived ultimacy." Religions offer a theory to four major human questions:

- What is human nature?
- What is the structure of the universe?
- What is the relationship of humans to the universe?
- What is death?

Religions can be oral or written. Oral traditions are based on inherited wisdom passed down through the ages by word of mouth or through songs and stories. Written traditions are based on one or more official texts. Religions typically include: sacredness, mythology, ritual (a symbolic acting out of religious beliefs), taboos (prohibitions), doctrine (the official beliefs of a religious group), sacred seasons or calendars, holy people, and ethical codes.

Common characteristics of most religions include: submission to the perceived will of the divine powers or gods, selflessness or service to others, and some degree of self control.

VALUE OF RELIGION TO HUMANS

Religion offers its believers:

- Comfort (knowing that another world is morally fair if this one is not)
- Community and belonging (a sense of obligation toward one's fellow believers)
- Identity and structure (a sense of purpose)
- Answers about the unknown (it satisfies people's need for existential meaning when the world does not)

Psychological theories about the origin of religion speculate that religion results from a human brain making attempts to close the cognitive gaps in a world it does not fully understand. According to these theories, mythologies about creation and the natural world offered comfort to primitive peoples seeking to understand the world around them without the benefit of science. Religious rituals helped communities to hedge their bets against a world in which they struggled and often failed to survive for long. However, these psychological hypotheses fail to explain why religion retains widespread significance in a world saturated with science, suggesting these explanations may be incomplete.Immanuel Kant offered a moral argument for the existence of religion. People behave better, he wrote, if they expect their good behavior to be rewarded by a merciful god. A community's religion offers an incentive for people to behave morally and thus achieve social cohesion.

Origin of Religion

The following are major theories regarding the origin of religion:

- The animistic theory: Edward Burnett Tyler, a nineteenth century anthropologist, believed that early man's exposure to dreams death led him to believe in the existence of another, spiritual, world. This belief led to the worship of dead ancestors as well as a belief in animism.
- The nature-worship theory: Max Müller, a nineteenth century thinker, believed that primitive people, aware of the regular nature of some aspects of nature (for instance, the four seasons), attributed personal qualities to these aspects of nature, a mythology that later evolved into religious belief.
- The magic theory: Sir James George Frazer, observing the Scientific Revolution, declared that religion evolved from the use of magic in an attempt to control nature directly (for instance, rain dances), and that eventually humans began to ask the gods to intervene in nature rather than trying to control it themselves. Once humans began to rely on scientific reason to control nature, Frazer argued, religion would die away.

Characteristics of Religions

Most religions have at least a few things in common, such as:

- They address the relationship of humans to the unknown world of the dead, ancestors, and spirits.
- They have myths for understanding this unknown world and rituals for interacting with it.
- There is an organized system of rituals, holy people, sacred places, and possibly sacred texts.
- They contain a belief about what happens to humans after death.
- They contain guidelines for living morally.
- They have, at some point, attracted large numbers of followers.

This list is not all-inclusive and may not be applicable throughout the entire history of a particular religion. However, religions do tend to create some means by which to address the issues listed above.

The basic characteristics of religions originating in Africa and the Americas, India, East Asia, and the Middle East are explained as follows:

- Africa and the Americas: an oral tradition as opposed to a written one, animism, totemism (association of a group of people with a particular animal or natural symbol), and polytheism
- India (Hinduism, Jainism, Buddhism, and Sikhism): a pantheon of deities (Sikhism is an exception), a belief in cyclical time, a monastic tradition (Sikhism is an exception), a belief in reincarnation, and distant gods who do not intervene in human affairs or provide for their salvation
- East Asia (Taoism, Confucianism, and Shinto): worship of ancestors, world of nature (and, in the case of Shinto, reverence for the nation-state as well), and polytheism
- Middle East (Judaism, Islam, Christianity, Zoroastrianism, and Baha'i): a written tradition relying on the wisdom of sacred books, a linear view of time, disbelief in reincarnation, and a single god who actively intervenes in human affairs and sits in judgment of human actions

Ritual

A ritual is a formalized ceremonial expression of religious belief. These rituals may use symbolic object, mark rites of passage, or reinforce values. All religions have rituals:

- Native American religions: Many tribes have a "vision quest" ritual, which is a journey a person must undertake alone, often accompanied by a fast, in order to receive a vision from a spirit guide. Vision quests are undertaken at important times, such as puberty or in times of decision-making.
- Judaism: A bar mitzvah is a coming-of-age ritual given to boys (bat mitzvahs are given to girls sometimes as well in modern society) when they reach the age of puberty. Participants demonstrate their knowledge of the Torah and are formally initiated into adulthood.
- Christianity: Baptism is a symbolic second birth of infants (in certain denominations) or older converts, symbolizing the cleansing of their innate sinfulness through their savior, Jesus Christ.
- Islam: All capable Muslims are expected to make a pilgrimage, known as hajj, to Mecca, Islam's holiest site, at one point in their lives. Symbolic acts are performed during the visit, including the sacrifice of a sheep or goat and kissing of the sacred black stone in the shrine.

Myths Within Religion

Myths are stories that reveal truths to a society in a metaphorical way. All religions contain mythology. Myths may or may not be literally believed by the communities that create them, or they may be viewed simply as a poetic story with a greater significance. Myths can:

- Provide moral instruction to a community (for instance, through a tale of a great hero's sacrifice for his society)
- Explain the significance of a person (for instance, the Japanese sun goddess Amaterasu illustrates the perceived divine nature of the emperor)
- Explain the significance of a holy day
- Reinforce social standards (such as social class, race, and gender roles)
- Explain the unexplainable (most cultures, for instance, have creation myths that explain how the world came into being)

Eastern and Western Religions

In general terms, there are some major differences between Eastern and Western religions, though there are notable exceptions within each grouping. Western religions are characterized by:

- A linear view of time (time has a beginning and an end and progresses in one direction only)
- Monotheism (a worship of a single god)
- A defined role for humans (they should worship and serve God)
- Humans bear similarities to god (created "in God's image")
- Humans are superior to nature and their relationship to it is one of stewardship or "dominion"
- Exclusivity (only one God ought to be worshiped, and there is only one path to God)

Eastern religions are characterized by:

- A cyclical view of time, often incorporating beliefs in reincarnation
- The role of humans is not limited to the service of God
- Humans are interconnected with nature rather than apart from it
- Inclusivity (one's own religion is not necessarily viewed as the only means to the divine)

Creation Story

A creation story is the founding myth of a religion. Through creation stories, religious practitioners tell themselves how the world came into being.

- Judaism, Christianity, Islam—God created the heavens and the earth. Then God created all creatures and an original couple (Adam and Eve), who lived in an earthly paradise.
- Hinduism-All creation comes from the word aum.
- Jainism—The universe was not created and cannot be destroyed, but changes continually in a fixed series of cycles.
- Taoism—All creation comes from the Way, which led to the Unity, which then divided to create all creatures and things.
- Mayan religion—The prehistorical world consisted of water. Creator gods made the world in three stages: first land, then animals and plants, then humans (three attempts, from mud, then wood, and finally from maize).
- Australian Aboriginal religion—In the Dreamtime, a time that predates earthly time, totemic ancestors made the Creation.

Taboo

A taboo is a prohibition against an action, object, or person. Taboos are common in most societies. Violation of sacred taboos (for instance, touching the person of a chief or mixing with the community during menstruation) is believed to provoke supernatural wrath. The forbidden objects or people can be taboo either because they are considered unclean (e.g., pork to Jews or Muslims) or because they are considered sacred (e.g., cows to Hindus). If a taboo is broken, even accidentally, confession and/or rites of penitence are usually required. Some other taboos are as follows:

- Christianity: Catholics once were forbidden to eat meat on Fridays.
- Judaism: eating shellfish or pork is taboo.
- Native American religions: killing the animal that is the totem of one's clan was considered taboo.
- Islam: eating pork is taboo, as is drinking alcohol, gambling, and charging interest.

Critiques of Religion

Karl Marx

Karl Marx was one of many psychologists and sociologists interested in the origin of religion. He argued that religion was a tool used by the powerful in order to oppress the powerless, as well as a crutch the powerless used for comfort. "Religion is the sigh of the oppressed creature, the heart of a heartless world, and the soul of soulless conditions. It is the opium of the people."(Contribution to Critique of Hegel's Philosophy of Right, 1843)

Marx argued that in their efforts to control the working classes, society's powerful create a value system that convinces the oppressed that ultimate power resides not with people but with God. Therefore, the poor and oppressed turn to prayer to ease their struggles, rather than demanding social change. Furthermore, Marx asserted that the powerful use religious rhetoric to persuade the oppressed that the social order has God's approval and that to question it could have spiritual consequences.

Emile Durkheim

Emile Durkheim, one of the founders of the field of sociology, was interested in the social function of religion. In his book, The Elementary Forms of Religious Life, Durkheim asserted that the primary function of religion is to reinforce the cohesiveness of the community. Religion reinforces class, ethnic, and gender roles, dictates moral and immoral behavior, and identifies when it is and is not acceptable to employ violence. Durkheim argued that the community's behavior does not conform to the dictates of its religious laws, but vice versa. Religious laws and practices evolve to reflect the practices of the community. To examine a religion was to understand the values of the community that practiced it. To experience religion, Durkheim argued, was really to experience what it meant to be part of the community. The community's common beliefs and practices result in a common social identity, a source of significant meaning for its members.

Sigmund Freud

Sigmund Freud, the founder of psychoanalysis, wrote a great deal about the unconscious mind and its expression, through dreams, of repressed feelings and desires. In his books Future of an Illusion and Moses and Monotheism, Freud argued that religious rituals and myths allow an individual's repressed urges to be expressed in a way that is socially acceptable. Freud offered the example of ritual sacrifice. An individual might have repressed fantasies about committing an act of violence, and religious rituals allow the expression of this desire in a way that is considered not only acceptable but holy. However, the act is done within a very tightly scripted context, outside of which it remains taboo. Freud argued that religion is a crutch used by individuals for coping with their disturbing urges. He claimed that a strong individual would not need religion.

Approaches to Religion

Philosophical

The philosophical approach to religion is a way of studying religion by analyzing the actual beliefs and attitudes of practitioners of a particular religion. What attitude do these believers have about the world, man's place in it, and the proper way to behave? What do these practitioners believe about the nature of the universe? What do they believe about the nature of the deity they worship and the way they are supposed to interact with other human beings and with nature? What do critics of the religion say about its belief system? To apply reasoned analysis to the beliefs of a particular spiritual system is not to advocate it or to deny its validity. It is simply to understand and articulate the philosophy to which the advocates of a religion adhere.

Literary/Historical

Most modern study of a religion is done through textual analysis. By reading and understanding the texts of a religion (whether the actual holy books, supplementary texts such as scholarly analysis, or the texts used during religious rituals), a scholar can attempt to understand how a religious community functions or functioned in the past. Analysis of a religion's myths, as well as its functional texts, can help historians piece together what a religious community was like and what its values were. The anthropologists Edward Burnett Tylor and James George Frazer, both working in the late nineteenth and early twentieth centuries, developed theories about the evolution of religion among various societies. Both anthropologists' theories relied heavily upon the descriptions of religious practices and rituals around the world written by missionaries and colonial administrators.

Anthropological

The anthropological approach to religion takes as its starting point the methods and practices of anthropology: firsthand participant observation and objective analysis. Specifically, the anthropological approach is interested in religious institutions and how they interact with other social institutions, as well as how religious practices are both similar and different across different cultures. The earliest proponent of this approach was the eleventh century scholar Abu Rayhan Birun. Sir Edward Evans-Pritchard's work Theories of Primitive Religion argued that most anthropologists project their own attitudes onto the peoples they study, resulting in a patronizing analysis of other cultures' religious practices. Accurate analysis of religious practices, he argued, cannot be accomplished without understanding the social function of those practices.

Theology

Theology is an area of study devoted to the application of rational analysis to religious teachings. Through theology we can:

- Understand one's own religion more thoroughly
- Compare religious traditions
- Locate a justification or defense for a particular religious practice
- Identify areas of a religion in need of reform and offer a religious-based justification for reform
- Help to spread a particular religious tradition by teaching it to others
- Identify for members of a religious community the proper religious-based response to a crisis or problem

The theological approach to religion, however, takes as its starting point a preexisting devotion to one particular set of religious teachings and analyzes other religions in light of what it believes to be a particular religious truth. For example, a Muslim theological analysis of Judaism and Christianity will analyze the religious teachings of these religions in the context of Islam, identifying some aspects of the other religions as legitimate and other aspects as false (since they contradict Islam).

Arguments for the Existence of God

The cosmological, teleological, ontological, and moral arguments for the existence of God are explained as follows:

- The cosmological argument: The universe exists, ergo something (God) must have created it. Also known as the "prime mover" or "first cause" argument. Associated with thirteenth century Christian St. Thomas Aquinas.
- The teleological argument: The universe is so complex that a super-intelligent being must have designed it. This argument was first posited by Plato.
- The ontological argument: If God is the greatest thing that can be conceived, and it is greater to exist than not to exist, then God must exist. First proposed by Christian St. Anselm in the eleventh century and elaborated upon by French philosopher Rene Descartes.
- The moral argument: If all good and evil are relative to each other, then there must be a god who represents maximum goodness. The philosopher Immanuel Kant argued that behaving morally leads to humans' happiness, because there must be a god who represents the highest good.

Orientations to Religion

Orientations to religion can be organized into sets of opposing binaries. For example, intrinsic vs. extrinsic orientations may be described as follows:

- An intrinsically oriented religious person finds deep personal motivation to be religious. The satisfaction they derive from their religion is motivated by their own emotional connection to it. Religious feeling motivates their behavior in all aspects of life.

- An extrinsically oriented religious person compartmentalizes their religious life: it is but one aspect of their life, not the sum of it. They use their religion for what it adds to their life but do not necessarily view it as integrated with the rest of their life.

For example, an intrinsically motivated person might identify their reason for prayer as establishing a personal connection with the divine, whereas an extrinsically motivated person might say they get relief from prayer. An intrinsic motivation relies on religion for its own sake, whereas extrinsic motivation uses religion as a means to an end.

(These opposing orientations are identified in Allport and Ross's Religious Orientation Scale, 1967.)

The prophetic, sacramental, and mystical orientations are explained as follows:

- Prophetic—The prophetic orientation to religion stresses that contact with the sacred is maintained through adherence to set rules of moral and ethical contact. This may require going through an intermediary, such as a shaman, or it may be entirely personal. A prophetically oriented religion stresses the personal revelations given directly to a believer from a deity.
- Sacramental—The sacramental, or priestly, orientation emphasizes the importance of carrying out set rituals in order to maintain contact with the divine. Sacramentally oriented religions place great importance on sacred objects.
- Mystical—The mystical orientation is somewhat pantheistic at its core, seeking a personal connection with the universe often described as "oneness," a breaking down of the illusions that people and the universe are separate.

Fowler's Six Stages of Faith

The following are Fowler's six stages of faith:

- Stage 1: Intuitive-Projective Faith—This stage affects young children who observe the religiosity of adults around them. Their imaginative abilities allow them to identify with religious stories on an intuitive and perceptive level. Children unconsciously accept the truth they receive from their communities.
- Stage 2: Mythic-Literal—The development of reasoning skills allows children to start asking logical questions about the nature of the universe and to order their perceptions about religious stories and lessons. Their sense of religious morality begins to develop, but focuses on reciprocal fairness and justice, and lacks nuance. Their gods are nearly always anthropomorphic.
- Stage 3: Synthetic-Conventional—The literal understanding of the universe begins to break down as adolescents sense contradictions in their understanding of the world. They develop an ideology: a more or less consistent grouping of rules and beliefs. They do not, however, reflect on or analyze these values. This stage is characterized by conformity.
- Stage 4: Individuative-Reflective—Some adults reach stage 4, in which unignorable contradictions among their held beliefs must be confronted. The individual becomes aware of his or her belief system as one among many possible worldviews and takes personal responsibility for their beliefs.
- Stage 5: Conjunctive—In stage 5, middle-aged adults grasp a paradox: the value of their own belief systems coupled with their subjectivity. They become open to the teachings and possibilities of other belief systems.

- Stage 6: Universalizing—Stage 6 is extremely rare. In this stage, a very few people become alive to the universal. Their sense of a universal truth or love incorporates all beings and values their particularities as expressions of the universal experience. These people try to influence others to accept this universality, and many in stage 6 are martyred in the attempt to spread social change. This stage parallels, but is not limited to, what is referred to as "enlightenment" in certain Eastern religions.

Animism

Animism is an idea originally associated with Edward Tylor. Animism is the belief that objects in nature, whether living or nonliving, have personal spirits, which can be appeased or offended by human actions. There are four types of spirits:

- Human spirit: ghosts, the spirit of the dreamer
- Animal spirits: humans' allies, associated and protected through totemism
- Plant spirits: sacred plants and herbs (e.g., peyote to many Native American communities)
- Spirits of inanimate objects: rocks, mountains, sacred rivers (e.g. the Ganges to Hindus)

Important Terms

Doctrine—A doctrine is a teaching of a particular religion. Official doctrine attempts to organize the religious thought of a community in an elegant and coherent way.

Canon—A canon is the officially sanctioned set of sacred texts of a particular religion, excluding texts of questionable merit or that are considered outside the mainstream of the religion's thought.

Dogma—A dogma is an official opinion of a religious group, often laid down authoritatively in a way that makes it unacceptable to question it. Often dogmas are understood by members of the religious community to be absolutely true.

Fundamentalism—Fundamentalism is the strict adherence to a group of religious principles to the exclusion of other schools of thought. Usually a fundamentalist group believes that their interpretation of their religion's principles is correct and unchanging and is intolerant to alternative viewpoints.

Ideology—An ideology is a product of consciousness that answers metaphysical questions for an individual (e.g. what their place in the universe is and how they should behave).

Agnosticism—a belief that humans lack sufficient evidence to prove or disprove the existence of God

Atheism—a belief that there is no God

Deism—a belief in a god that exists but who is not personally involved with the world. A common metaphor is "God the watchmaker."

Determinism—a belief that all events are determined by external causes (thereby denying the existence of human free will)

Henotheism—a hierarchical polytheism with one main god and multiple lesser deities

Humanism—a belief that people are essentially good and have no need for a god to intervene in the world on their behalf

Materialism—a belief that nothing exists apart from matter

Monotheism—a belief in a single, personal god

Nontheism—a belief in a spiritual reality but not in personal deities (for example, in Buddhism and Confucianism)

Pantheism—a belief that everything is God and that there is nothing apart from the deity

Polytheism—a belief in more than one personal god

Theism—a belief in a personal god who responds to prayer

Magic—Magic is the effort made by holy people (priests and shamans) to control nature, for instance by performing a rain dance. This is distinguished from "religion" by the fact that in religion, holy people make efforts to persuade the gods to intervene on their behalf, rather than controlling nature directly.

Divination—Divination is the prediction of the future, using magical practices, and is usually performed by the holy people of a society. Examples: the I Ching, the Greek oracle at Delphi.

Shaman—The holy person of a religion. Often possessed by spirits and a performer of healing rituals.

Indigenous Religions

Native North American Religions

Vision Quest

A vision quest is a ritual used by many diverse North American religions. Its purpose is for an individual to seek visions from the spirit world, often at significant times in an individual's life, such as puberty. Typically, a vision quest requires a person to go alone into the wilderness and fasting for several days. Often they will wear shabby clothes in order to appear humble before the spirits; occasionally, they will inflict injuries upon themselves to prove their earnestness to the spirits. They remain in the wilderness until a guiding spirit appears to them. Once the spirit has appeared to them, the individual returns to the community. Often they will receive the totem of the spirit that has appeared, and sometimes their name is changed to reflect this guiding spirit. Vision quests are used as a rite of passage to mark the transition to adulthood, or to aid an individual in times of hardship or decision making (for instance, an individual having marital or financial troubles may go on a vision quest to receive wisdom in their crisis).

Problems with Analysis

Analysis of past cultures relies on textual evidence and that of artifacts left behind by them. Although native religions of American Indians are alive and well today, it is very difficult to identity which aspects of these religions are native to American Indian culture and which have developed as a result of contact with European settlers. It is challenging to analyze North American religions accurately because, for the most part, they have come from oral cultures without a written tradition. (The Cherokee are one of several obvious exceptions.) Therefore, most written accounts of these religions have come from early European settlers, who were not always intimately involved in firsthand experiences with these religions, and who may not have been inclined to describe their rituals in an unbiased light. In fact, a large percentage of the written accounts of Native American religious life came from Christian missionaries whose explicit goal was to convert Native Americans. Therefore, these accounts may not be entirely unbiased.

Characteristics

Although it is difficult to generalize about all North American religions, since there are many and they are diverse, there are several characteristics that are generally shared across a wide spectrum of them. Among them are:

- A reverence for nature bordering on animism. For many Native Americans, nature is alive with spirits who must be respected.
- Polytheism in the general sense. These nature spirits are living manifestations of a Mother Earth figure.
- A primary deity. Though many godlike figures exist, there is usually a "high god" or "Great Father" spirit who is considered supreme.
- Connection: the Native American worldview emphasizes the universe's connections rather than ownership over it, or separation (good vs. evil, mind vs. body).
- A personal, nonhierarchical religious experience. A shaman figure in many tribes performs rituals but is not an intermediary between an individual and the divine.
- Circularity, not linearity: there is a focus on the cyclical nature of the universe, rather than on cause and effect.
- A serious taboo about the dead.

Relationship Between Living and Dead

In many Native American societies, the dead are a major taboo. It is considered taboo to touch the bodies or clothing of dead people or to disturb their burial sites. Their spirits are feared out of the belief that they may attempt to take others. Those individuals appointed to bury the dead are often considered ritually unclean for a short period of time afterward. Because of this taboo, it is considered highly disturbing to many Native Americans that the bodies of their ancestors are held in archaeological museums, away from their intended resting places. Many Native American societies believe in a dual soul. One, the mortal soul, dies with the body. The other is a soul that coexists with the mortal soul, wandering away during dreams and illness, and after death lives on for a period, but not indefinitely. Usually the belief is that this soul fades away and eventually dies as the person is gradually forgotten by others. All dead people go to the same land for the duration of the life of this second soul; there is no concept of Hell.

Changes Resulting from Contact with European Settlers

From the earliest days of European settlement in North America, indigenous religions have competed with and coexisted with Christianity. In the lives of many Native Americans, both traditions coexist with no seeming contradiction. The Native American Church evolved in the late nineteenth century and represents an amalgam of Christianity and indigenous religious practices. Rituals may involve the taking of peyote, a hallucinogenic cactus, a practice that has historically been done by Native Americans in Mexico and has gradually moved northward. Members of the Native American Church have a complicated relationship with Christianity and vary widely in their adherence to one or the other set of beliefs. For some, they are Christian in all but name. For others, the two belief systems coexist happily; for instance, some churches will use peyote in a ceremony not unlike the Christian communion ceremony. Many have a special reverence for Jesus as a martyr, but incorporate the traditional symbolism of the deer to stress their similar martyrdom.

Mayan Religion

Mayan religious tradition was characterized by a spiritual reverence for the land and its soil. The maize that formed the Mayans' staple diet was revered as holy. Mayans believed that humans were created from maize, after attempts with clay and wood. Tepeu and Gucumatz were the Mayans' original gods, who thought things into existence. The gods ordered and controlled all human events on earth. Mayan religion was a complicated polytheistic system in which many gods are each associated with particular colors, directions, days, months, and omens. Mayans sacrificed to them, including human sacrifice on occasion. Ancestors were worshipped. Mayan religion contained an obsession with fate and avoiding it. Offerings were made for good fortunes, and horoscopes used to foretell the future. Mayans made personal sacrifices before farming or sowing maize, and their prayers consisted of an explicit request rather than praise. There is no natural conception of goodness; Mayans sacrifice in order to receive from the gods. Much influence of Mayans' personal superstitions and direct contact with deities can be seen in the popular Christianity of Latin America today.

Incan Religion

Incas believed that they descended from the ancestor-gods Inti and Quilla, who represent the sun and moon, respectively. Incas believed in a three-part world, with a mortal world (Kay Pacha, the present) and two underworlds: Uku Pacha (an afterlife for the unrighteous, representing the interior past) and Hanan Pacha (an afterlife for the righteous, representing the superior and future). Incan religion was polytheistic. Because the Incas ruled an empire, they absorbed many other cultures, allowing the colonized people to keep their local gods. Possibly for this reason, there are several creation myths in Incan mythology. In all of them, the god Manco Capac is the primary founding god of the religion. Apu were spirits of the mountains, each mountain having its own patron apu. Incas also believed in huacas, animistic entities who dwelled in sacred sites. Incas sacrificed humans and animals to these deities. For Incas, the world was dualistic in nature: the concept of Hanan represented the right, superior, and masculine, while Hurin represented the left, inferior, and feminine. There were cults to individual gods, including Quilla and Inti.

Aztec Religion

Aztecs believed in the concept of teotl, a fundamental unity connecting all things, both positive and negative. More than 100 deities personified various aspects of Aztec religion, but Aztec priests accepted them as all part of the same ultimate unity. Huitzilopochtli was the main god in the Aztec system of belief. He personified the sun and war, though prior to the Aztec empire he was associated with hunting; regardless, he remained at the center of Aztec social life. Other important deities included Quetzalcoatl (the god of civilization) and Tlaloc (the god of rain). All gods required constant appeasement. There were three parts to the Aztec universe: the mortal world, an underworld, and a celestial world. Sacred places such as caves represented places of access from one plane to another. Aztecs envisioned time as cyclical and believed in human reincarnation. As with other Mesoamerican religions, Aztec religion associated gods with particular aspects of life, with directions, and with colors. Aztec religious ritual involved ritual human sacrifice and the recreation of mythological events.

Native West African Religion

Death

In West African traditions, the line between the living and the dead is not clear-cut. In some cultures, death is always seen as an unnatural event that must have been caused by an external force. The dead are often greatly feared. Once dead, people become sacred and powerful ancestors who must be appeased by the living. Bodies are eased into the next life with objects designed to make the next world more comfortable. Part of the purpose is to ensure that the dead do go on to the next life and do not haunt the living. Ancestors are powerful spirits in West African religions. Like the High God, they are spirits, but unlike the High God, they affect daily life and are often malevolent. They may be sacrificed to, because African ancestors are not only revered but also feared for their ability to do unpredictable harm.

Major and Minor Gods

Although it is difficult to generalize about all West African religions, most do share some major characteristics. For instance, in most West African societies, there is a High God, who is a creator god in the deist sense of the word: he created the world and then withdrew, and his influence is no longer directly felt, though at times of crisis he may be prayed to. In addition to the High God, there are often lesser deities. Most African religions are animistic: that is, practitioners believe that the natural world is full of spirits, both harmful and helpful. Believers can pray to these spirits to seek protection and favor. Often societies have elaborate rituals for contacting ancestors. These rituals include dances, masks made in sacred spaces, and ritual art objects.

Rites of Passage

Birth rituals are observed throughout West Africa, but are often not celebrated until the baby has lived for a week. Naming ceremonies are common. Puberty rites include seclusion of the celebrants for a period of time, as well as physical trials for boys. Ritual circumcision for boys is very common and is typically performed at puberty. Female genital mutilation, also called circumcision by the participants, is performed in many cultures as a puberty rite as well. Marriage rites are usually secular in West African societies. It is a contract between families rather than a spiritual matter. The dead are buried quickly, frequently with items such as money and weapons designed to make life in the next world more comfortable. Religious rituals often involve water, and this water must be sacred "living" water—that is, from a spring or a river and not treated in any way.

Sumerian/Akkadian Religion

The ancient Sumerians were a polytheistic society that worshipped over two thousand deities, both major and minor. Deities represented various aspects of nature, and large settlements had a patron deity, though all gods were welcome everywhere. Akkadian culture later adopted the pantheon of Sumerian gods; Akkadian mythology is better preserved. Ishtar was the major goddess figure of Sumerian religion. She was widely worshipped, and eventually her cult spread far beyond the Fertile Crescent. She represented fertility, femininity, and war. The six major gods in the Sumerian/Akkadian pantheon were:

- An/Anu: the sky god, technically the "pristine king and ruler" of all the gods
- Enlil/Bel: god of wind and flood, conferred power upon rulers
- Nanna/Sin: son of Enlil, the moon god
- Utu/Shamash: sun god
- Enki/Ea: god of water and wisdom
- Ninhursag/Aruru: the mother goddess

Gods typically had a female consort. Akkadians divided the major gods into significant families. For instance, Anu, Bel, and Ea divided the powers of the physical universe among themselves.

Myths of Babylonian Religion

Creation

Two creation myths exist. In one, heaven and earth (associated with An and the earth god Ki) united, emerged from the primordial sea, and reproduced into aspects of nature associated with various gods: the air, the moon, the sun, plants, animals, and humans. In the second, the world as we know it was formed by a primeval struggle between the gods of order and the dragons of chaos.

The Flood

The angry gods decided to flood the earth, but Ea revealed their plan to one man, Utnapishtim, who built an ark to survive it.

Return of Ishtar

Ishtar (associated with fertility) ventured to the underworld to recover her dead lover (associated with the springtime sun), but was afflicted by diseases, rendering the world's people and animals unable to reproduce. Ea's messenger then ordered that Ishtar be returned to life, and life returned to the earth.

Journey of Gilgamesh

Gilgamesh, the ruler of the city of Uruk, died prematurely for offending Ishtar. He searched for immortality, found the herb of immortality, and then was robbed of it by a serpent.

Zoroastrianism

Zoroastrianism originated in Persia (now Iran), but in modern times its greatest number of adherents live in India. Zoroastrianism is monotheistic, worshipping Ahura Mazda ("Wise Lord"), a preexisting god of the Aryans (known to them as Varuna) who represents order and morality, perfect goodness and wisdom. Ahura Mazda created all things and is locked in an eternal struggle against evil. Zoroastrianism specifies a code of moral behavior, including obedience and correct thought. It emphasizes the struggle between good and evil, right and wrong. There is a fundamental good spirit and bad spirit in the world, and each human soul struggles in a battle between the two. Individuals are responsible for their moral choices. Unlike previous religions, Zoroastrianism retains only the rituals of worship (e.g., the sacred fire). Individuals are judged on their merits after death and sent either to paradise or to hell. At the end of the world, all souls will be resurrected and put to a test of fire; the evil will burn and the good will be unharmed. Zoroaster will triumph over evil in an apocalyptic battle.

Rituals

A hereditary priesthood regulates Zoroastrian life. Sacred fire temples are tended by a special class of priests. A complicated ritual creates the sacred fire, which is made of sixteen specific fires from various sources. It is a symbol but is not itself divine. Worshippers give offerings at the fire temples in return for ashes made from this fire, which they rub on their faces. Zoroastrians pray five times a day, ideally at the fire temples. Priests recite holy scriptures in Avestan, the original, now-dead language of Zoroastrianism. The most important ceremony in Zoroastrianism is the extraction of the juice of the haoma, a sacred plant. New Year's Day is an important religious day, with worship and alms-giving. In India, Zoroastrians dispose of their dead in dakhmas, or towers of silence. These towers are placed on remote hilltops, where bodies are left exposed for vultures to eat, then bones are cast into a well. In this way Zoroastrians avoid contaminating the soil.

Ancient Egyptian Religion

Ancient Egyptian religious beliefs included a semidivine status for the pharaoh, or king. They had animal totems that represented human ancestors and told a broad collection of myths about the world. Their beliefs about the afterlife are particularly notable in that they believed an individual's body remained with them even after death. Therefore, bodies were embalmed and mummified, in order to remain preserved for eternity, before being sealed in tombs surrounded by money, treasures, and, depending on social status, live servants. It is possible, however, that the afterlife was reserved only for kings. Egyptian mythology included two creation stories, in both of which the first humans originate in tears of joy falling from the sun god. Their main god was the sun god, Ra, but they worshipped a pantheon of other gods as well, including the wife and husband pair Isis and Osiris, as well as their son, Horus.

Greek Religion

Relationship of People to Gods

The ancient Greeks' religion was one in which gods were powerful but immediately accessible in daily life. The gods' approval was needed for all human activities, but human addresses to them were direct rather than fearful. Public festivals celebrated the most powerful gods, but most human interaction with the gods occurred in an immediate, quotidian fashion. Even the dwelling places of the gods were both real places on the earth and simultaneously otherworldly. Sacrifices were made. Formal occasions and rituals necessitated the invocation of a god, and gods were prayed to in hopes of healing from illness. Some gods were known to respond to human requests, but others were known to be distant from human affairs. Gods were individually the patrons of various cities, functions of nature, and human occupations. Gods, though more than mortal, were not omnipotent. They had many human failings, conflicts with each other, and familial relationships. Gods were limited in the scope of their powers. Moira, or fate, had ultimate control over human lives. The drama of human lives was ultimately a source of the amusement of the gods.

MAJOR DEITIES

Major deities of Greek religion were frequently Olympian gods—the main family of gods who were said to live on Mount Olympus. These include:

- Apollo: god of light and truth, associated with the sun, the most handsome of the gods
- Ares: god of war
- Artemis: goddess of the wild, the hunt, and the moon
- Athena: goddess of wisdom and warfare, patroness of Athens
- Aphrodite: goddess of love, the most beautiful of the gods
- Demeter: goddess of fertility and agriculture
- Dionysius: god of wine and celebration
- Hades: god of the underworld
- Hephaesthus: god of fire
- Hera: Zeus's wife, who was the goddess of women, marriage, and childbirth
- Hermes: a messenger god who guided departed souls to and from Hades. God of trickery, flight, commerce, and travelers
- Hestia: goddess of the home and hearth
- Poseidon: god of the sea
- Zeus: chief deity, the controller of weather, and the father figure for all the gods

Other important Greek gods and demigods included:

- Achilles: warrior hero
- Eros: god of love and sex
- Pan: god of shepherds and pastures
- Persephone: Demeter's daughter, goddess of fertility and queen of the underworld

ROMAN RELIGION

NUMEN

The Romans described their early religion as "the religion of Numa," their lawgiver. It was based in magic, spells, and omens. Numen were supernatural forces, but rather than being a vague supernatural force, numen were the result of the individual will of the gods. Numen were sacred forces that existed within people, places, and objects, as determined by the gods. Early Roman gods were not named, nor did they have human characteristics until Roman culture was sufficiently influenced by the Greeks. The personification of Roman gods evolved only as Romans named the numen in order to distinguish their functions. Specific gods came to be associated with particular numen in the world. For instance, Saturnus was associated with sowing, whereas Consus was associated with harvesting, and each god came eventually to be anthropomorphized and would be prayed to in turn for divine aid in a particular stage of farming.

DEITIES

Roman religion had many deities, each the personification of some particular aspect of home, nature, or agriculture. Some of the major deities include:

- Jupiter: father figure, god of light, determiner of human affairs, responsible for rain and sunshine (Greek = Zeus)
- Janus: two-faced numen of the doorway and of beginnings
- Mars: god of war (Greek = Ares)
- Vesta: numen of the hearth (Greek = Hestia)

- Genius: a personal guardian spirit that bestowed numen on an individual man
- Juno: the equivalent of Genius for women, later becoming a personified goddess of women and married to Jupiter (Greek = Hera)
- Diana: goddess of the moon and the hunt (Greek = Artemis)
- Minerva: goddess of wisdom, patroness of arts (Greek = Athena)

Influence of Etruscan and Greek Religion

Roman religion evolved greatly over the centuries, from a religion respecting the vague, genderless, powers known as numen to personifying and anthropomorphizing those numen and creating a mythology of family relationships for them. Many of these changes are due to the influence of Etruscan and Greek culture. From the Etruscans, the Romans borrowed the practice of engraving temples with images of their deities, which reinforced the new personification of their gods as human-like deities with distinct personalities. Gods originating in Etruscan religion include Juno and Minerva. From the Greeks, Roman religion gained poetry, astrology, and humanity, as opposed to the heretofore-abstract qualities of their gods. The Sibylline Books, a collection of oracles introduced from Greece to Rome during the sixth century B.C., are largely responsible for the introduction of many of the Greek gods and myths to Roman religion.

Shinto

The origins of Shinto are aesthetic rather than abstract or intellectual. It is, at its root, a love of the land of Japan itself. In the Shinto system, the land is now filled, and was once exclusively filled, with kami, which are powerful spirits of nature and the ancestors of Japanese people. The Japanese emperor is said to be a direct descendent of Amaterasu, the sun kami. Invaded by the Chinese in the fifth century B.C., and influenced by Buddhism, Shinto eventually codified its mythology in the Kojiki, or Chronicle of Ancient Events. Shinto recognized the bodhisattvas of Buddhism as revelations of the kami. Gradually, Buddhism and Shinto began to overlap and influence one another, and to coexist harmoniously, with Buddhism responsible for the afterlife and Shinto responsible for daily life. Over time, Shinto began to disappear as a separate religion. In the seventeenth century, the Tokugawa regime revived Shinto as an explicitly nationalist religion. Today, Shinto in Japan is state-supported, but other religions are allowed to exist

The three main forms of Shinto are:

- State Shinto: The state of Japan supports hundreds of thousands of Shinto shrines and employs their priests, as well as supporting patriotic rituals there. The grand shrine at Ise is dedicated to the mother goddess of Shinto, Amaterasu, and Japanese people are expected to visit the shrine at least once. Anyone may visit the outer shrine, while only priests are allowed in the inner shrine, since it contains religious objects.
- Sectarian Shinto: During the Japanese imperial era, Shinto came to be a nationalistic and militaristic institution. Sectarian Shinto became a separate practice and is divided into three categories: the mountain worship sects, shamanistic sects based in peasant tradition, and sects practicing traditional Shinto, emphasizing purification rituals, chanting, fasting, family, cleanliness, worship, and ethical guidelines.
- Domestic Shinto: Domestic Shinto is a simple form that takes place in Japanese homes. Many homes have shrines with religiously significant objects, where offerings of flowers, incense, and food are left. The shrine may be the site of a daily prayer or for special occasions—but not for funerals, which are a Buddhist affair.

Major Myths

The land of Japan was created specially by the kami after a primal chaos. One original male, Izanagi, and female, Izanami, conceived the solid land itself, then conceived other kami, including the kami of wind, the tree, the mountain, and the plains. However, Izanami was badly burned while giving birth to the kami of fire, and died. Izanagi sought her in Hades, but ran away after seeing her putrefied body. He washed his eyes to purify his body, and from his eyes and nose came Amaterasu, the sun kami, Tsukiyomi, the moon kami, and Susanoo, the ocean kami. Later, Susanoo offended Amaterasu, and in apology, the eighty myriads of kami brought her gifts, including singing birds, a 500-branched tree from Mount Kagu, a string of Yasaka jewels, a mirror, and blue and white objects. As well, a dance was performed using a spear wrapped in Eulalia grass. These myths illustrate some of the common themes of Shinto: the importance of purification and the sacred symbolism of certain objects.

Hinduism

Influence of Pre-Aryan India

Around 2000 B.C., Aryans from the west invaded India, bringing with them their religion. The India they encountered had its own native religion, and while much remains unknown about it (in part because their written language has yet to be translated), their archaeological artifacts tell us that Hinduism may have inherited its use of the lotus position of meditative Hinduism, as well as fertility gods and goddesses that may be the basis for later Hindu deities like Shiva. In addition, these pre-Aryan Indians (known by the Aryans as Dasas) were agricultural, possessing cattle—a fact which probably later led to the Hindu reverence for cows. There was in this pre-Aryan religion a suggestion of the later idea of karma, the linked cause-and-effect structure of the Hindu universe.

Aryan Invasion of India

Aryans invaded India from what would later be known as Iran. They were a nomadic, tribal people without permanent settlements. They were a warlike society who migrated in horse-drawn chariots, and they easily subdued the native peoples of India before settling into a pastoral life themselves. Each tribe had a hereditary chieftain, who maintained an army to protect his tribe. Women were relatively free. The three essential social classes of Aryan society were known as varnas. They included: Brahmins, who were priests; Kshatriyas, who were chieftains and warriors; and the lowest class, known as Vaishyas. A fourth servant class was known as Shudras (and may have been exclusively made of conquered non-Aryans). These social classes would comprise the basis for the later caste system of Hindu India.

Vedic Religion

The four Vedas, or collections, of writings, are the principle source of contemporary knowledge about Indo-Aryan, or Vedic, religion. It is not easy to say for certain which aspects of Vedic religion were native and which were influenced by the pre-Aryans, but many aspects do bear a certain similarity to European religions. Vedic religion was partly animistic, believing in gods (similar to those of Greece or Rome) who personified various aspects of nature. Sacrifice was the main means of worship; along with animals burned on open fires, milk and butter were also offered to the gods. Soma, a sacred plant, was drunk as well as shared with the gods.

Vedas

The four Vedas are the oldest sacred books of Hinduism. They were written sometime between 1500 B.C. and 600 A.D., though the earliest hymns may predate the Aryan invasion. The books, in order, are:

- The Rig-Veda: the most important book, a collection of more than 1,000 hymns that describe basic Aryan mythology. Consists of praise for the gods and prayers requesting blessings.
- The Yajur-Veda (knowledge of rites): a collection of chants to be read during rituals.
- The Sama-Veda (knowledge of chants): verses from the hymns read by the priests during sacrifices.
- The Atharva-Veda (knowledge given by Atharva, the sage): rituals used in the home, along with spells.

Each book consists of four parts:

- Mantras: hymns to the gods
- Brahmanas: instructions to priests about how to perform rituals
- Aranyakas: "forest treatises," instructions for hermits
- Upanishads: philosophy

The Vedas are used in modern Hinduism as a scholarly work and are respected by Hindus, but are not known intimately by ordinary Hindus.

Upanishads: The Upanishads, the fourth and last section of each of the Vedas, form the basis for Vedic philosophy. They are the last part of the Vedas to have been written, and there are two hundred surviving Upanishads, about fourteen of which are primarily important. The Upanishads are mainly focused on the god Brahman (though he is an abstraction and not anthropomorphic), in contrast to the clear polytheism of the rest of the Vedas. Unlike the focus on priestly rituals throughout earlier portions of the Vedas, the Upanishads emphasize meditation as the means to true knowledge and ignorance as the sole problem of humanity.

In the Upanishads, Brahman is reality; all that is not Brahman is false. All living souls are part of Brahman, and their seeming individuality is an illusion (maya). In Upanishadic thought, all seeming reality, be it suffering or joy—the entire world—is maya. The curse of human existence is ignorance of this illusion, and it is the work of human beings to understand it. The Upanishads also introduce the concept of karma, that individuals' choices have personal consequences, either in this life or the next. Samsara, or reincarnation, is introduced here too: that souls do not die but move to another time and another body until the individual breaks the cycle of karma and achieves enlightenment. When an individual understands the illusory nature of life, he can be free of the burden of mortal life. This breaking free from potentially endless cycles of rebirth and redeath is known as moksha.

Deities Described in the Vedas

The following are primary deities, associated with phenomena of nature:

- Indra: the largest number of hymns is addressed to Indra, god of the thunderbolt, clouds, war, and rain, and the ruler of heaven. He conquers Vitra (chaos).
- Vishnu: less important in the Vedas than in later Hinduism. In the Vedas he is one of a number of sun gods.
- Rudra: later to be known as Shiva, Rudra was a destroyer god who was greatly feared. He caused storms, brought destruction against the Aryans, and was prayed to humbly for his mercy.
- Varuna: god of order, law, and the sea.
- Yama: god of the dead; supposedly the first man to have died.

The following are liturgical deities, associated with rituals:

- Agni: god of fire, and of the priest. Also has a priest-like role among the gods. He brings burnt sacrifices to all the gods and blesses.
- Soma: the god of the sacred soma plant.
- Brahmanaspati: the god of sacred words.

Law of Manu

The Law of Manu is a classical piece of Indian literature offering instruction in proper living. It was written between 300 B.C. and 300 A.D. It identifies the ideal characteristics of a moral person:

- Pleasantness
- Patience
- Control of one's mind
- Not stealing
- Purity
- Control of one's senses
- Intelligence
- Knowledge
- Truthfulness
- Nonirritability

It expounds on the varna class system of the Aryans. Within the varna system, there is no class mobility in a lifetime; only through reincarnation (after performing their expected duties as a member of their current class) could an individual change classes. The three top classes are known as "twice born", the Shudras "once born." The Law of Manu also codifies the expected stages of life for men of the upper castes:

- Student of the Vedas
- Householder (marrying within his caste)
- Hermit, living and meditating in the forest
- Wandering beggar

The role of women by this stage of Aryan society is much more limited. Women are expected to be devoted daughters and then wives and mothers. There is no independence for them at any stage.

Role of Women

Until the Law of Manu, women in Vedic society enjoyed relative freedom. The Law of Manu, however, codified a set of rules for appropriate female behavior. According to the Law of Manu, women are to remain wholly dependent on the men closest to them for their entire lives. First, they depend on their fathers, then their husbands, and later, if they are widowed, their sons. All important decisions are to be made for their benefit by these men. Women's sphere of influence is wholly domestic. The total role of women is to serve the men in their lives, indeed to worship them as gods. There is a hierarchy within female society, and lower-ranking women must defer to higher-ranking ones. Women, however, are considered objects of worship, representing goodness and beauty.

Bhagavad Gita

The Bhagavad Gita is an epic poem written within a larger epic called the Mahabharata that tells the story of two warring families from early India. In the poem, Arjuna, the young warrior, contemplates his role in the imminent war between the two families. Arjuna hesitates, realizing he must kill loved ones in the battles. His charioteer, Krishna, instructs him in proper living: they must follow the obligations of their castes, which Krishna says are religious duties, not simply social ones. He explains the five basic truths:

- Ishvara (The Supreme Controller)
- Jiva (the soul)

- Prakrti (matter)
- Dharma (duty)
- Kaala (time)

The advice Krishna offers to Arjuna is a summary of Hindu thinking. He advises Arjuna that attachment to his mortal body is preventing his enlightenment and instructs him that there are various paths to enlightenment: service, action, meditation, and knowledge.

Several concepts in Indian religion appear for the first time in the Bhagavad Gita. Vishnu appears for the first time in this poem as a loving god who will appear on earth to intervene in human affairs. In addition, Krishna advises Arjuna that moksha can result from various paths: meditation, asceticism, devotion to gods, or proper obedience to caste laws. It reinforces the obligation of individuals to perform their castes' duties. Generally speaking, the Bhavagad Gita offers a more inward-facing orientation than had previously existed in Indian religion. The emphasis on meditation and interior struggle for knowledge is new, as is the narrower focus on a handful of key deities.

Change from Brahmanism to Hinduism

The evolution of Indian religion is often divided into two eras, Brahminism and Hinduism, separated by the completion of the Bhagavad Gita. Brahminism involved priestly ritual sacrifices to a myriad of deities. The very gradual change to Hinduism was marked by a more selective focus on a few deities—but, simultaneously, an expansion of the number of ways they could be worshipped. Personal devotion to these gods was a new development, and the gods were seen to have human qualities and foibles, and to take a personal interest in human lives. Goddesses became more important. A pessimistic worldview developed. In Hinduism, life is a burden that ends only with enlightenment. The advent of Hinduism brought with it a new focus on the philosophical, the internal, and the mystical. Ritual sacrifices were replaced by the personal sacrifice of asceticism.

Shankara and the Aducita System

Shankara was the most outstanding Hindu scholar of the medieval period. Shankara founded the Advaita system, a branch of Vedanta, the Upanishad-based philosophical school. Advaita means "nondual" and is a monistic worldview. It declares that all is Brahman. There is only one reality. The curse of humanity is not sin but ignorance of the fact that all material reality is an illusion. People are thus stuck in the cycle of death and rebirth until they realize that they are not apart from Brahman. Shankara was known for his opposition to Buddhism and led it to be driven out of India. He was a personal devotee of Shiva and is believed by other devotees to be an avatar of Shiva himself.

Ramanuja and Madhva

Ramanuja and Madhva were medieval Hindu philosophers. Both were devoted to Vishnu and believed in the importance of personal devotion to the gods. In the medieval debate over the Vedas' significance, each offered an important counterargument to the teachings of Shankara. Ramanuja offered that true devotion to gods was impossible if all was Brahman; separation from Brahman was necessary in order to worship it. He proposed a dual system in which both humans and Brahman were united but were not the same, thus enabling worship. Madhva took this thought a step further, arguing that, in order to worship a god properly, humans must be both separate from Brahman and individuated from one another. His Advaita system is greatly influenced by Islam and Christianity and posits that salvation is achieved through Vayu, the son of Vishnu. In Advaita, the righteous are rewarded with an eternity in the presence of Vishnu, while the wicked are punished with an endless life of transmigration.

Soma

Soma was both a deity and his symbol, a sacred drink made from a plant that remains unidentified to this day. Soma was drunk in public rituals as a sacrifice to the god. Soma the deity also acted as a transporter of received offerings to the other gods, and so was critical in sacrificial rituals. Every part of the soma ritual was carefully scripted and considered sacred, from the procurement of the plant to the pressing of the juice to its drinking. The plant, though unidentified, was possibly hallucinogenic, leading worshippers to the belief that they communed more directly with the gods when under its influence. The soma ritual bears a strong resemblance to a ritual used in Zoroastrianism, but its accompanying mythology changed as the Aryans settled in India and their religion evolved.

Hinduism

Hindu literature can be divided into Vedic and non-Vedic types. Vedic literature includes:

- Samhita: the collections of Vedic hymns
- Rig-Veda: collection of more than 1,000 hymns that describe basic Aryan mythology
- Yajur-Veda: collection of chants to be read during rituals
- Sama-Veda: verses from the hymns read by the priests during sacrifices
- Atharva-Veda: rituals used in the home, along with spells
- Brahmanas: commentaries on the Vedas. These emphasize the importance of ritual and the Varna system
- Upanishads: the last section of each of the four Vedas, and the basis for Vedic philosophy

Non-Vedic literature includes:

- Vedangas (scholarly methods for understanding the Vedas)
- Dharma Shastras (including the Law of Manu): religious and legal duties
- Nibandhas: commentaries on Dharma Shastras
- Puranas/Epics:Bhagavata Purana: story of Krishna as a child
- Ramayana: epic of Rama and his wife Sita
- Mahabharata (including the Bhagavad Gita): origin story of India
- Darshanas: literature of the six philosophical schools: Sankhya; Nyaya; Vedanta; Yoga; Vaishesika; Mimamsa;
- Agamas or Tantras (divinely revealed techniques for self-realization)
- Philosophical writings of Hindu scholars: Shankara: medieval; Ramanuja: medieval; Madhva: medieval; Ramakrishna: A.D. 1800s

Brahman, Maya, and Avidya

According to the Upanishads, Brahman is the only reality. There is nothing apart from Brahman, who is divine, but who is a totally impersonal god. The illusion that there is something other than Brahman is a persistent one, but it is false, and when humans believe that Brahman is distinct from anything else, they have maya, or false knowledge. Avidya means ignorance, and it is avidya that humans suffer from when they do not realize the maya they live with. Only through realization of their avidya will humans come to enlightenment. One problem that the concept of Brahman creates is the relationship between Brahman and humans. The Upanishads clarify this by drawing a distinction between "manifest" and "unmanifest" Brahman, or "He/She" and "It." "He/She" is the personal god whom people can address, while "It" is the true Brahman, the source of all things, but basically so pure as to be indescribable and unknowable.

Four Permissible Goals

The four permissible goals in Hinduism are:

- Dharma: Dharma is duty. Dharma includes ethics, virtue, and righteousness. All pursuit of other goals must be done within the bounds of dharma.
- Artha: Artha is wealth and glory, material possessions, and money. Artha is a legitimate aim but must be conducted within the ethical laws of dharma.
- Kama: Kama is worldly pleasure, aesthetic pleasure, and sexual pleasure. So long as one's pursuit of pleasure is bound by the ultimate bounds of dharma, kama is a fully legitimate goal.
- Moksha: Moksha is liberation. Moksha is the primary goal of human life and means to become liberated from the cycle of death and rebirth. Moksha is the final desire of human life because it can only be achieved once an individual realizes that the other three goals can never bring complete satisfaction.

These four goals, if attained, represent a satisfaction of all human needs. They correspond to the four stages of life: student life, household life, retirement, and renunciation or asceticism.

Caste System

The caste, or varna, system of Hinduism is dictated by the Law of Manu and has its origins in the original social divisions of the early Aryans. The strict division of society did not appear until the seventh century B.C., however. There are four social castes:

- Brahmanas: Brahmins, who were scholars and priests. Expected to live a religious life. "Twice born."
- Kshatriyas: Warriors. "Twice born."
- Vaishyas: Traders. "Twice born."
- Shudras: Manual workers. "Once born."
- Dalits: Social outcasts or untouchables. "The oppressed."

One's caste represents one's place in the universe and is dictated by karma. By living a virtuous life (i.e., by accepting the dharma of one's caste) one can gradually make one's way up through the system.

Every aspect of life is dictated by one's caste. There are different dietary and social rules for each caste. Greater contact with pollution and impurity means a lower social position. There is little social interaction between members of different castes, particularly within a traditional village setting, and the Dalits are considered "untouchable," literally doing the dirty work of society and coming into contact with sources of pollution (cleaning clothes or latrines, handling the dead, etc.). Various reformers, including Mahatma Gandhi, have agitated for the reform of the caste system and its treatment of the Dalits, and the 1948 Indian constitution officially forbids caste discrimination.

Shraddha Rites

Shraddha is a Sanskrit word meaning anything done in full sincere faith. The shraddha rites are rituals of remembrance of ancestral spirits. During the ritual, individuals offer food and often money to their ancestors as an act of both remembrance and thankfulness for their assistance. These offerings are thought to keep the ancestral spirits alive in the universe. Pinda, or rice balls, are the typical offering. They are offered to parents and those who have not died at home, and are performed on the anniversary of the death. They must be performed by male descendents; therefore, if one does not produce sons, one's spirit will cease to exist in the afterlife.

Great Five Daily Sacrifices

The five great daily sacrifices of Hinduism are designed to help humans increase their awareness of their relationships with the entire universe. They are:

- Brahma Yajna—sacrifice to Brahman. Hindus should study the scriptures and share their spiritual knowledge with others.
- Deva Yajna—sacrifice to the celestials. Hindus should offer sacrifices to the deities.
- Pitri Yajna—sacrifice to the manes. Hindus should make offerings to ancestors.
- Bhuta Yajna—sacrifice to the creatures. Hindus should feed animals.
- Manushya Yajna—sacrifice to men. Hindus should feed the poor and otherwise serve suffering people.

Bhakti Marga

Hindus are free to choose any path to enlightenment that speaks personally to them. One of the many paths is bhakti-marga, which means "the way of devotion" and describes the path in which practitioners choose to devote their worship energies to one or more individual deities. In return, the god in question may help the worshipper in life. All gods can be seen as manifestations of all the characteristics of Brahman. Bhakti yoga, or the discipline of bhakti, developed in the lower castes of Hindu society independently of the intellectual religious work of the Brahmin. Bhakti emerged relatively late in the development of Hinduism, partly in response to the personal relationship of Christians and Muslims to their religion. The Way of Devotion is more accessible to non-Brahmins, but is neither inferior nor superior to the Way of Works or the Way of Knowledge.

Brahma, Shiva, and Vishnu

Brahma, Shiva, and Vishnu are known as the Trimurti, or Triad, of Gods and represent the three functions of the one and only reality, the supreme god Brahman.

- Brahma: Brahma is the creator god, who created the world but is not mentioned in the Vedas. He is the least worshipped of the gods and maintains an aloofness from the world, having finished the work of creation.
- Shiva: Shiva is the destroyer god and, like Brahma, does not appear in the Vedas. He represents disease and death, and is commonly worshipped by ascetics. He is also the god of reproduction, however, and the destructive nature of his character is seen as not wholly negative, as destruction also clears the way for progress and a new life. He is male but has androgynous aspects.
- Vishnu: Vishnu is the preserver god and is loving and benevolent. He has appeared in nine different forms on earth (including as the Buddha). At the end of time, Vishnu will appear for the tenth and final time, rewarding the good and punishing the bad.

Mahadevi, Kali, Parvati, Durga, Saraswati, Ganesha, and Lakshmi

Hinduism contains only one reality, the impersonal god Brahman, but many incarnations of God known as devas (male) or devis (female), who themselves have aspects personified in other devas or devis. Though these gods have different names, they are merely personifications of aspects of the one supreme god, Brahman, according to Upanishadic Hinduism.

- Mahadevi is the supreme goddess of Hinduism and represents the feminine principle present in all things. She is the female equivalent of Brahman.
- Kali, Durga, and Parvati are variations of Mahadevi. Kali is the goddess of destruction and the consort of Shiva. Parvati is the opposite, a gentle maternal figure, a fertility goddess and an ascetic. Durga embodies feminine creative power and compassion.
- Saraswati is the consort of Brahma and the goddess of knowledge and music.
- Ganesha is the son of Shiva, depicted with an elephant's head. He is the god of obstacles and beginnings.
- Lakshmi is the consort of Vishnu and the goddess of wealth.

Astika and Nastika

Loosely speaking, astika means "theist" while nastika means "atheist," or "orthodox" and "heterodox," respectively. Hindu philosophical schools are differentiated according to whether they accept the divinely revealed nature of the Vedas. The astika schools are the six darshanas:

- Nyaya
- Vaisheshika
- Samkhya
- Yoga
- Vedanta
- Mimansa

These nastika schools are rejected by Hindu orthodoxy as being heretical:

- Buddhism—rejects the atman, or permanent personal soul
- Jainism—emphasizes nonviolence and immediate consequences for human behavior
- Charvaka—rejected the idea of an afterlife

All three of the nastika schools reject a creator God as well.

Three Ways of Salvation

According to the Code of Manu in orthodox Hinduism, there are three ways to achieve moksha:

- Karma Marga, the Way of Works. This way is the oldest of the three. It is marked by ritual rather than intellectual study or emotional connection, making it accessible to many. Making sacrifices and holding appropriate ceremonies at different stages of life can help an individual to accumulate the good karma necessary to transcend death or to move upward in caste.
- Jnana-Marga, the Way of Knowledge. All schools of Hindu thought maintain the premise that wrong action comes from ignorance rather than moral failure, and studying the Upanishads helps individuals to understand their ignorance and improve their chances of moksha.
- Bhakti Yoga, the Way of Devotion. By publicly and privately worshipping individual gods, a Hindu can curry favor with the gods.

Avatar

An avatar is a human incarnation of a Hindu god. According to convention, there are ten avatars of Vishnu, though there are countless others according to different sources. Vishnu has appeared as

Krishna, Rama, and the Buddha, and will return at the end of time to dispense justice and end time. The most popular avatars, who are worshipped in their own right, are Rama and Krishna. Rama is the ideal man in Hindu epics and is married to Sita, the ideal woman. The epic of their relationship, the Ramayana, is enormously influential in Hindu culture. Rama is worshipped as both an avatar of Vishnu and as a symbol of devotion. Krishna is a complex character. One epic characterizes him as a serious and resourceful war hero. The other describes him as both a mischievous child and an erotic hero.

DARSHAN

Darshan means system of philosophy. Hinduism offers many paths to enlightenment, and most people who choose the Way of Knowledge devote themselves to one of these six darshans. All of them aim to achieve moksha, and claim their origin in the Vedic scriptures. Variations of these six main systems exist as well. The six major systems are:

- Sankhya: Sankhya recognizes no personal gods and believes in dualism, the force of spirit and the force of matter, with nothing else in the universe.
- Yoga: Yoga is sankhya put into practice and focuses primarily on meditation.
- Mimansa: Mimansa involves close reading of the Vedas.
- Vaisheshika: Vaisheshika believes that there are nine eternal elements in the universe and that no gods are necessary.
- Nyaya: Nyaya focuses on logic and reason as means to achieving truth.
- Vedanta: Vedanta believes only in Brahman and bases its beliefs on the transcendent messages of the Upanishads.

WAY OF KNOWLEDGE

The Way of Knowledge dictates a set of four expected stages of life for the Brahmin men who choose this path to enlightenment:

1. The Student: From an early age, the student works with a teacher to study and understand the Vedas and his caste duties. He is expected to beg for food during this period. (Girls in this stage learn domestic duties from the senior women in their home.)
2. The Householder: Once studies are completed, the young man marries and starts a family, ideally producing a son. He is still obligated to make sacrifices to the deities and not to break any caste rules.
3. The Hermit: Once he is a grandfather, a man concentrates on renouncing earthly desires. (This stage no longer exists in the extreme form it once did, when men were expected to take to the forest for this period.)
4. The Sannyasin: In the last stage, a man is expected to wander homeless, renouncing all possessions and familial ties.

SANKHYA SYSTEM

The Sankhya darshan is atheistic. It is a dualistic philosophy, believing in a separation of spirit and matter. It is the oldest darshan. Both spirit and matter, according to Sankhya, are real. The world of nature is composed of 24 principles, including the mind, the intellect, and the ego; they resemble spirit but are in fact physical realities. Three gunas, or features, of the natural world are present in all people, in various degrees, which indicate their personalities. All souls are independent, rather than part of one reality. Through thoughts, humans can realize that souls have no need for their association with bodies and the physical world, thus allowing for their liberation from earthly reality.

Yoga System

Yoga is considered a practical application of Sankhya philosophy. It focuses on the attempt to join the spirit to Brahman. Its primary method is through meditation, which helps the individual to develop mentally and spiritually and eventually to transcend the body in order to join the spirit to the one reality. Unlike Sankhya, Yoga allows a place in the universe for the deity Ishvara, a pure spirit accessible to yoga practitioners. Breath control, physical postures, and psychological methods all allow the yoga practitioner to disengage the soul from the body and cleave to the one reality. It is the mind itself that suppresses its consciousness, allowing for a thoughtless and sensationless state of freedom.

The eight stages of yoga are:

1. Yama: taking the vows of restraint—against harming living creatures, against unchastity, against deceit, against stealing, and against materialism
2. Niyama: learning self-discipline in order to achieve self-control and an inner sense of calm
3. Asana: learning the physical postures of yoga
4. Pranayama: learning to control one's breath, in order to reduce the physical processes to two—the in and out of the breath
5. Pratayama: learning to control one's senses, or shutting out the outside world
6. Dharana: concentration on one idea or object to the exclusion of all else
7. Dhyana: meditation
8. Samadhi: achieving a stance of trance in which the individual loses all awareness of self and becomes one with Brahman

Vaisheshika and Nyaya Systems

The Vaisheshika and Nyaya systems are often paired philosophically. The Vaisheshika system is very different from the other darshans, in that it teaches that there are nine distinct elements composing the universe: earth, water, air, fire, soul, mind, ether (nothingness), time, and space. It is an atheistic system: except for these nine elements, nothing else in the universe exists. Modern Vaisheshika accepts the existence of a Supreme Being. The Nyaya school was founded by Gautama, the "Aristotle of India." Nyaya privileges reason and logic above other modes of knowledge, and believes that individuals can achieve true knowledge through reasoned and logical analysis.

Mimansa and Vedanta Systems

Purva Mimansa, the full name for the Mimansa system, means "early examination," and involves a close reading of the Vedas in a search for full understanding of the Vedas' laws. Originally an atheistic system, modern Mimansa accepts the existence of gods. It focuses on ritual. Vedanta believes that the cause of human suffering is humans' persistent illusion that the world of materials is real. Knowledge of their ignorance can free them from it and allow them to achieve moksha, or enlightenment. Vedanta is the basis for much of modern Hindu ritual. Vedanta has within it three varieties:

1. Advaita (monism): Advaita argues that the world consists of Brahman, the one and only reality.
2. Vishisht-advaita (qualified monism): Vishisht-advaita argues that the human and divine souls are separate but united.
3. Dvaita (dualism): Dvaita argues that both souls and the physical world are real and that humans can be saved by the presence of Vayu, the wind god and the son of Vishnu.

Hindu Festivals and Holy Days

Hindu holy days can involve either feasts or practicing fasting, feeding the poor or giving charity, visiting temples, acting out sacred stories, processions of holy figures, and decorating streets and temples with flowers and fruit. Holi is a festival celebrated at the beginning of spring each year. It is a fertility celebration and a celebration of Krishna. Like many other spring festivals in other religions, Holi lays aside many of the caste duties and rules for the duration of the holiday. Divali is the Hindu new year and the festival of lights. Pilgrimages to the holy sites of Kali and Lakshmi are common in order to ensure good fortune the following year. Dussehra is a celebration of the god Rama's victory over the evil demon-king of Lanka. Particularly in eastern India, Dussehra may be observed as a part of the larger holiday of Durga Puja in which the goddess Durga defeated the Buffalo demon. Dances and processions are held, along with gift-giving.

Tantric Shaktism

Shakti, or cosmic energy, is personified in Hinduism in the goddesses Kali and Durga. Some bhakti marga sects are devoted to the goal of moksha through specific practices to harness the power of shakti. There are two types of this Tantric Shaktism:

- Right-hand Shaktism: This form focuses on the benevolent and creative energy of nature in the form of the mother goddess.
- Left-hand Shaktism: This form is full of magical rites, often secret ones, where the hedonistic side of creative energy is indulged in through dancing, drinking alcohol, sexual rites, and even blood drinking. This embrace of what is forbidden aims to increase the participant's self-control to the point where these pleasurable acts hold no appeal, thus enabling the participant to identify fully with nonphysical reality.

Practice of Worship in Hindu Daily Life

In Hinduism, symbols and manifestations of the divine are everywhere, and all representations of Brahman can be worshipped at any time. There are countless deities, arguably millions, and any shrine can be visited regardless of whether a particular family has chosen a patron deity for their home. Different deities can be invoked before any task that they have special power over. For instance, if obstacles are preventing a task from being accomplished, a visit to a shrine to Ganesha, the remover of obstacles, is in order. Homes often have shrines to a particular deity the family is devoted to, and individual acts of devotion can take place here or at a public temple. In addition, priests can conduct rites at either a family or a public temple. Community worship takes place at a temple in ceremonies led by a priest.

Pilgrimage

There are two types of sacred places in Hinduism: inherently holy places (rivers and hills) where temples were built to honor the site's holiness, and places made holy by the temples placed there. Many places are holy because they are mentioned in Hindu literature, and it is a great pilgrimage to travel to them. Pilgrimage gives expression to a Hindu's faith and allows them to celebrate in company. They may also travel to the sites of holy leaders. On pilgrimage, Hindus may offer charity at temples, listen to talks, perform specific rites, circumambulate holy places, or do spiritual penance. The seven holy rivers are associated with particular goddesses. The Ganges is the holiest. There, pilgrims can be purified and have their sins removed in its waters. Four cities are the sites where the elixir of immortality is said to have overspilled its pitcher, and large public festivals are held in each city every four years.

Classes of People Considered Holy

People of the Brahmin caste are considered holy by virtue of their righteous birth. While a badly behaving Brahmin may be despised individually, his status is still respected, and non-Brahmins continue to aspire to it in the next life. Gurus are appointed to provide Hindus with religious instruction. They may be employed in an individual household or serve in a community generally. They have the authority to provide children with the ceremonial cord that marks their transition to adulthood. Yogins in pursuit of enlightenment through yoga are holy. Sannyasins, the elderly beggars in the fourth stage of life, are so holy that the dust displaced by their footprints is holy to those who touch it.

Cows

Cows are venerated throughout Hinduism and are a special taboo, according to the Vedas. They are celebrated at festivals, represent a good omen for the dying, and wander freely through the streets. Cows are a symbol of motherhood, of purity, and of ahimsa, or nonviolence. They are not eaten, but their products (dairy and excrement) are used daily. In the Vedic age, cows were consumed, but the influence of Buddhism and Jainism later on led Hindus to adopt a cow taboo. Cows are symbolic of all animals to Hindus, and remind Hindus of their obligations of nonviolence and respect for nature. Cows have also come to be a maternal symbol due to the abundance they provide.

Dharma

Dharma means "duty" but also suggests the integral nature of something. For instance, the dharma of fire is to be hot. Dharma is divided into three main types:

- Sanatana Dharma: another name for Hinduism, Sanatana Dharma means "the eternal law," and is a universal guideline for the proper relationship of humans to the universe. The dharma of atman, or individual conscious beings, is to perform service. Hinduism is a religion very tolerant of other paths to god, and Sanatana Dharma applies to Hindus and non-Hindus alike when they are pursuing service to god.
- Varnashrama Dharma: the duties specific to the particular circumstances of an individual's life. Members of different castes and different stages of life have different varnashrama dharma, though Sanatana Dharma applies universally.
- Sadharana Dharma: Sadharana are specific moral duties, according to the Law of Manu:
    - Dhairya (steadfastness), Kshama (forgiveness), Dama (self-restraint), Chauryabhava (nonstealing), Shaucha (cleanliness), Indriyanigraha (sense control), Dhi (high-mindedness), Vidya (learning), Satya (truth), Akrodha (absence of anger)

Rituals of Hindu Life

The currently performed sanskaras, or rituals, of Hindu life are as follows:

- Garbhadharana: A ritual to ensure conception
- Jatakarma: This ceremony is performed to ensure a safe birth.
- Namakarana: A naming ceremony is performed eleven days after birth after consultation with an astrologer.
- Annaprasana: The feeding of the first solid food
- Karnavedha: Both boys and girls have their ears pierced on their first birthday.
- Vidhyarambha: Children ritually write the first letter of the alphabet in a tray of rice to mark their initiation into formal learning.
- Choodakarana: Shaving a child's hair represents a symbolic separation from the mother.
- Kesanta Kala: The first shaving of a boy's facial hair.

- Ritu Kala: A girls' first menses.
- Upanayanam: A sacred thread is ceremonially presented to a young man when he begins to study the Vedas.
- Samavartana: This ceremony marks the end of student life and a young man's choice to pursue either family or monastic life.
- Nischitartha or Vagdana: A formal betrothal ceremony
- Vivaha: Marriage
- Anthyesthi: Funeral rites, including cremation and remembrance

Major Denominations

Although there are sects devoted to the worship of many Hindu gods, the four major denominations, practiced by the majority of Hindus, are:

- Vaishnavism: Vaishnavites believe that only Krishna or Vishnu can bestow moksha on a believer.
- Shaivism: Shaivites believe that only Shiva can bestow moksha on a believer.
- Shaktism: Shaktas believe that Devi, the goddess, is the supreme Brahman, the creator of the world and the energy that governs the world. They worship shakti, or power, and believe that all other gods are simply her manifestations.
- Smartism: Smarta Hindus believe in the "essential oneness" of six different deities and are free to worship any of them.

Monotheism, Polytheism, or Pantheism

It is not easy to say whether Hinduism fits into the category of monotheism, polytheism, or pantheism. It contains elements of all three. Ultimately, Hinduism believes in one reality: Brahman. All is Brahman and nothing is apart from Brahman. Hindu gods are considered a symbol or manifestation of Brahman on earth, rather than deities unto themselves; however, in practice, Krishna and Vishnu are worshipped nearly in their own right. Calling Hinduism a monotheistic religion, however, is problematic. Most monotheistic religions are dualistic, in the sense that the physical world and God are very much separate. Hinduism teaches that all is Brahman, and that there is no differentiation between the two—indeed, that there is no "two" to be differentiated. In that sense, pantheism is a better description of Hinduism, but clearly there are elements of both monotheism and polytheism as well. Even among Hindus there are differing worldviews that fit more neatly into one category than another.

Hindu Symbols

Aum—The most sacred sound in Hinduism. Composed of three distinct but connected sounds, this triad is symbolic of many triads, including earth, atmosphere, and heaven, and the three most sacred Vedic scriptures.

Shiva linga and yoni—Stylized, abstract sculptures of the male and female sex organs, representing creative energy. These objects are the focus of worship in Shivaite homes and temples.

Tilaka—Marks on the foreheads of Hindus, made from sandalwood paste or other materials, designating the third eye, which is the focus of Hindu meditation. Tilaka vary in design by sect and region.

Swastika—A cross with its arms bent at right angles. Represents the two forms of the god Brahma, and, facing all four directions simultaneously, represents groundedness and stability. Used as a good luck symbol as well.

Lotus—A flower that represents transcendence. It is beautiful but grows in mud; it rests on water without contact.

GURU

In Hinduism, figures known as gurus are powerful teachers of religion. They are spiritual guides for others and are considered to have great spiritual insights to share with their pupils. It is a common belief that without the guidance of a guru, an individual cannot achieve enlightenment. After finding a guru, a student treats them with service, with humility, and with sincere inquiries; the attitude is one of near-worship. (To touch the foot of a guru is a sign of great respect.) The guru is believed to awaken pre-existing spiritual knowledge within the student and allow him to access it. The ultimate goal is for the student to learn all of the guru's accumulated knowledge and become as wise as the guru. There are four main types of gurus:

- A spiritual advisor who performs rituals for high-caste individuals
- An enlightened master who has achieved wisdom through experience
- An avatar, or incarnation of God
- A book that guides the disciple as a living guru might

Buddhism

Siddhartha Gautama

Siddhartha Gautama was a member of the Kshatriya class, from the wealthy Gautama family in ca. 500 B.C. He lived a sheltered and happy life until his thirtieth year, when he became increasingly aware of the ugliness in the world, and became aware of the constant presence of suffering and pain in human life. Leaving on a quest for answers, he tried studying with a guru, then living an ascetic life. Realizing that neither life brought him true happiness, he finally meditated until he achieved enlightenment. He began to preach that nirvana is found not in the life of indulgence nor in one of ascetism, but in the "middle way" that avoids extremes. He spent the rest of his life preaching this message and attracting followers.

Four Passing Sights of the Buddha

Kept in luxurious seclusion by his father in the hopes that he would (as foretold by a soothsayer) become "a universal monarch" of all India, Siddhartha Gautama was not allowed to see ugliness or decay in his youth. As a young man, riding in his chariot, Siddhartha saw four sights, gods in human form, that led him to understand that life is full of suffering:

- An old man, leading Gautama to realize that all people age.
- A diseased man, leading him to realize that physical illness and misery is always with people.
- A dead man, leading him to the realization that every person dies.
- An ascetic, calm and peaceful, leading him to realize that freedom from the three aforementioned horrors can be attained.

Renunciation, Six Year Quest, and Great Enlightenment

After the Four Passing Sights, Siddhartha Gautama renounced his comfortable life and family and embarked on a homeless quest for enlightenment. He quested for six years, studying first with two ascetic yoga teachers. Then he began a five-year period of asceticism by himself, disciplining his mind through discomfort, pain, and starvation. He failed to find enlightenment. One day, Gautama fainted, then lay in a shallow stream, realized that self-mortification was not the correct path, and renounced it. At the foot of a fig tree, later called the bodhi tree, he meditated, realizing that desire was the cause of his suffering, and by eliminating desire he could achieve enlightenment. He remained unmoved through a series of natural, sensual, and evil provocations, and escaped from the burden of desire. From this point on he was known as the Buddha (the Enlightened One).

Philosophy of Early Buddhism and Reform the Vedic Approach

The Buddha rejected the notion of a creator god. The goal of life is still to achieve moksha, but one's ability to achieve it depends totally on one's own efforts. Women and people of any caste were equally capable of achieving enlightenment. Atman, or selfhood, has no place in Buddhism; the illusion of a self causes ignorance, which in turn causes all suffering. He adopted the Hindu practice of yogic meditation but made a fundamental change: unlike in Hinduism, where the goal is to achieve oneness with the universe, in Buddhism, there is no higher object. The goal is instead to practice mindfulness at all times. The Buddha rejected the Vedas and the various darshans dealing with the Upanishads. He rejected all animal sacrifices as violent and unnecessary, emphasizing instead the idea of internal sacrifice. The Buddha rejected the caste system; he also sought followers, whereas Hinduism has no interest in conversion.

First and Second Buddhist Councils

Not long after the Buddha's death, his followers began to debate the meaning of his teachings. The first Buddhist Council was called within a year of his death and failed to unite Buddhist followers in a single doctrine. Fifty years later, a second Council was called. By this time, differing opinions on Buddhist teachings had resulted in sixteen separate Buddhist factions. At the second Council, a unified group of conservatives decreed their interpretation to be correct and the others heretical. Their faction came to be known as Hinayana Buddhism, and the larger, more liberal faction as Mahayana.

Spread of Buddhism

Unlike Hindus, Buddhists actively recruited converts, traveling into the world to spread their message. When the Indian emperor Asoka converted to Buddhism in the third century B.C., his influence led to a rapid growth of Buddhism. Asoka sent missionaries around Asia: to Ceylon, Burma, Thailand, and possibly the Middle East. The strands of Buddhism that settled in these places were gradually influenced by local religions. Because the spread began before the Second Buddhist Council, it was the Theravada school whose influence was felt in other parts of Asia. Beginning in the second century B.C., Buddhism began to spread east to China, then to Korea and Japan. It spread into Tibet beginning in the eighth century A.D.

Development and Decline of Buddhism in China

Buddhism reached China in the first century A.D., through Chinese trading routes with Central Asia. With Emperor Ming's blessing, Buddhist monks were allowed to establish a monastery. Early Buddhism in China relied on concepts already present in Taoism. By the fifth and sixth centuries, the Pure Land and Ch'an schools of Chinese Buddhism began to emerge. The T'ang Dynasty in the sixth century was considered the golden age of Chinese Buddhism. Under later emperors, however, persecution of Chinese Buddhists took place, and by the ninth century A.D., the emperor Wu-tsung forbade all Buddhist establishments. The decline of Chinese Buddhism began, and the Buddhism that remained was consolidated under the Ch'an and Pure Land schools. During the Cultural Revolution of the 1960s, Buddhist establishments were sacked, though in recent decades the policy has somewhat liberalized.

Spread of Buddhism to Japan and Zen Buddhism

Buddhism spread to Japan from India, via Korea, in the sixth century A.D. Buddhism was officially supported by the state, under the protection of Prince Shotoku. Buddhism and Shinto existed side by side, with Shinto gradually taking a more daily, domestic role, and Buddhism being the religion of serious occasions (for instance, funerals). During the ninth century, Chinese schools of Buddhism arrived in Japan. By the twelfth century, under the Samurai rulers, distinctly Japanese forms began to emerge: Jodo Shinshu, Nichiren, and Zen. Zen Buddhism, a Japanese offshoot of Chinese Ch'an Buddhism, focused on the discipline of the mind and body. It stressed that an individual could rely only on his or her own inner self and that anyone had the potential to become a Buddha. Zen Buddhism greatly influenced Japanese popular culture, from dance forms to painting styles to Noh theatre.

Tibetan Buddhism

Buddhism gained a foothold in Tibet during the eighth century A.D., when the king who unified the country took Buddhist wives. Due to its relatively late arrival, Buddhism developed unique characteristics in Tibet, though it is technically a subset of Mahayana Buddhism. In addition, it took some qualities from the native Tibetan religion of Bon. Buddhism was not initially successful in Tibet but was reintroduced by two scholars from India who encouraged the building of monasteries, where Tibetan scholarship flourished. There are four schools of Tibetan Buddhism: Nyingma, Kagyu, Sakya, and Gelug. Nyingma is the oldest, though over the centuries Gelug has come to dominate. Under Chinese occupation beginning in 1949, Tibetan Buddhism has been very tightly controlled by the state, and the current Dalai Lama has been exiled.

Hinayana and Mahayana Sects

After the Buddha's death, Buddhists began to debate the theological meaning of his teachings. Two Buddhist Councils were held to settle doctrinal differences, but shortly after the Second Council, around 100 A.D., the religion divided into two camps, which in subsequent centuries have subdivided further. The first sect, known as Hinayana, was known as the exclusive way, but within it were many schools (of which Theravada Buddhism remains today). The second, Mahayana, was a larger sect and more liberal. Hinayana Buddhism advocated a monastic life as the superior way. Only monks, through devotion, could be released from the cycle of death and reincarnation. Women could not be monks. All efforts toward enlightenment are entirely within the control of the individual, not any gods or divine forces. The Buddha, therefore, was simply a man. Mahayana Buddhism believed that the Buddha was a divine figure, that anyone could become a Buddha, and that Buddhas could be appealed to for help on the path to enlightenment.

Decline of Buddhism in India

After the death of the Buddha, Buddhism spread throughout Southeast Asia, and became the largest religion in India for centuries. By the end of the nineteenth century, however, it had nearly disappeared in India. There are several reasons for this. Firstly, the Brahmin caste, which controlled the flow of money to Buddhist monasteries, gradually took on more and more power within India. In subsequent centuries, the White Huns invaded India from the west, bringing their own religions with them, and the consolidation of the (Muslim) Mughal Empire in the twelfth century contributed further to Buddhism's decline. At the same time, Hinduism, influenced by Buddhism, became more accessible to average Indians, and its appeal grew as a consequence. Hinduism was more appealing to others than Buddhism because Hindu ceremonies were available to the average person, unlike in Buddhism, where practitioners were expected to support the monasteries that remained largely isolated from the community. In some parts of rural India, Buddhism survived in a syncretic version heavily influenced by Hinduism.

Changes During Twentieth and Twenty-First Centuries

Buddhism spread widely across Asia after the death of the Buddha, but once it had done so, its membership numbers remained stagnant for many centuries. In the twentieth century, however, its popularity surged again. What began as a campaign to restore destroyed Buddhist temples in India led to a growth in popularity there. Across Asia more generally, the collapse of colonialism and the advent of the nuclear age led to a revival of Asian nationalism and interest in the nonviolent teachings of Buddhism. Western study of Buddhism led to its increased presence in Europe and North America, especially through Zen, and many members of the Dalit caste in India also found refuge in the supposed non-caste-based structure of Buddhism. In addition, the exile of the Dalai Lama from Tibet led to additional worldwide awareness of Buddhism.

Schools of Buddhism

The two main schools of Buddhism are:

1. Theravada—Conservative school, broke away from the Mahayana school around the time of the Second Buddhist Council. Monastic life is central; monks are closer to enlightenment than laypeople are. The Buddha was an enlightened human. The individual is responsible for his own enlightenment. Theravada Buddhism is prevalent in Southeast Asia.

2. Mahayana—Oldest school. Buddha is a divine figure. Mahayana Buddhism is prevalent in lands influenced by China. Mahayana Buddhism has several subschools, including:
   a. Tantric or Vajrayana—Emphasizes ritual. All practice is undertaken with the explicit goal of achieving Buddhahood. A distinctive form has developed in Tibet. Learning is passed directly from teacher to student, giving Tantric Buddhism an air of secrecy.
   b. Shingon—A form of Mahayana in Japan that emphasizes the possibility of enlightenment in this lifetime through body and mind training.
   c. Pure Land—Emphasizes worship of the Buddha, who reigns over the afterlife paradise.
   d. Ch'an/Zen—Emphasizes the importance of personal, nonrational insights to achieve enlightenment.
   e. Yogacara—Emphasizes the use of yoga to empty the mind of conscious thought. It is influential on many of the other Mahayana schools, especially Zen.

THERAVADA BUDDHISM

Theravada is the more conservative branch of Buddhism. All Buddhas are merely enlightened humans. Therefore, anyone can become a Buddha. The goal of Buddhist practice is to liberate oneself. Deities are of no use to the individual seeking liberation, and ritual is not emphasized in Theravada tradition, as the path to enlightenment is entirely self-directed. Even the Buddha himself is of no use to Buddhists in their quest, as he has achieved nirvana and therefore cannot intervene in human affairs. Theravada emphasizes the importance of a solitary monastic life, and monks are closer to enlightenment than laypeople are. Theravada tradition does not subscribe to a belief in Bardo, the in-between state after death. Its influences are Indian (pre-Vedic and Hindu), which can be seen in the Theravada concepts of karma and sangha (the monastic community).

MAHAYANA BUDDHISM

Mahayana Buddhism is the more liberal of the two main branches of Buddhism, and it contains several subschools of thought. Mahayana emphasizes the importance of helping other beings to attain enlightenment, in addition to achieving enlightenment oneself. It also accepts the existence of several bodhisattvas in addition to Maitreya. These enlightened beings help others to achieve liberation themselves and can be appealed to for help.

Sunyata, or emptiness, the indivisible nature of reality, is a central tenet of Mahayana. Sunyata is a rejection of dualism, emphasizing the interconnectedness of all things instead. Language is therefore inadequate in spiritual matters. Mahayana subscribes to the concept of trikaya, or the three bodies of Buddha (physical, celestial, and "truth body," or the body of enlightenment). It emphasizes ritual more than does Theravada. Mahayana's understanding of death includes the concept of Bardo. Its foreign influences are northern: Taoism and Confucianism, as well as Shinto in Japan. Mahayana emphasizes the Buddha nature of all beings and the divine nature of Buddha, though Buddha is not a god: Buddha is the essence of all things, and anyone can become a Buddha.

TANTRIC OR VAJRAYANA BUDDHISM

The most distinctive characteristic of Vajrayana, or Tantric, Buddhism is deity yoga, a form of yoga in which the practitioner meditates on the unity of himself and the meditating Buddha. Tantric practice centers on the Four Purities:

- Purity of body. The practitioner conceives of his body as the body of the deity being meditated upon.
- Purity of environment. The practitioner visualizes his surroundings as the Pure Land (the celestial dwelling place of a Buddha).

- Purity of resources. The practitioner perceives his feelings of pleasure as not relating to worldly attachments.
- Purity of action. The practitioner performs all actions for the sole benefit of others.

Practitioners of Tantric Buddhism study with a guru, abiding by tantric vows.

Pure Land Buddhism

Pure Land Buddhism, known alternately in Japan as Jodo and in China as Chin-t'u, focuses on the celestial realm known as the Pure Land—a heavenly paradise presided over by the Buddha Amitabha, who vowed to save all sentient beings. Pure Land followers ascribe great significance to the mere uttering of Amitabha's name, with some believing that that act alone may grant the speaker entrance to the Pure Land. Monks do not live a separate life from that of the average Pure Land Buddhist and may marry and have families. The emphasis in Pure Land Buddhism on enlightenment through grace leads to a rejection of individual efforts toward enlightenment, which are seen as insulting to Amitabha, representing as they do a lack of faith in his power. Pure Land Buddhist practice bears many similarities to Christianity: the focus on a heavenly afterlife as the eternal reward for the virtuous, the gathering of worshipper in congregations, and the rituals of prayers, religious instruction for children, and sermons.

Zen or Ch'an Buddhism

Zen Buddhism (as it is known in Japan) and Ch'an Buddhism (its equivalent in China) are known as the "intuitive sects" of Buddhism. Zen was founded in the fifth century A.D. in India by the monk Bodhidharma and spread through China, Korea, and Japan. Zen practitioners believe that study of religious traditions and scriptures is not the source of enlightenment—that enlightenment comes from direct personal experience and sudden insights (satori, or epiphanies, into the nature of reality), as the Buddha had under the Bodhi tree. Meditation is key for Zen practitioners. Only direct experience can lead individuals to enlightenment, and meditation clears the mind of rational thought in order to achieve the "truth beyond reason." One famous aspect of Zen practice is the use of riddles known as koans, designed to help clear the mind of distractions. In Japan, the focus on simplicity in Zen has influenced everything from tea ceremonies to architecture.

Nichiren Buddhism

Nichiren Buddhism is a Japanese sect founded in the thirteenth century A.D. by followers of the monk Nichiren. Nichiren Buddhism is a sect of Mahayana Buddhism and an offshoot of Tendai Buddhism. Nichiren taught that all texts besides the Lotus Sutra were unnecessary and dangerously misleading to Buddhists, and that devotion to the Lotus Sutra could earn enlightenment for a devotee. Nichiren Buddhism has always been a small and persecuted religion, due to its being actively hostile to other sects, such as Zen and Pure Land. It is strongly patriotic and recruits converts—a rarity among Buddhist sects. Through its Soka Gakkai form, it is now popular in Japan.

Shingon Buddhism

Shingon Buddhism was imported to Japan from China, where it was known as Chen Yen. Its origins are in Tibetan Tantrism, where it relied heavily on mysticism. Practitioners appealed to past Buddhas as savior figures for help in this world, both on the quest to enlightenment and in mundane goals. Upon import to Japan, its mysticism was toned down and it assumed a more rational outlook, incorporating many features from Tendai. It believes in the possibility of an individual's enlightenment within the present lifetime, and incorporates meditation, study, and mantras (sacred words) to help the practitioner on his or her quest.

Tibetan Buddhism

Because of its relatively late development and the influence of Bon, the native Tibetan religion, Tibetan Buddhism has unique features. Among them is the person known as the tulku, or the reincarnated religious leader. The Dalai Lama is the head of Tibetan Buddhism. A large percentage of Tibetans have historically become monks, or lamas, and they have held great political power as a group. Tibetan Buddhists emphasize magic in their practice. They rely on the practices of tantra—ritual meditation and chanting in order to identify fully with an archetypal deity. There are two major groups of Tibetan Buddhists:

- The Gelugpa, or Yellow Hat school: the larger and more conservative of the two. This school is led by the Dalai Lama, as is the nation of Tibet. The Dalai Lama is a reincarnated position; a young boy is identified several years after the previous leader's death as his reincarnated successor.
- The Kagyupa, or Red Hat school: the smaller sect, and one that places more emphasis on tantric practice rather than scholarship and traditional monasticism.

Tendai Buddhism

Tendai, or T'ien-t'ai, Buddhism, was founded in the sixth century A.D. in China by the monk Chih-I, and later spread to Japan. Tendai Buddhism does not disregard the importance of meditation, but emphasizes the importance of reading and studying Buddhist texts in order for the practitioner to understand Buddhist teachings for himself. Tendai evolved as a reaction against the anti-intellectualism of the esoteric Buddhist schools (Zen and Chan, for example). Chih-I evolved an inclusive doctrine that respected the many points of view of Buddhist philosophy, arguing that the Buddha had adapted his message to best reach his various listeners. The Tendai school is most strongly attached to the Lotus Sutra, the teachings of the Buddha that reveal him to be a manifestation of an eternal cosmic principle, present everywhere and in all things. Tendai Buddhists interpret this Sutra to mean that all beings can become Buddhas because of their inherent Buddha-nature.

Yogacara Buddhism

Yogacara Buddhism is a Buddhist sect originating in India, evolving from the questions posed by the Madhyamika school. Yogacara Buddhists practice meditation as a means of destroying impure dharmas and releasing their minds from the bondage of rational thought. Nothing exists outside consciousness in this school, and everything that passes through consciousness (which is to say everything) is only an idea. Therefore, the universe is mind only. One famous Yogacara tenet is the eight layers of consciousness:

- The five consciousnesses of sense
- Ideation consciousness (the consciousness of distinctions between things)
- Manas consciousness (that consciousness which apprehends the impermanence of all things)
- Store or seed consciousness (the basis for all the other seven consciousnesses and the store of karma)

The store consciousness contains impressions of the world shared by all people. It is the store consciousness that is ultimately responsible for the individual's fate. One by one, the consciousnesses of an enlightened individual fall away, until the store consciousness contains only pure "seeds" and no polluted ones, and the Buddhas are liberated into nothingness.

Nagarjuna and the Madhyamika School

In the early centuries A.D., the scholar Nagarjuna took an intermediate view to the three Theravadin schools of thought. Nagarjuna argued that no object exists at all, that they are no more than the illusions of unenlightened minds. While perceptions may be real, the objects perceived by the mind are false. In fact, Nagarjuna argues, all knowledge and opinions created by human minds, including his own writings, are themselves illusory, as human minds themselves are clouded by the everyday, relative, world. Nagarjuna concludes that all that is actually real must be nonmaterial. He then points out two paradoxes:

- If all things that appear to humans, including the Buddha, are illusory, then entrance to nirvana is entrance to a void, where nothing exists, including nirvana.
- If both nirvana and samsara (the world order) are apprehended by humans, they are both equally subjective, and neither one can be desired by humans. Therefore, the best course of action is not to desire anything, and nirvana will be reached.

Early Theravadin Schools of Thought

The three main early Theravadin schools of thought are:

- Sthaviravadins—The sthaviravadins were early followers of the Buddha. They believed that as the human self was a skandha, or constantly changing state of being, as were all things. All objects are in constant flux, composed of elements called dharmas. As all objects are impermanent, one should strive to avoid being attached to them.
- Sammatiya—The sammatiya school believed as the sthaviravadins did, with the exception of living things. According to this school, in every living thing there is a semi-permanent conscious person who moves from body to body through transmigration until nirvana.
- Sarvastivadins—The sarvastivadins believed, in contrast to the other two schools, that everything exists simultaneously, including things from the past and future, aggregating temporarily to form consciousness.

"Middle Way" of Buddhism

According to the Pali canon of Theravada Buddhism (a canon of literature named for its original language), the "middle way" was the path advocated by the Buddha in his sermon in the Deer Park. He rejected the notion of giving one's life over to sensual pleasures, gluttony, and sloth. On the other hand, he said, devoting oneself to a life of painful asceticism profited the individual nothing. Instead, the correct path is between the two extremes. More specifically, this middle path is the Eightfold Path. By following the middle path, a Buddhist avoids the extremes that would drive him away from his search for enlightenment, retaining a calm and peaceful stance, receptive to insights.

Eightfold Path

The Eightfold Path is the path followed by Buddhists in their quest for enlightenment. By cultivating an acute awareness of their actions and thoughts, Buddhists can develop wisdom. The eight aspects of this path are:

1. Right view: a correct vision of the nature of reality and the path before one
2. Right attitude: acting from a standpoint of love and compassion toward others
3. Right speech: speaking truthfully, compassionately, and clearly
4. Right action: living the five precepts (not killing, not stealing, not committing sexual misconduct, not lying, and not becoming intoxicated), refraining from exploiting oneself or others
5. Right livelihood: performing work honestly and with integrity

6. Right energy: consciousness of performing actions with compassion and creative energy
7. Right mindfulness: self-awareness, respect for others
8. Right concentration: enlightenment

The word "samma" is often translated to English as "right" but really means something more like "complete" or "whole." These eight qualities are not narrowly moralistic, but general qualities that guide the Buddhist on the path to spiritual development.

Four Noble Truths

The Four Noble Truths are the foundation of Buddhist teaching and outline the path to liberation. They are:

- Life is suffering (dukkha).
- Suffering is caused by desire.
- Suffering can be overcome. Happiness is possible.
- The Eightfold Path is the way to overcome suffering.

The first truth acknowledges that life is full of misery, illness, and finally death. "Dukkha" means a variety of things—frustration, disappointment, sadness—anything resulting from the reality of impermanence. The second truth states that the cause of this suffering is desire, because a lifetime of desire results in an individual whose desire to be born again cannot be overcome. Desire creates suffering because all is illusion; there is nothing really to desire and no one to do the desiring. The third states that suffering can be overcome. Understanding the limitations of desire leads the individual to abandon it, thus laying the path for enlightenment. The fourth is that the Eightfold Path is the way. The path is a process by which one's true nature can be realized, eliminating the obscuring desires that usually prevent seeing it.

Three Refuges of Buddhism

The Three Refuges, also known as the Three Jewels, of Buddhism, are central tenets of Buddhism. They are the three binding principles that guide a Buddhist's spiritual development. Often, a Buddhist commits himself to the Three Refuges in a formal ceremony, whether he is a layperson or a monk. The Three Refuges are:

- The Buddha. A Buddhist commits to follow only one teacher, the Buddha. In Mahayana Buddhism this may mean taking refuge in the Buddha-nature itself by committing oneself to enlightenment.
- The Dharma, which refers to both the Buddha's teachings and to the law of karma. To take refuge in the Dharma is to commit to living fully in the moment and trusting one's practice of Buddhism.
- The Sangha, or monastic community. In a larger sense the Sangha is also all Buddhists in the world, so committing oneself to the Sangha means embracing the Buddhist community at large.

Five Precepts of Buddhism

The five precepts of Buddhism are the principles for moral conduct. They are:

- To avoid the killing of living beings, human and otherwise (in the Mahayana tradition this includes vegetarianism)
- To avoid taking things not given
- To avoid sensual misconduct (both sexual misconduct and overindulgence generally)

- To refrain from false speech (not simply lying, but also avoiding speech that hurts others)
- To abstain from intoxicants (the principle being that indulging in them may encourage the breaking of the other precepts)

The aim of these precepts is not to avoid feelings of guilt, but to maintain a clear mind. These precepts apply to all lay Buddhists. In addition, three more precepts which are normally applicable only to monks can apply to all Buddhists in the Theravada tradition:

- To abstain from inappropriate foods (i.e. fasting)
- To abstain from entertainment and adornment
- To abstain from luxurious beds

ROLE OF THE BUDDHA(S)

The historical Buddha, Siddhartha Gautama, is an example of an enlightened human soul. He is not a creator God. The Buddha himself taught that individuals must not take his word on faith, but must test his teachings for themselves. Theravada Buddhism believes that the Buddha was merely a human who became enlightened, but have developed a religious practice that looks very much like worship. There is an unlimited number of potential Buddhas, since Buddha status is obtained through one's own efforts. Mahayana Buddhism believes that the Buddha was a manifestation of a divine essence and was destined to become a Buddha before he was born. In this way, he is more than simply human. In addition, Buddhas can aid humans in their quest for enlightenment.

KARMA, WISDOM, AND COMPASSION

Karma is the Buddhist law stating that all actions have effects. The Eightfold Path suggests that individuals pursue good karma by assessing whether their actions have positive effects on others and on oneself and what the intention is behind the action. The middle path results in wisdom. Knowledge must be accompanied by kindness, and patience and flexibility must accompany one's quest for wisdom. Without compassion, there can be no true wisdom. Bodhisattva vows are undertaken to ensure that enlightenment is not for oneself alone, but for all sentient beings.

BODHISATTVA

A bodhisattva is one who has committed to becoming a Buddha. The Theravada and Mahayana schools view the nature of a bodhisattva differently. In Theravada Buddhism, there are only two bodhisattvas: Siddhartha Gautama before his enlightenment, and Maitreya, the next bodhisattva, who will only appear when all the Buddhist teachings have been lost in an age unfathomably far in the future. In Mahayana Buddhism, bodhisattvas have the merit to enter Nirvana but refuse out of their desire to help other sentient beings. Instead they sit in the heavens aiding humans in need, sometimes appearing on earth in angel form. The goal of Mahayana Buddhism is to become a bodhisattva oneself. The four bodhisattva vows are:

- To rescue living beings from suffering
- To end the afflictions of living beings
- To "learn the measureless Dharma-doors"
- To realize the path of the Buddha

Death and Afterlife

Buddhists believe in a cycle of death and rebirth, but it is not the same as the Hindu belief in reincarnation. The Buddhist universe is divided into ten realms:

- Buddhas
- Bodhisattvas
- Pratyeka (a "Buddha for himself")
- Sravka (a discipline of Buddha)
- Heavenly beings
- Human beings
- Asura (fighting spirits)
- Animals
- Preta (hungry ghosts)
- Hellish beings

The accumulated karma of an individual will lead him to return to a life after death in one of these realms; the experience in a hellish realm is transitory and purifying. The human soul is an illusion, but its apparent cohesion (through memories, emotions, habits, etc.) is persistent until individuals realize its illusory nature. This new person is not necessarily the same, nor necessarily different, from the one who lived the previous life. Both the person and the body are illusory. Only through enlightenment can one pass out of the earthly realm and into Nirvana.

Prayer

Buddhist prayers are inward-directed. They do not address a creator god in an attempt to connect in relationship or have a wish fulfilled. Rather, Buddhists sit in calm meditation in order to call up in themselves inner reserves of strength, tolerance, and kindness. Buddhists believe that in order for prayer to be effective, it must originate in a place of compassion and be used for the benefit of all beings, not for oneself. Two common types of Buddhist prayer are:

- Radiating loving-kindness: a prayer focusing on sending positive thoughts and feelings toward others in particular, or toward all living beings
- Sharing of merit: the rededication of one's life to the benefit of all living beings

In Pure Land Buddhism, practitioners do pray in a form of wish fulfillment, directing requests for heavenly assistance to Buddhas. Even in Pure Land, however, Buddhists believe that all that they are praying to already exists within themselves. In Tibetan Buddhism and some other forms, mantras are repeated. Mantras are sacred words that, when spoken, are believed to summon positive energy and open up the believer to higher consciousness.

Dependent Arising

From the suffering cycle of life and rebirth comes Dependent Arising. Ignorance of the Dependent Arising is the ultimate cause of suffering in the Buddhist worldview. It is the interdependence of all phenomena, which are all, of course, illusory. Twelve causes lead to the coming-into-being of each individual. Each cause leads to the next in a constant cycle that can only be broken by enlightenment. The twelve causes are:

- Ignorance (of the illusory nature of the world and the self)
- Predispositions (one's set personality)
- Consciousness (awareness of the world)
- Traits (one's individuality)

- Senses (the expression of individuality)
- Contact (with other things)
- Feelings
- Desire
- Clinging (to existence)
- Becoming (bringing on a new state of being)
- Birth
- Death

Monastic Life

The Buddha founded the first monastic order, and later an order of nuns, within his own lifetime. Its purpose was both to transmit the Dharma to others while at the same time allowing a space for the monks and nuns to achieve nirvana. A Buddhist monastery is a center for Buddhist life and teaching for the whole community. Over two hundred rules govern a monk or nun's life, including abstention from sexual contact, theft, killing, and proclaiming miraculous powers. Monks and nuns shave their heads and wear the robes of their order. They spend days in study, meditation, work at the monastery, and religious services in the community. Because they have renounced worldly life, those in monastic orders are often able to counsel laypersons while maintaining insightful objectivity. The Buddhist monastery is provided for by the community. Monks eat only during the morning, accepting offerings from laypersons.

Bardo and the Tibetan Buddhist Understanding of Death

Bardo is a dreamlike, liminal state in Tibetan Buddhism. It exists after death as well as in dreaming and meditative states. One unique feature of Tibetan Buddhism is its relationship with death. Like other Buddhist sects, Tibetan Buddhism believes in reincarnation (or, alternatively, enlightenment, delivering the Buddhist from the cycle of death and rebirth). One's behavior in life influences whether reincarnation or enlightenment follows one's death. However, in Tibetan Buddhism, one's soul (that is, one's accumulated karma) lives in bardo for forty-nine days following death, and karma determines whether they are pulled back into life or into nirvana. The concept of bardo is introduced in the Bardo Thodol (known in English as The Tibetan Book of the Dead) is a Red Hat school contribution to Buddhist literature that describes the influence that trained Tibetan monks can have over the dying. It is believed that rituals for the dying can increase the chances of the dying individual's being received into nirvana.

Three Marks of Existence

The three marks of existence, or Dharma seals, are:

- Impermanence
- Suffering
- Atman, or not-self

These three characteristics mark everything in the physical world. All things are illusory in their current form; everything is in a constant state of flux and nothing that appears to be real is stable. All existence is relative. All living things suffer. Nothing in the physical world, due to its impermanence, can bring true satisfaction. In addition, there is no real selfhood to physical beings. By cultivating an acute awareness of the three marks of existence, a Buddhist can change his worldview, achieve wisdom, and find his way to nirvana.

Arahat

An arahat is a Buddhist who has escaped the cycle of rebirth. He has overcome the "three poisons" of Buddhism: desire, hatred, and ignorance. By following the five precepts and the ten unwholesome actions, the arahat purifies body, mind, and speech. This lays the path to nirvana, a path consisting of four stages:

1. The stream-winner: removing the first three of the ten fetters (belief in a permanent self, doubt in the Triple Gem, and the belief that actions alone can lead to nirvana). After this stage, he will not be reborn in the lower realms of existence.
2. The once-returner: partly removing the next two fetters (attachment to sensual desire and ill will). After this stage, he will be reborn once more as a human.
3. The nonreturner: completely removing the fourth and fifth fetters. After this, he will only be reborn in the higher realms.
4. The arahat: he has broken the last five fetters (desire for existence in the formed or formless worlds, conceit, restlessness, and ignorance). At this point, he becomes enlightened.

Buddhist Literature

There are different Buddhist collections of canonical texts, depending on geography, but the major collections are the Chinese canon, the Tibetan canon, and Pali Canon. What is and is not considered canonical is widely debated. The fundamental collection for all Buddhists is the Tipitaka (or Pali Canon). These works are associated with the Buddha himself and comprise over fifty volumes. The Pali Canon consists of:

- Sutras (Buddha's discourses)
- Vinaya (rules for monastic life)
- Abhidharma (analysis and philosophical discussion)

Mahayana Buddhism adds to the list of canonical literature the Mahayana Sutras, consisting of over two thousand additional sutras. Some of the best known include the Heart Sutra, the Lotus Sutra, the Sutras of the Perfection of Wisdom, and the Land of Bliss Sutra. Tibetan Buddhists also use a collection of tantras and the Bardo Thodol, outlining their belief in the bardo state. In addition, Zen Buddhists reject texts altogether as a false path, believing that only through direct experience can one achieve enlightenment.

Important Terms

Buddha—One who has attained perfect enlightenment. According to Theravada tradition, a Buddha can only develop, without a teacher, in a time where the Eightfold Path and Four Noble Truths do not exist in the world, teaching the path to others before death and nirvana. Mahayana Buddhists believe that Buddhahood is a property of wisdom that is revealed to all.

Bodhisattva—One who has committed to the path of enlightenment. In Mahayana Buddhism, all Buddhists are encouraged to become bodhisattvas.

Bodhicitta—The wish to attain enlightenment in order to aid all sentient beings

Dharma—The teachings of the Buddha. Alternatively, "dharma" (with a small D) means a constituent part of human experience.

Confucianism

Life of Confucius

What we know about Confucius comes from his Analects, the book about his life and teachings that was compiled about a century after his death. Kong Fu-zi (Latinized as Confucius) was a real historical figure who lived in the sixth century B.C. He came from faded gentry and held a minor position in government. He later became an acclaimed teacher, so respected that in later life he was offered the position of the region's prime minister. He saw firsthand the effects of poor government on human society, and his writings focused on his sociological concerns about proper government. He became convinced that China was out of balance because its citizens were not living properly, and his writings offer a theory about how to rebalance society.

Development of Confucianism

Confucius's writings were sociological in nature. He was nonreligious and his philosophical writings pay little attention to matters of spiritual concern. After his death, the small group of disciples he had gathered spread to the far regions of the Chinese empire, where his philosophy gradually split into two major camps: the religious and the nonreligious. Confucius himself had advocated a return to feudalism, and his philosophy might have died out had additional scholars not refined it. Two important Confucian thinkers were Hsun-tzu and Mencius. Where Confucius had rejected religious institutions, Hsun-tzu advocated religious rites as being socially important to keep humans, who were naturally evil, behaving morally. Mencius softened Confucius's advocacy of feudalism, making an important distinction between a benevolent leader and a tyrant.

Teachings About Human Goodness and Government

Confucius had great faith in human nature but believed that only through proper behavior could society run smoothly. Human goodness without social order was worthless. He advocated a return to feudalism, believing that a strong but benevolent leader was necessary to create the conditions necessary for human perfectibility. Confucius believed that the Tao, the ineffable balancing force of the universe, was expressed through benevolent leaders, who had a celestial mandate for their rule and possessed the te, the sacred power of the Tao. Confucius, however, was not interested in rewards and punishment as a means to change human behavior. He believed that virtue was its own reward and that the important issue was to create the social conditions conducive to their being able to express virtue.

Mencius

After Confucius, Mencius is the most important Confucian philosopher. Tradition states that Mencius studied under Confucius's grandson. The Book of Mencius, written a hundred years after his death, expresses his views. Mencius, like Confucius, was not interested in religion, but in the state and in social order. Even more than Confucius, he believed that human beings were basically good and that it was a bad environment that led them to be less than virtuous. He was opposed to war, because it created a bad environment that made it impossible for humans to express their natural goodness. Significantly, he believed that it was the right of the people to overthrow an oppressive government.

Hsun-Tzu

In the generation after Mencius, Hsun-tzu arose as a great Confucian teacher. His thinking represented a major departure from previous Confucian tradition. Hsun-tzu believed, quite opposite to the beliefs of Confucius and Mencius, that human beings were basically evil. Goodness expressed in humans was a function of their being properly trained. Hsun-tzu was the most nonreligious of all the Confucian scholars, yet he believed strongly in the importance of social rites as a means for humans to connect and be educated. Influenced by Taoists, Hsun-tzu argued that the universe tends toward perfection, and that humans should follow the moral order of the universe, rather than expecting deities to respond to human needs.

Han Dynasty

After many centuries of political upheaval and instability, the Han dynasty consolidated power in the second century B.C., inaugurating an era of calm and peace. A large government needed civil servants, and these were drawn from the ranks of Confucian teachers. Importantly, Confucians were put in charge of the education of Chinese children, ensuring Confucius's legacy for the ages. With Confucius such an omnipresent figure, there arose a cult of Confucius, with people revering him nearly as a deity. Temples were built to him and sacrifices were made. In this way, he became a semi-saint, and a symbolic patron of Chinese scholarship.

Decline of Confucianism

In 1503, the Chinese government under the Ming dynasty attempted to rein in the cult of Confucius, removing images of the man from temples and replacing them with tables inscribed with his teachings. The honorific titles he had been awarded posthumously were removed, and the official focus was redirected to his philosophy rather than his saintly status. Sun Yat-sen, in the nineteen century, reasserted Confucian values as part of a neo-Confucian revival, but any success was short-lived. The Cultural Revolution of the 1960s officially eliminated recognition of all religions and took an especially hard-line stance against Confucianism, viewing it as antiquated and fascistic. After 1977, the People's Republic of China liberalized its policy toward religion; however, of the native Asian religions, only Buddhism and Taoism have been officially recognized.

Neo-Confucianism Movement

Beginning in the ninth century A.D. and in full swing by the eleventh, neo-Confucianism was an attempt to maintain the distinctive face of Confucianism in response to the growing popularity and influence of Buddhism and Taoism in China. The two most important figures in this movement were Chu-Hsi and Wang Yan Ming. Chu-Hsi adopted the Tao principle to Confucianism, turning the calm, passive Tao of Taoism into an active, energetic force. This principle he called the Tai Ji, the "great ultimate," a combination of physical and rational forces working in concert to create the changes of nature and of souls. Influenced by Buddhist metaphysics, Chu-Hsi argued that moral development leads to the individual becoming one with all. Wang emphasized the importance of the mind in constructing reality for an individual. By disciplining the mind, one would naturally practice goodness. No concessions were made to organized religion in this movement. Wan advocated meditation, but its purpose was for moral clarity, not spirituality.

Distinguishing Traits of Confucianism

Unlike most other major religious traditions, Confucianism is unusual in that it claims no theological basis for its belief system. It does not believe that its texts are sacred, merely important, and it does not provide a role for God in dispensing its wisdom. Its words are not divinely revealed, but rationally created by a man who claimed no divine assistance. There was originally no monastic tradition. Additionally, Confucian scholars, while believing in a general idea of heaven as an impersonal but positive place, had little interest in an afterlife. While divine figures may exist, the chief value of religion, according to Confucians, is a social one.

Li, Jen, and Shu

Li: propriety. For Confucius, li is a social behavior that is concerned with courtesy and ritual (everyday ritual, not religious rituals). Translated roughly as "life as it is supposed to be lived." According to Confucius, li lies at the heart of social order. A society whose members act with li create an earthly and cosmic harmony.

Jen: love, goodness, the inner dimension of li. It is benevolence and an internal effort to perform one's social duties properly.

Shu: reciprocity. The principle of treating others as one would wish that they themselves would be treated. One should act with shu in all matters.

Important Texts

Confucian texts can be divided into the Five Classics and the Four Books. The Five Classics are:

- Shu Ching (Classic of History)—A later compilation of speeches and various documents
- Shih Ching (Classic of Odes)—An early collection of poems and songs
- I Ching (Classic of Changes)—A collection of texts offering guidance for divination
- Ch'un Ching (Spring and Autumn Annals)—A history book attributed to Confucius
- Li Ching (Classic of Rites)—An examination of the concept of li

The Four Books include:

- Analects—A composite book containing the life story and sayings of Confucius. It is the most important source of information on Confucius's life.
- (Doctrine of the Mean)—A book elaborating Confucian philosophy, specifically clarifying the relationship between humans and the universe.
- Great Learning—Written from Hsun-tzu's point of view (though not written by him), this book sets forth the principles of Confucian education.
- Mencius—Written by Mencius, this book is the first systematic compilation of Confucian thought.

Divination

The I Ching, one of the Five Classics of Confucianism, is a book dealing with divination. It predates Confucius by thousands of years, though it has become associated with his philosophy due to its inclusion in the Five Classics. The book consists of sixty-four hexagrams, combinations of six broken or solid lines, and their associated meanings. To use the I Ching, some means of random generation is used: either flipping three coins, tossing sticks, or using similar tools, while meditating on a question or concern. Then the individual reads the associated section of the I Ching for insight into his issue. In this way, Confucianism has a vaguely spiritual element, though it is typically viewed as a secular philosophy rather than an organized religion.

Death

As in Taoism, Confucianism focuses its interest almost exclusively on the present life. Confucius was criticized during his own time for ignoring the issue of the afterlife, but he fails to mention spirits or gods, positively or negatively, in any of the writings attributed to him. Though he mentioned spirituality very little, he did believe that all human endeavor was under the auspices of Tien Ming, or the regulation of heaven. Death does not seem to be feared or desired in Confucianism. In fact, Confucius holds social order and integrity in such high esteem that he advocates a "death before dishonor" mentality that holds martyrdom as righteous.

Golden Mean and Superior Man

Chung Yang, or the Golden Mean, is a moderate lifestyle advocated by Confucius. Like the Taoists, Confucianism advocates avoiding extremes, not out of passive acceptance of the world, but out of loyalty to social order and propriety. This concept is not dissimilar to the Buddhist "middle way." A chin-tzu, or the superior man, exemplifies Confucian principles. He practices the Golden Mean and avoids excess. He has five constant virtues: self-respect, magnanimity, sincerity, earnestness, and benevolence. The superior man demonstrates an important Confucian principle: people should not conform to the rules of li, but should cultivate jen in themselves so that they have a natural desire to behave properly. A superior man is motivated internally and is naturally virtuous.

Five Basic Relationships and Rectification of Names

In Confucianism, family is of supreme importance and deserving of special loyalty. Consequently, the major ethical principles are based in family relationships. Confucius outlined the five major relationships in life, specifying the behavior with which each party should act:

- Friend and friend: Both friends should treat each other with respect and devotion.
- Elder brother-younger brother: The elder brother should act with gentility, while the younger should treat the elder with humility.
- Father-son: The father should be kind to the son, and the son should treat the father with filial piety.
- Husband-wife: The husband should be righteous in his behavior toward the wife, while she should be obedient to his will.
- Ruler-subject: The ruler should be benevolent, and the subject should be loyal.

These are the major five, but not the only five mentioned. The goal of maintaining proper relationships is to create a cosmic harmony that will put into effect the Tao. Confucius stressed the "rectification of names," or the shaping of people into their proper social roles, in order to create order.

Taoism

Pre-Taoist Chinese Religion and Historical Origins of Taoism

The early Taoist text The Classic of Great Peace is the source of much contemporary knowledge about the early origins of Taoism. It contains the Chinese religious concepts of polytheism and ancestor worship that made their way into Taoism as well. The pre-Taoist Chinese greatly respected the aged and believed in the immortality of their ancestors' souls, paying homage to them in a practice known as "filial piety." There were other spirits in addition to ancestral ones, including beneficial ones known as Shen and malevolent ones known as Kuei. Pre-Taoist beliefs also include the harmony of the yin and yang (represented by the taijitu symbol), principles that are present in different proportions in all things and all people. The yin is a feminine force, associated with coolness, wetness, darkness, and evil, and the yang is a masculine one characterized by warmth, dryness, light, and goodness. The harmonious interaction of these two basic elements governs the universe. Elements of divination were also present in pre-Taoist China, such as the reading of grain stalks and the cracks in tortoise shells.

Lao-Tzu

Lao-tzu, the founder of Taoism, remains a mystery to modern scholars. He is said to have lived during the sixth century B.C. and is associated with the writing of Taoism's fundamental text, the Tao te Ching, but he is certainly not responsible for its entire content—if he even ever existed as anything other than mythology. According to legend, Lao-tzu was a famously wise thinker employed in the royal court until his retirement, when he wandered west but was stopped by a guard and forced to write his collected wisdom. The second most important figure in Taoism, Chuang-zhu, is said to have been Lao-tzu's disciple, but his historical existence has been proven.

Political Background of China and Taoism

The China of the early Taoist period was marked by social unrest and political insecurity. The feudal system was collapsing. Against this background, several schools of thought developed, each offering a theory about the best social structure to maintain order and human happiness, and they competed for popular support. Each had an alternate viewpoint on the role of religion and government in human lives. The Confucians advocated the return of feudalism, the Legalists believed that human nature was essentially lazy and in need of a strong and ruthless Machiavellian government, and the Mohists believed in a strong government, but one founded on the principle of human goodness and traditional religious principles. Taoists believed in as little government as possible. Ideas moved fluidly among the three groups, despite their rivalry, and Lao-tzu is traditionally believed to have been a teacher of Confucius. Confucian ideas about the goodness of human nature greatly influenced Taoism, but they split on the issue of the role of religion in human life, with Confucians believing it united people while Taoists despised its rituals and organization.

Philosophical and Religious Taoism

Though early Taoism was explicitly antireligious, not long after the period of Lao-tzu and Chuang-zhu, Taoism began to develop a distinctly religious element very much opposed to the philosophy of the early leaders. Traditional Taoism, what we now call philosophical Taoism, continued, while other Taoist leaders began to focus on magical efforts to extend life. The philosophical camp focused on living one's life in harmony with the Tao, and while it appealed to a few intellectuals, religious Taoism was much more accessible to the masses, becoming far more popular. Because Taoism had never been explicitly interested in the afterlife, focusing instead on enjoying the present life, so religious Taoism naturally focused on staving off death for as long as possible. In some respects the two schools were diametrically opposed; whereas philosophical Taoism stressed the spiritual transcendence of its philosophy and advocated a distrust of government, religious Taoism valued loyalty as well as the extension of physical life.

Although Taoism began as an explicitly antireligious philosophy, religious Taoism made many compromises as it gained popularity. As it evolved, religious Taoism developed a system of rituals thought to increase harmony with the Tao, and eventually led to the development of a pantheon of specific deities, including Shang Di (the lord of heaven and ruler of ancestral spirits), the Tao Shen (the god of the stove, to whom sacrifices were offered), and the three purities (Lao-tzu, Ling Bao, and the Jade Emperor, the supreme deity of Taoism). Taoist practice includes rituals influenced by Buddhism, virtues taken from Confucianism, meditation practice, and traditional Chinese medicine. Religious Taoists practiced sacrifices, exorcisms, and vegetarianism, and abstained from alcohol. They also invented T'ai Chi Ch'uan, a system of meditative movements designed to improve health. Their interest in alchemy was strong, and they believed that if they could master the Tao they could achieve immortality, extending the present life indefinitely.

Relationship with Buddhism

Theravada Buddhism entered China with the emperor Asoka, but its influence was not great. Chinese Buddhism increased in popularity only when the missionary Bodhidharma brought Mahayana Buddhism to China, where it and Taoism mutually influenced each other. Differences between the two abound, however: unlike Buddhism, which has thousands of pages of canonical and noncanonical texts, Taoism has only one short treatise and no set rituals or doctrines. From Buddhism Taoism adopted rituals, an interest in the afterlife, and the idea of post-life judgment, as well as monasticism, which had not previously existed in Taoism. In return, Buddhism accepted the Chinese folk gods as bodhisattvas. While the two religions coexisted, gradually Taoism became associated with commoners, while Buddhism was associated with upper class intellectuals.

Major Schools of Taoism

After Taoism split into the philosophical and religious camps, it developed various competing schools of thought about the proper way to come into harmony with the Tao. Among these schools were:

- Ch'uan Chen: influenced by Buddhism, emphasized monasticism and asceticism.
- Wou Tou Mi Tao: the "five pecks of rice way" evolved in the first century A.D. It allowed the full participation of women in leadership roles and emphasized rituals and the confession of sins.
- School of Pure Conversation: originating in the third century A.D., a reaction against the more populist strain of religious Taoism. It emphasized a rigid philosophy and the public responsibilities of Taoists.
- Monastic Taoism: developed in the seventh century A.D., accepting both monks and nuns for the monastic life.
- Teaching of the Tao: had the broadest appeal of all early schools.
- Orthodox Unity: emphasized healing rituals. It is one of two modern branches of Taoism, now known as Southern Taoism.
- Completely Real: emphasized monasticism and "internal alchemy," i.e., meditation. It is the other modern branch, now known as Northern Taoism.

Yang-Zhu, Shen-Dao, and Chuang-Zhu

Yang-zhu was a pre-Taoist thinker whose philosophy arose during a period of political unrest. He advocated turning one's back on society, which was uncaring. He wrote that men should become self-sufficient instead of relying on society. Shen-dao was another pre-Taoist thinker whose philosophy emphasized the importance of having an easygoing, impartial attitude, accepting the inevitable and avoiding too much self-assertion. His antipathy for knowledge was a forerunner to the Taoist ideal of the innocent child. After Lao-tzu, Chuang-zhu is Taoism's most important thinker, writing the Chuang-zhu, a major Taoist text. He elaborated on Lao-tzu's thoughts about the Tao, and the reciprocal causality of yin and yang forces. He also advocated relativism; all things he wrote, have equal right to exist and nothing is inherently good or bad. The only duty is to be true to one's own nature.

Tao Te Ching and Teachings of Early Taoists

Lao-tzu's Tao te Ching, meaning "The Way and Its Power," advocates that life itself is the greatest possession, making it an unusual religion far more concerned with this life than what comes after. The Tao te Ching teaches that the universe's governing unity is an ineffable, mysterious force called the Tao, and that the way to happiness is to live in harmony with the Tao. Everything outside of the Tao, including society, family, and money, is an illusion and worthless. The Taoists rejected achievement, wealth, and privilege, which are the cause of strife. They also rejected war, not out of morality, but out of the sense that it was pointless. The Taoist ideal is that of an innocent child. The ideal society is a small, self-contained village, with as little government as possible. Taoists also believe that the human body is a microcosm for the universe, with the five basic organs corresponding to the five elements, seasons, and directions. There is a corresponding emphasis on physical health to strengthen the connection to the Tao.

Three Jewels of the Tao Te Ching

The Three Jewels of Taoism are the ethical precepts of Taoism, the means by which a person can come to live in harmony with the Tao.

- The first jewel is translated as "compassion" or "love," like a mother's. All actions should be undertaken out of love.
- The second jewel is translated as "economy" or "simplicity." This is marked by simplicity of desire and nonwastefulness.
- The last jewel is translated as "humility" or "modesty." To stand out is to be vulnerable to the destructive forces of the world. Taoism advocates blending in and not being too extreme in desire or action.

Death and Afterlife

Taoists are remarkable among religions for their apparent lack of interest in the issue of life after death. Death is not feared or desired; it is simply one additional stage of life in which individuals continue, in some sense, as they always have. People are always of the Tao and this does not change after death; as the Tao continues, so do people. In addition, people's bodies continue in the creatures of the earth and their personal memory continues for those who knew them. Lao-tzu made vague suggestions that death was in some way inauspicious and to be avoided if possible. In religious Taoism, this led to a fascination with alchemy and extending the present life. Later Taoism has evolved into a religion with more in common with others than it began with. There are now notions of an afterlife in which souls are eternal in either sacred mountains or a punishing hell. Taoist priests have the power to extract departed souls from hell. The most important issue for Taoists, both philosophical and religious, is maximizing the joy of this life; the afterlife is an afterthought.

Texts of Taoism

The following are important texts of Taoism:

- Tao te Ching—the most important book in Taoism. Compiled over several centuries beginning near 800 B.C. This short 81-section book sets forth the major concepts of Taoism. This book is addressed to a benevolent ruler.
- Chuang-zhu—the second most important book in Taoism. Presents several discourses attributed to Lao-tzu, addressing its instructions about the proper conduct of private life to the individual reader. Sets forth the characters of the Immortals, metaphorical examples of proper living, who were later worshipped by religious Taoists.
- Lieh-tzu—argues that all worldly activity is controlled by neither free will nor fate.
- Kuan-tzu—emphasizes the submission of the body to the heart in order to achieve harmony with the Tao.
- Classic of the Sacred Jewel—reveals the deities that later became central to religious Taoist worship.
- Classic of Great Peace—the fundamental text of the alchemy-based cults of Taoism

Important Terms

Tao—"The way" or "the path." The Tao is the flow that balances the universe. Like water, it is calm and passive, but mightier than everything, even stones and buildings. The Tao is subtle, quiet, cyclical (in that all things return to their origins), and nurturing.

Te—Translated variously as "power" or "integrity," te is Tao put into action, the conscious application of Tao to one's life.

Wu wei—Accomplishment without active assertion, "doing without doing." Those who act through wu wei are ultimately more successful than those who are aggressive. The way to act with wu wei is not to resist the Tao, but to humbly accept its flow.

P'u— "Uncarved block," a metaphor for the state of wu wei, in which one is passively receptive to all. P'u is the ideal Taoist state of pure direct awareness. Taoist sages, in an innocent state of p'u, look foolish to outsiders.

Ch'i—The life force that animates and sustains matter and life. Taoists believe in the importance of cultivating ch'i in oneself, through nutrition, physical activities, and breath control.

Judaism

Jewish Identity

"Jewish" is not an easy category to define. Whereas other religions' members are clearly identified by subscribing to a particular set of religious beliefs, there is great diversity in Judaism. A Jew can be someone who practices Judaism, whether born a Jew or converted, but there are many types of Jewish practice. Over thousands of years, there have also come to be ethnicities associated with Judaism, though these ethnic and Jewish identities are not coterminous. There are Jews of every race, and members of the Sephardic and Ashkenazi ethnic groups who are themselves irreligious. Some define themselves as Jewish because their families are historically Jewish, though they do not practice. In addition, it is traditional among Jews to say that Jewish identity is inherited from one's mother. Even among practicing Jews, there are only a few core beliefs shared by all: the existence of one god who takes a personal interest in the lives of individuals and who has indicated that the Jewish people are his chosen ones on earth.

Jewish Book of Genesis

The Jewish creation story is traditionally dated 3760 B.C. In the beginning, God created the heaven and earth, the water and land, and plants, animals, and the first man, Adam, out of dust. God made a woman, Eve, from Adam's rib, and she became his companion. Both Adam and Eve were created in God's image. Adam and Eve lived in an earthly paradise called the Garden of Eden, but when they rejected God's only law and ate fruit from a forbidden tree, they were cast out of Eden and forever separated from God. After several generations, God became displeased with people's wickedness, and created a massive flood. This flood wiped out all living creatures except for Noah, whom God had commanded to build an ark to save himself, his family, and the representative animals they have taken on. From Noah are descended all people, including Abraham, the father of the Jewish people.

Abraham and His Lineage

Abraham was a devoted follower of El, the ancient Hebrews' name for God. God called Abraham to lead his family into Canaan, where God promised Abraham that he would become the father of a great nation and be a blessing to his people, who are the chosen protectors of Canaan. In return, Abraham and his descendents must comply with God's moral laws and must circumcise all males as a sign of their commitment. God appeared to Abraham several times, renewing this covenant. Abraham had two sons. His first, Ishmael, is said to have fathered the Muslim nations, and his second, Isaac, the Jewish nation. God tested Abraham's faith by asking him to offer Isaac as a sacrifice, but at the last minute sent an angel to intervene and substitute a ram instead. In return for Abraham's obedience, God renewed the covenant, forbidding human sacrifice from this point. Abraham's immediate male line (first Isaac, then his son Jacob, then Jacob's twelve sons) is known as the Patriarchs.

Religious Practices of Early Judaism

The Patriarchs are described as nomadic shepherds, and their theology is notable for its monotheism. Judaism is, in fact, one of the world's oldest monotheistic faiths. There was an element of animism to their worship; they revered trees, stones, and pillars, offering animal sacrifices in the open rather than in temples. Jews practiced circumcision from the time of Abraham's covenant with God, and may have predated it. Resting on the Sabbath is also believed to be part of early Jewish practice. God in early Judaism was referred to by many names. The most common was Elohim, or "gods," the emphasis being on the fact that this god was the only god, replacing all the other local gods worshipped by other societies. Zoroastrianism influenced Judaism in several key ways: the notion of clean and unclean foods, monotheism, and a last judgment of humanity.

Moses

Moses is the greatest Jewish prophet and one of the most significant figures in Judaism, because God chose him as the human recipient of the Torah. Moses was born as an Israelite in Egypt during the Israelite enslavement. A decree was given to kill all male Israelite babies, but Moses was miraculously saved and raised as an Egyptian. As an adult, he became aware of his true identity, and after killing an Egyptian, escaped across the Sinai Peninsula, only to return when God instructed him to free the Israelites. Moses led the Israelite people across the Red Sea, and on the journey received from God the Torah, or Jewish law, on Mount Sinai. God spoke to Moses, telling him that he would not see the Promised Land himself, and Moses died on the far side of the River Jordan after reminding his people of God's law and blessing them. Joshua then led the Israelite people to the land of Canaan.

Exodus of Judaism

The Exodus is the most significant event in ancient Judaism. The Jewish descendents of Abraham were enslaved in Egypt for forty years outside Canaan, the land promised to them by God through Abraham. God, through his instructions to Moses, miraculously delivered them from slavery. God spoke to Moses through a bush that burned but was not consumed, telling him to deliver the Jews to Canaan. After ten miraculous plagues on Egypt, Moses secured the release of the Jews and when he was pursued by the pharaoh, who had changed his mind, God parted the waters of the Red Sea so that the Israelites could cross. The waters closed behind them, enabling their deliverance. The Israelites then spent forty years wandering in the desert before being able to enter the land of Canaan.

The Book of Exodus describes Moses' encounter with God On Mount Sinai. The Israelites stopped near Mount Sinai on the return to Canaan. There, Moses received from God instructions to carve two stone tablets. He did so, and received from God ten commandments, which were to form the basis for all Jewish law. These stone tablets were placed in a specially made chest known as the Ark of the Covenant. During this encounter, God revealed his true name to be YHWH and renewed his covenant with the Israelites, reaffirming that they were his chosen people and that the land of Canaan was theirs by holy decree. After receiving the commandments from God, including one not to have any gods before YHWH, Moses discovered that the rest of his people had, in his absence, made an idol of a golden calf. Moses was outraged and asked those who were on the Lord's side to join him, and they put to death the idolaters.

Jewish Ark of the Covenant and the Tabernacle

The Ten Commandments that God gave to Moses on Mount Sinai were inscribed on two stone tablets, which were carried in a wooden box known as the Ark of the Covenant. The Ark was a sacred relic to Jews (and, later, to Christians as well). In addition to the commandments, the Ark also contained some of the sacred manna from the Exodus (which had rained from the sky when supplies ran low), as well as a rod of Aaron, a magical staff used by Moses' brother Aaron. The Ark was built at the request of YHWH, and in addition to being a container for the commandments was also possibly a symbolic throne for him. In addition to the Ark, the Tabernacle, a portable house of worship for the Jews, was constructed during this time. The Ark was placed in the first temple when it was built in the tenth century B.C. When the Babylonians destroyed the temple in 586 B.C., the Ark was lost to history.

Saul, David, and Solomon

Eleven generations after the Patriarchs, Saul is appointed the first king of the Israelites by Samuel, the Judge. Saul, however, is disobedient and does not kill all the members of a neighboring tribe, as God has commanded, with whom the Israelites are at war. According to differing stories, David, a poor shepherd, is sent to work for Samuel, and he becomes a successful warrior and a political threat to Saul. When Saul is killed in battle, God appoints David king instead, and he joins the kingdoms of Israel and Hebron. As an effective and powerful king, David conquers Jerusalem, but God forbids him, as a man of war, to build a temple. He represents the first consolidated Jewish kingdom. His son Solomon, having amassed wealth and power, builds the first temple in Jerusalem and formalizes Jewish worship practices.

First, Second, and Third Temples of Judaism

King Solomon, the son of David, completed the First Temple in Jerusalem in 960 B.C. The Ark of the Covenant was contained inside, and for the first time, there existed a formal ritualized worship process for Judaism, including, at the time, sacred dancing and animal sacrifices. The First Temple was destroyed and looted by the Babylonians in 586 B.C. when they sacked Jerusalem. After the Babylonian Captivity, beginning in 516 B.C., the Second Temple was built, more magnificent than Solomon's. The Ark of the Covenant, however, was not recovered. Under King Herod, the temple was torn down and rebuilt in 19 B.C., but this is still considered part of the Second Temple. The Romans destroyed both Jerusalem and the Second Temple in 70 A.D. during the Jewish rebellion. The Third Temple has not been built. Its future building is the source of much prayer among, especially Orthodox, Jews. There are organizations agitating to construct it, but many Jews believe that its construction can only be brought about by the Messiah or otherwise guided by God.

Israelites' Settlement of Canaan

Sometime around 1400 B.C., Joshua, Moses' successor, led the Israelites to the land of Canaan after forty years in the wilderness. Joshua led a military campaign to conquer Canaan, destroying the cities of Jericho and Ai, and, with God's favor, finally conquering the Canaanite society. At one point, the battle of Gibeon, God makes the sun and moon stand still so that Joshua can fight a battle in daylight. After the settlement of Canaan, there are two conflicting accounts: according to the Book of Joshua, the Israelites destroyed the Canaanites, while according to the Book of Judges in a theory that is more widely supported, the two societies lived side by side.

Israelites' Prophetic Movement

The First Temple had two classes of religious leaders: priests, who led Jews in their first formal religious rituals, and prophets, whose role was that of mysticism and ecstasy. They led ecstatic dancing, singing, and trance experiences, as well as healing the sick and blessing worshippers. Prophets in Judaism are considered to have been especially chosen by God in order to spread a message of social change that will lead to obedience to God's laws. Many claimed to have had religious visions of the future or of God. Some of the best-known prophets are:

- Nathan
- Elijah
- Deborah
- Jeremiah
- Malachi
- Miriam
- Samuel
- Ezekiel

- Isaiah
- Amos
- Micah
- Hosea

Split of Israel and Judah, and the Babylonian Captivity

In 922 B.C., a group of Israelites rejected the rule of Solomon's son Rehoboam (a rebellion resulting from high taxation), and Israel was split into two nations—a northern nation, called Israel, and a southern one, called Judah. The Assyrians, a neighboring nation, destroyed Israel in 721 B.C., and these Israelis were gradually assimilated, enslaved, or killed out of existence, to be known from that point as "the Ten Lost Tribes of Israel." In 586 B.C., the Babylonian empire destroyed Jerusalem and Solomon's temple. Jews were exiled to both Egypt and Babylon. Jews in Babylon maintained their traditions even in this captivity, and when the Persians invaded Babylon in 538 B.C., the Jews were freed and many returned to Israel, where the Second Temple was constructed. The Babylonian Captivity is important because it marks the beginning of the Jewish Diaspora, the last high point of the prophetic tradition (with Ezekiel), and the reaffirmation of Jews' destiny to be continually punished and saved by their God.

Jewish Communities During the Second Temple Period

Various political factions existed in Israel during the period of the Second Temple. Their disagreements carried important theological weight for future Jews of the Diaspora.

The four communities were:

- Sadducees: Strict conservatives on the literal authority of the Torah. Rejected all laws not written by Moses. Believed in complete human free will. Associated with wealthy classes. Rejected life after death.
- Pharisees: Unique among the five in their advocacy of other oral laws (the "traditions of the elders") in addition to the Torah. Strict adherents to Torah law. Forerunners of the rabbinical tradition. Believed in the resurrection of the dead.
- Essenes: Focused on strict personal morality and were especially sexually conservative. Lived a monastic life in isolation, rejecting both the authority of the Jerusalem priests and the legitimacy of temple worship. Waited expectantly for the Messiah. Probably responsible for the Dead Sea Scrolls.
- Zealots: Extreme nationalists, advocating violent opposition to Roman rule. Those who engaged in acts of sabotage and revenge against Jewish collaborators were known as sicarii.

Jewish Diaspora and Synagogues

The Jewish Diaspora is the exile of Jews, whether voluntary or not, from Israel. When Jews were scattered as a result of war and political troubles, they developed new traditions and even, to a certain extent, the characteristics of ethnic groups. Jewish populations evolved around the world, including Ashkenazi Jews in Eastern Europe, Sephardic Jews in North Africa, Beta Jews in Ethiopia, and Mizrahi Jews in Central Asia and the Middle East. According to the Torah, the temple can only ever be in Jerusalem. However, Diaspora Jews had to adapt to their new circumstances in order to worship properly. Consequently, synagogues became the standard house of worship for Jews. A synagogue is defined only by the presence of a Torah and a minyan (a quorum of ten adult Jewish men). Each community, or kehillah, had a synagogue to gather for worship. The development of the synagogue led to the need for trained religious leaders to study the Torah and act as spiritual teachers for Diaspora Jews. This led directly to the rabbinical movement.

Jewish History Under Roman Rule

When Jews returned from the Babylonian exile, Israel was no longer a political power and fell under the Roman Empire in 63 B.C. Under direct Roman rule, Jewish belief in the cult of the Messiah grew. Jews began to adapt their interpretation of the coming Messiah, believing that a warrior hero would be sent by God to save them from their oppression. Romans tolerated Judaism at first, but after the Jews rebelled in 66 A.D., the Romans conquered Jerusalem, enslaved and slaughtered Jewish revolutionaries, imposed direct rule, and destroyed the Second Temple. After the rebellion, Yohanan Ben Zakkai, a rabbi, asked the emperor Titus for permission to start an academy at Yabneh. There, rabbis discussed the future of Judaism, and fixed the Jewish canon of literature permanently. Two more rebellions took place over the next century, culminating in the Bar Kochba revolt of 132–136. Led by Simon Bar Kochba, a messianic figure, the rebellion was quashed by the Romans, who thereafter expelled all Jews from Palestine, prohibited Torah law, and renamed Israel "Syria Palaestina."

Ezra

Ezra was a Jewish priest who lived around 428 B.C. He led Jews, after the Babylonian Captivity, back to Jerusalem, bringing with him a book of scripture, the "book of the law of Moses," whose contents are now lost to history, and led a public reading of the Torah. After this, Jews in Jerusalem experienced a religious awakening and reformed their lives in response to his influence. From this point forward, Jews became known as the "people of the book." It became part of the Jewish doctrine after Ezra to believe that God no longer spoke through people, but through books, and it was the duty of the individual to understand the meaning of the books in order to live one's life in proper obedience to God. His leadership also established the Jewish traditions of the feast of Purim, the sacredness of public Torah reading, and the Amidah, the central prayer of Jewish daily life.

Impact of Early Islam

After the death of Muhammad in the seventh century A.D., Jews throughout the Middle East and North Africa came under the rule of various Muslim governments. Because of their monotheism and their reliance on sacred books, both Jews and Christians were initially treated with tolerance by Muslim rulers. The Abbasid Caliphate, centered in Baghdad beginning in 762, ushered in a "golden age" of religious tolerance and learning in the Middle East. Jews, Muslims, and Christians worked together in academies on scholarship and translation projects that were of lasting intellectual and religious significance. Beginning in the ninth century A.D., however, persecution began against Jews by Muslim rulers, leading to heavy taxes levied on non-Muslims, as well as internal divisions in the academies. The academies declined shortly thereafter.

Medieval Spain

Throughout Europe, Diaspora Jews were required by law during the medieval period to live in ghettoes, segregated neighborhoods apart from the Christians of the cities. Jews had been living in Spain since the first century A.D., and after the Muslim conquest of Spain in 711, had experienced religious freedom. As Babylonian power declined elsewhere, slowly Spain became the center of the Jewish world, producing great Jewish thinkers, such as Maimonides and Moses ibn Gikatella. In the thirteenth century, however, Muslim rule began to decline and Christianity regained power. For two centuries Christians, Muslims, and Jews lived in relative harmony, but by the fifteenth century, violent persecution of Jews and Muslims had begun in earnest. Converted Catholics falsely thought to have converted from Judaism or Islam were executed, and in 1492, a royal decree expelled all Jews from Spain.

Impact of the Crusades on Jews in Europe

The Crusades were an effort by medieval European Christians to regain Christian control of the Middle East, particularly the Holy Land of Israel (Palestine). As Jewish populations were expelled from Spain, many Jews settled elsewhere in Europe, often being required by law to live in ghettoes. Beginning in 1095 under Pope Urban, European armies gathered support to win back Palestine for Christianity, and although the Crusades were unsuccessful, they sparked a revival of religious fervor in European Christians. The fallout from this fervor was earnest and violent persecution of Jews. Across Europe, Christians killed Jews, forced them to convert to Christianity, and drove them to suicide. By 1296, many Jews had left Western Europe for Poland or for the Middle East, finding Muslim rule far more tolerant than Christian.

Zionism

Zionism was the historical political movement that agitated for a national Jewish homeland in Israel. Beginning in the 1890s, Austrian reporter Theodor Herzl argued that Jewish people needed a homeland of their own in order to truly enjoy the same rights as others. The Zionist movement began shortly thereafter. In the early 1900s, land settlements by Jews began in Israel. After World War I, Palestine was designated a British protectorate, and massive waves of Jewish aliyah (immigration to Israel) began. Arab Christians and Muslims already living in Palestine panicked, urging the British to limit immigration, which they did with the White Paper of 1939, restricting Jewish immigration to fifteen thousand people a year at the height of the Holocaust. After World War II, the modern state of Israel was founded as an explicitly Jewish nation.

Shoah

The Shoah, or Holocaust, was the twentieth century genocidal extermination of six million Jews in Europe by Nazi Germany. In 1933, Adolf Hitler came to power as Chancellor of Germany and quickly turned Germany into an anti-Semitic dictatorship. Jews' legal rights were methodically stripped away, making many of them refugees. Simultaneously, Germany was on an imperialist march through Europe, conquering much of Europe and exposing millions of non-German Jews to the Nazis' plans. Jews were sent to labor camps, and then, beginning in 1941, to extermination camps where they were annihilated as part of the Nazis' "final solution" to the "Jewish problem." The anti-Semitism that motivated the German elites was a result of two widespread conspiracy theories; both were outlandish and incorrect. The result of the Shoah was that the worldwide Jewish population declined by one-third, including 78% of European Jews. In addition, up to seven million other groups (Romani, gypsies, the disabled, Soviet POWs, Polish Christians, and Jehovah's Witnesses) were murdered.

Modern State of Israel

The state of Palestine was a British protectorate beginning after World War I. Zionists agitated for the establishment of a Jewish homeland there beginning in the late nineteenth century, and after the Shoah and the massive displacement of Jews worldwide, the United Nations proposed partitioning Palestine into two states, one Jewish and one Arab, with Jerusalem to be an international city administered by the U.N. In 1948, a day before the end of the British Mandate, Jewish authorities declared the whole of Israel an independent state, which was immediately invaded by five neighboring nations. After a ceasefire, temporary borders were drawn, with Jordan and Egypt annexing some of the land designated by the U.N., and 80% of the Arab population fled or was expelled from the country. The founding of Israel was highly controversial, and questions persist about the right of return for Arabs, many of whom have now lived their entire lives in refugee camps, and about political control of the West Bank and Jerusalem, a holy city to Muslims, Jews, and Christians alike.

Baal Shem Tov

In the eighteenth century, Baal Shem Tov (also known as Israel Ben Eliezer) led a popular movement among Polish Jews that became known as Hasidic Judaism. During a period when European Judaism focused strongly on Torah study and the inward, intellectual experience of religion, Baal Shem Tov preached the importance of joy in Judaism. God, he argued, was not to be found in literature, but in simple faith, and experiencing the mystical side of faith was attractive to many Jews, especially those from the lower classes, who did not have access to Torah study. Making Judaism a compelling religion to individuals, he believed, was the way to keep it accessible, and to help it thrive as a minority religion in a society overwhelmingly Christian.

Mendelssohn

Mendelssohn (born Moses Dessau) was an eighteenth century Jewish scholar in what would become Germany. Born poor, he was self-taught in many subjects, and eventually became famous in German courts for his poetry and philosophy. He Germanized his name and spent his latter years focusing his scholarly work on Judaism. He published several works in German arguing for the rights of Jews, and encouraged Jews to learn more about high culture. He espoused integration, not separation, of European Jews. Mendelssohn is credited by his admirers with ushering in a European Jewish renaissance, and charged by his detractors with encouraging Jewish assimilation at the cost of their identity.

Reform Judaism

Reform Judaism began as a response to the Enlightenment, arguing that Jewish historical practices were out of date and that Jews should integrate with secular society. In 1843, Reform Jews published the following:

> "1. There is a continuation in the development of Judaism.
>
> 2. The Talmud has no authority for the modern Jew.
>
> 3. We seek no Messiah, and we know no homeland but the land of our birth."

This represented a major departure from Jewish tradition. In addition to not practicing Zionism, Reform Jews began calling their synagogues "temples," emphasizing the nonsupremacy of Jerusalem in their lives. Today, Reform Jews emphasize the ethics of Judaism and a personal connection to the religion over specific Torah laws. They do not follow kashrut, have choirs and organ music as part of their services, and hold temple services on Friday evening in the vernacular rather than Hebrew. In addition, Reform Jews do not cover their heads in temple, ordain female rabbis, and emphasize the universalism of their religion, social activism, and interfaith outreach. Reform Judaism is the largest denomination in the United States.

Orthodox Judaism

Orthodox Jews hold that the Torah was written by God and dictated to Moses, and that its laws are eternal and literal. Orthodox Judaism is basically identical to pre-Enlightenment Judaism. Orthodox Judaism is split into two main branches:

- Modern Orthodox Judaism: relatively accepting of modernity and society in general, though not welcoming of it
- Haredi Judaism (also known as ultra-Orthodox, and includes Hasidism): unwelcoming of modernity, very strict rules about morality and gender, often living in isolation from non-Haredim

Orthodox Jews often wear full Jewish garb: women often cover their hair with a scarf or wig, and men wear either a skullcap or a tall brimmed hat, formal suits, and grow peyos (long curls of hair from the temples) and long beards. Orthodox Judaism is the most popular denomination in Israel and in most other countries with Jewish populations, the United States being a notable exception.

Conservative Judaism

Conservative Judaism (also known as Masorti Judaism) was founded in the nineteenth century in Germany by Sabita Morais as a reaction against Reform Judaism. It is, consequently, more conservative than Reform and less conservative than Orthodox Judaism. Conservative synagogues make thoughtful concession to modernity; they neither obediently follow the Torah nor dismiss its relevance to modern life. Its intellectual center is the Jewish Theological Seminary in New York. Conservative Judaism emphasizes the rabbinical tradition, kosher laws, and the scientific study of the Bible. The main tenets of conservative belief are:

- Nonfundamentalism
- Acceptance of modernity
- Acceptance of both rabbinical and modern textual interpretation of the Torah

Reconstructionist Judaism

Reconstructionist Judaism is an American Jewish movement emphasizing the cultural nature of Judaism over its religious nature. Begun by Mordecai Kaplan in the 1930s as an offshoot of Conservative Judaism, Reconstructionist Judaism focuses on Jewish history, laws, and arts, and the center of Reconstructionist life is in Jewish Community Centers. One important difference between Reconstructionist sects and other Jewish sects is that Reconstructionist Jews do not accept the Torah as the word of God. This movement emphasizes Jewish historical wisdom but does not require believers to follow Talmudic decrees. It also contends that Judaism is an evolving culture and that it can and should be influenced by developments in modern life, such as scientific discoveries that may contradict the teachings of the Torah. Their position on Jewish law is that an individual's starting place of morality should be Jewish teachings, unless there is a compelling reason to follow different laws. Modern secular thought is a priority, however.

Role of Women and Homosexuals

Orthodox Judaism subscribes to very strict laws regarding the roles of men and women. Women are not ordained as rabbis, both men and women must cover their hair in synagogue, and men and women are separated during services. Women are often not allowed to study the Torah in some Orthodox sects. Homosexuality is condemned. Conservative Judaism allows individual congregations a great deal of discretion in applying Jewish law. Women may be ordained as rabbis, and homosexuals may be permitted commitment ceremonies, though same-sex marriage ceremonies are not performed. Reconstructionist Judaism allows individual congregations to determine their own stance on Jewish identity; some congregations contend that Jewish identity is patrilineal as well as matrilineal. All positions in the synagogue are open to women as well as men; gay men and lesbians play a full role in the congregation as well. Reform Judaism ordains women, allows women and men access to the same roles in temple, and allows rabbis to perform same-sex marriage ceremonies.

Shabbat Worship Practice Among Major Jewish Denominations

Orthodox Judaism services take place on Saturday morning. Women and men are separated; only men may touch or read from the Torah. The heads of both men and women must be covered. Orthodox sects emphasize the importance of ritual, reading scripted prayers for all occasions. Conservative Judaism services are held on Saturday morning. The value of ritual in conservative synagogues is as an expression of values, and conservative congregations vary widely in their orthodoxy. Some or all of the service will be in Hebrew. Reconstructionist Judaism ordains both men and women as rabbis, calls its meeting places synagogues, hold services in Hebrew rather than the vernacular, and Reconstructionist men cover their heads with yarmulkes during services. Reform Judaism calls its meeting places temples, holds services in the local language on Friday evening, and requires neither men nor women to cover their heads during services. It emphasizes the actual experience of God's creation over set rituals, believing that set rituals can alienate a Jew from God.

Religious Practices of Early Israelites

Before the First Temple, Jews were a nomadic people, pasturing sheep and wandering the land. Until Solomon's time, there were no temples at all; instead, people made animal sacrifices upon altars in the open. Beginning with the Exodus, however, there were tabernacles—large tent structures consisting of an outer and an inner area, where Israelites would gather for worship. Only the priest was allowed in the inner area, and then only once a year. Circumcision is a ritual that has been featured in Judaism from the beginning, and may have predated it. The tradition of resting on the Sabbath, as God did after creating the world, also has its origins in the earliest days of Judaism. From the beginning, Judaism was a religion of historians, with a strong focus on recording the story of their people, and their history has been proven to be basically accurate.

Jewish Religious Service

Jewish religious services vary by denomination, but the basic structure is:

- Amidah—salutations and prayers of praise
- Sh'ma—the pledge of faith, including Deuteronomy's Shema Yisrael prayer, the central prayer of Jewish life
- A public reading from the Torah led by a member of the congregation. (It is considered an honor to be selected to read.)
- The canter leads the congregation in song. (In Reform congregations this may include instruments, but in more conservative denominations instruments are forbidden on Shabbat.)
- The rabbi leads the service, offering religious instruction or illumination on a particular aspect of the Torah.

There are variations, depending on the occasion and the time of day services are being held. Orthodox services are done entirely or mostly in Hebrew, and other denominations are done mostly or entirely in the local vernacular. If it is the day of a young person's bar or bat mitzvah, they may do the reading from the Torah or lead some of the service. On holidays, services may be much longer and incorporate elements used only on particular days.

Torah, Pentateuch, and Tanakh

The Torah is the holiest book in Judaism. The Torah consists of the Pentateuch and the books of oral law (including the Talmud). Pentateuch is another term for the first five books of Moses, which are:

1. Genesis
2. Exodus
3. Leviticus
4. Numbers
5. Deuteronomy

Tanakh is the entire Hebrew Bible, consisting of the Torah, the Nevi'im ("Prophets") and Ketuvim ("Scriptures"). The Nevi'im consist of: Joshua, Judges, Samuel, Kings, Isaiah, Jeremiah, Ezekiel, and The Twelve Prophets: Hosea, Joel, Amos, Obadiah, Jonah, Micah, Nahum, Habakkuk, Zephaniah, Haggai, Zechariah, Malachi. The Ketuvim consist of: Psalms, Proverbs, Job, Song of Songs, Lamentations, Ecclesiastes, Esther, Daniel, Ezra and Nehemiah, and Chronicles.

Talmud, Mishnah, and Gemara

The Talmud is the central rabbinical text of Judaism. Judaism began as an oral tradition, but after the Babylonian Captivity and the destruction of Judea in 70 A.D., rabbis began to codify Jewish law, culminating in the Talmud. There are two slightly differing versions, compiled separately: the Babylonian Talmud and the Palestinian Talmud (the Babylonian is authoritative). The Talmud consists of the Mishnah and the Gemara. The Mishnah is the first major rabbinical work, a systematic collection of oral law and political and civil laws. The Mishnah was consolidated in Galilee around 200 A.D. out of necessity; the beginning of the Diaspora meant that Jews far from Palestine needed a book available to them that would help them to understand the Torah. The Gemara is additional legal commentary on the Mishnah. The most important non-Biblical books in Judaism, the Gemara consists of haggadah (narratives) and halachah (legal writings).

Third Temple

The Third Temple has not been built yet, and its construction is a source of violent contention. Firstly, Jews disagree about whether building it will summon the Messiah, or whether it cannot be built until the Messianic Age. Once the Messiah appears on earth and the Third Temple is built, Jews believe, peace will reign on earth, Israel will be restored, and the World of Resurrection will be ushered in, so its construction, whether now or in the Messianic Age, is of supreme spiritual importance to Jews. In addition, the Dome of the Rock, a sacred site to Muslims, occupies the location of the Temples. To destroy it and build a Jewish temple in its place, as a vocal minority of Jews advocate, would be tantamount to sparking a holy war. Reform and Reconstructionist Jews do not believe in the necessity of a Third Temple, believing that its existence and associated sacrificial rituals are a primitive form of worship that do not apply to modern times.

Rabbi

The rabbinical tradition evolved out of the Jewish Diaspora. As Jews were scattered far from Israel, there grew a need for far-flung Jews to understand God's laws, and as the Torah grew more and more central in importance to Jewish life, people far from Israel needed some means by which they could understand it. The figure of the rabbi, someone dedicated to the study and interpretation of the Torah, became important. The rabbi is the head of a Jewish synagogue (or temple, as it is known in Reform Judaism). He or she has had extensive training in Torah study, and guides followers in the twenty-first century in understanding how laws written for a nomadic people thousands of years ago in the Middle East can apply to new times and situations. In addition, the rabbi officiates at significant life rituals, but their role is not super-human. The rabbi has no greater access to God than other Jews; he or she has simply devoted years of study to understanding the Torah and is in a position to help others understand it.

Rituals Surrounding Birth, Coming of Age, Marriage, and Death

Jewish babies undergo different ceremonies, depending on sex, on their eighth day of life. Girls undergo a naming ceremony called a brit hayyim, while boys are ritually circumcised as a symbol of Jews' commitment to their covenant. When girls are twelve and boys are thirteen, they undergo a ceremony called a bar mitzvah (for boys) or bat mitzvah (for girls), in which they willingly accept their responsibilities as adult members of the Jewish community and their obligations to know and follow Jewish law. Jewish weddings are called kiddushin (sanctification) and are held under a huppah (canopy). The couple drink wine together and the groom smashes a glass with his foot, symbolizing the destruction of the Second Temple and their commitment to the Jewish faith. After death, bodies are wrapped in a linen shroud, symbolizing the equality of all people in death. The body lies in its natural state for seven days and is never left alone, a ritual known as "sitting shivah." Traditionally, bodies are not cremated, so that they may be reunited with the person's soul in Resurrection.

Kashrut Laws

Kashrut, or Jewish dietary laws, are food taboos that are "make a fence around the Torah" in order to prevent inadvertent violations of Torah laws. Their origin is unknown, but they are detailed in the Book of Leviticus. Following kashrut serves the purpose of both accepting and following God's law, though humans do not understand it, and social cohesion with other kashrut-following Jews. Meat that is kosher (clean) may only come from particular animals—those that chew cud and have cloven hoofs. Pigs, for instance, are not considered kosher. Particular slaughtering procedures, overseen by rabbis, must be employed in the production of meat. Kosher seafood includes only fish that have scales and fins (not, for instance, shellfish). In addition, meat and dairy products (a category that includes fish) cannot be eaten at the same meal, nor can they be prepared using the same utensils, appliances, or sinks.

Sabbath

Sabbath day, or Shabbat, laws, guide Jews in acceptable and unacceptable behavior on the Sabbath. Shabbat in Jewish tradition lasts from Friday at sundown to Saturday at sundown. During this time, Jews are obligated to worship and rest, in homage to God's resting on the seventh day after creating the world. Reform Jews traditionally hold a Friday evening religious service, while other sects meet on Saturday morning. During this period, all work is forbidden, including the lighting and extinguishing of fires (including, in modern days, driving, which burns fuel), carrying objects, heating food, paying money, or completing circuits (e.g., by making telephone calls or turning on or off lights). At the beginning and end of Shabbat, a special short ceremony is held; the first is called Kiddush and the second halvadah. Candles are lit and sacred wine is drunk to demarcate clearly the sacred time.

Messiah

The Messiah is a human king of the Davidic line who will be sent by God but not immortal; God is so different from humans that he could never appear in human form. The Messiah will end history and create a new age of peace where the dead are resurrected and rejoined with their bodies, and Jews come home to Israel. The Jewish Messiah is not a savior in the godly sense. Debates abound about the conditions under which the Messiah could appear: when the world is most depraved or the most deserving? Haredi Jews tend to believe in Messiah's imminent arrival, while Reform and Reconstructionist Jews believe that the "Messiah" is shorthand for the Messianic Age itself rather than a reference to a specific person.

Kabbalah

The Kabbalah is the mystical sect of Judaism, which seeks to explain the relationship between God and his creation. It has existed in some form from the beginning of the religion, but its beliefs were codified during the era 500–900 A.D. as a response to the Diaspora and the persecution of Jews in Europe. Its most important book is the Zohar, the Book of Splendor, which was written in Spain in the thirteenth century. Kabbalah contends that the world was created through ten sensual forces and that humans have three souls: animal, spirit, and super-soul, or intellect. Its most important difference with mainstream Judaism is that it believes that evil and good are not separate forces but two sides of the same force—a tenet soundly rejected by most of Judaism. Kabbalah study is esoteric and persists mostly in Haredi sects. It uses numerology, dreams, and predictions to understand the secret code of the Torah and find clues to the Messiah's arrival. Because of its mysticism, it is rejected outright by Reform and Conservative Jews influenced by the Enlightenment.

Effects of the Shoah on Jewish Theology

Because six million Jews were specifically targeted for annihilation in the Shoah, many wondered afterward where God had been. A common assessment is that "God died in the Holocaust." Jewish theology teaches that Jews have a special covenant with God, and if God did not answer his people, there are several possible conclusions:

- God does not exist.
- God exists but is not omnipotent.
- God was displeased with the Jews and punished them.
- God revoked the covenant and abandoned the Jews.
- The Shoah was an attack on the message brought to the world by the Jews.
- The Shoah was an object-lesson in man's inability to understand the mind and motivations of God.
- It is the fate of Jews to suffer for the sins of the world.

After the Shoah, doubts drove many Jews away from faith entirely. The question of Job is a persistent one for Jews, especially after the Shoah: if there is suffering in the world, how does God exist, and if it is specifically Jews who suffer, what does that mean about their covenant with God?

Jewish Passover Festival

Passover, or Pesach, is a celebratory Jewish festival that remembers the Exodus from Egypt. It takes place each March or April by the Hebrew lunar calendar and lasts eight days. A Seder, or ritual meal, is held on the first two nights, and Jews eat foods associated with Exodus. The last of the ten plagues that struck Egypt before the Exodus was the Angel of Death, who killed the firstborn male of each house in Egypt. Because the Israelites smeared lamb's blood on their doorposts and lintels, they were spared. Before their departure from Egypt, God commanded Moses to prepare a great feast, and because it had to be prepared quickly, the bread was not leavened. Therefore, Jews eat lamb, unleavened bread (matzo), and bitter herbs. Traditionally, Jews sing songs, drink four glasses of wine, and follow a strictly scripted ritual for the Seder. Firstborn children fast the day before Passover.

Shavuot

The Jewish festival of Shavuot commemorates God's giving the Ten Commandments to Moses on Mount Sinai. The festival takes place in late spring, and is adapted from an ancient festival celebrating the first harvest of the season. During the festival, Jews abstain from work and serve special meals, with an emphasis on dairy products. Synagogue services include readings from the Book of Ruth and the Akdamut, a Passover poem. Homes and synagogues are decorated with greenery and flowers, with some synagogues even building a huppah to symbolize the marriage-like union of Jews and God.

Rosh Hashanah

Rosh Hashanah is the Jewish New Year festival. This important Jewish holiday takes place, according to the Jewish lunar calendar, on the new moon near the autumn equinox. It lasts two days (one in Reform Judaism) and is said to mirror the first two days of God's creation. The holiday is a day of rest, and Shabbat laws apply, no matter what days the holiday falls on. On Rosh Hashanah,

Jews pray, eat auspicious foods (apples, honey, pomegranates, round challah bread to symbolize the cyclical nature of the year, and foods specifically mentioned in the Torah), and attend services at synagogue. Rosh Hashanah begins a period of penitence for Jews that lasts until Yom Kippur, the Day of Atonement.

Yom Kippur

Yom Kippur, the Day of Atonement, is the holiest day in the Jewish year. On this day, Jews are absolved of their sins for the previous year and renew their commitment to the covenant with God, vowing to live by God's laws in the following year. Yom Kippur is a one-day holiday, lasting from sundown to sundown, and during this period Jews fast, abstain from work, give to charity, and spend most of the day in the synagogue, praying for forgiveness and reconciliation and hearing special descriptions of the rituals performed in the temples in Jerusalem. They are also required to abstain from sex, wearing leather shoes, bathing, and using perfumes.

Sukkot

Sukkot, or the Feast of Tabernacles, is a pilgrim festival recalling the Israelites' wandering in the desert after the Exodus. It is an adapted holiday originating in a Semitic autumn harvest festival. The festival lasts eight days, with no work allowed on the first or last days. Families build tents with three covered sides called sukkah, and for eight days take all their meals there. Some Jews choose to sleep in their sukkahs as well. Traditionally, each sukkah has seven spiritual guests: Abraham, Isaac, Jacob, Moses, Aaron, Joseph, and David, and prayers are said for them as they enter the sukkah. This tradition has extended to the practice of inviting guests, Jews and non-Jews alike, to share meals in the sukkah.

Chanukah

Chanukah was historically a relatively minor Jewish holiday, but in the West has taken on more importance since it falls so close to the Christian holiday of Christmas. The holiday is a celebration of the victory of the Maccabees, Jewish rebels, over the Syrians, and the retaking of the temple in Jerusalem. After Judas Maccabaeus took back the temple, oil meant to light the temple for only one day lasted instead for eight; thus, Chanukah is known as the "festival of lights" which Jews celebrate by lighting an eight-candled menorah, with an additional candle lit for each night of the festival. They give gifts, eat oil-based foods, and play games. In modern times the significance of Chanukah is also as a celebration of Israeli victories over foreign oppression.

Purim

The festival of Purim commemorates Esther, the queen of Persia during the Babylonian Captivity. The empire of Persia conquered Babylon during the Captivity, and Esther, who was secretly Jewish, married the king. When she learned of a plot to kill the Jews of the area, she shared this news with the king, confessed her Jewish identity, and the king allowed the Jews to battle the enemies, whom they defeated. The holiday is known as the "feast of lots" due to the lots that were drawn to determine the day of the planned massacre of the Jews. The holiday is one of merriment and is especially focused on children. People play games and wear costumes. Special services are held at synagogues, and Jews read from the Book of Esther. The day is preceded by a day of fasting and includes giving to charity.

Bat Mitzvah and Bar Mitzvah

The coming-of-age ritual in Judaism is known as a bar mitzvah (for boys) or a bat mitzvah (for girls). This is a modern rite, and was originally only done for boys. The ceremony takes place as part of an ordinary Shabbat service. For boys, it takes place after their thirteenth birthday, and for girls, after their twelfth. At this age, boys (as well as girls in more liberal sects) are considered old enough to constitute part of a minyan. The rite of passage represents a Jewish person's entry into adulthood and their acceptance of their responsibilities to know and follow the Torah. The ceremony follows years of religious instruction and consists of the honoree giving a blessing over the reading from the Torah, doing a reading themselves, and possibly a speech (traditionally beginning "Today, I am a man/woman...") Afterward, the honoree is typically the guest of honor at a party, where they are given gifts to celebrate their now being a "son or daughter of the commandment."

Death and Afterlife

According to the Talmud, the soul is judged by God after death. The righteous enter the "world to come," but some must wait in a shadowy place called Sheol for a period of approximately a year while they come to terms with their actions on earth. Judaism is at heart a nonexclusive religion that does not punish non-Jews after death. Non-Jews who are evil cease to exist after death, but virtuous non-Jews can also enter the world to come. There is another sense of an afterlife in Judaism as well. After the appearance of the Messiah and the Great Day of Judgment, bodies and souls will be reunited and live eternally in bliss in the World of Resurrection. This is a traditional Jewish view, which is now rejected by Reform and Reconstructionist sects. Fundamentally, Jews believe in the importance of following God's laws; for Jews, the performance of mitzvoth is a privilege. Jews are motivated less by the reward or punishment of an afterlife than by their duty to follow God's commandments.

Reincarnation

In the mystical schools of Judaism, there is a belief in "tikkun olam," or repair, that allows for the reincarnation of human souls if they have died with unfinished business on earth. Traditionally, this may happen up to three times for one human soul. In order to finish one's business on earth, one may reappear for only a short time, a doctrine that helps to explain those who die young. The Jewish belief that all Jewish souls were present during the receipt of the Commandments on Mount Sinai is made possible by this belief in reincarnation.

Covenant

Jews believe that they are a chosen people. By this, the vast number do not mean that they are superior to non-Jews or that they are any closer to God; rather, they believe that God chose them for a specific purpose—to be a light to other nations and a nation of priests giving praise to God. There have been several specific covenants with God in Jewish history:

- Noahic covenant: God promises never again to destroy the earth by flood.
- Abrahamic covenant: God promises the land of Canaan to Abraham's descendents, who are a blessed people.
- Mosaic covenant: God gives Moses the Ten Commandments.
- Davidic covenant: God tells David that he and his heirs are the rightful rulers of Israel (thus signifying that the Messiah will be a descendent of David's).

A minority of Jews disagree—particularly those (but by no means all) in mystical traditions. It is their belief that Jews do have a special and superior relationship to God than do others. This is not a mainstream Jewish view. Reconstructionist Judaism rejects the doctrine of chosenness altogether, arguing that it leads to judgment and racism against non-Jews

Conception of God

Strictly speaking, modern Judaism is a development of the religion of the Pharisees from over 2000 years ago, but the term "Judaism" can be taken to refer simply to the religion prescribed in the Old Testament. Modern Judaism arguably has a different conception of God than modern Christianity, but regardless, if we take "the God of Judaism" to be the God of the Old Testament, then He is the basis for all Abrahamic religions' conception of God. This God is a creator god, nonphysical, and genderless (though the Bible does refer often to God as male). God is omniscient (knowing all things), omnipresent (located everywhere), and omnipotent (all-powerful). God is both transcendent above the universe and available personally to individuals. God is also just, rewarding the good and punishing the wicked. Modern Jews disagree about the nature of God: whether God himself wrote the words to the Torah or inspired them, what sort of being God must be to allow evil in the world, and whether God is more vengeful or merciful. The Jewish God is a god of justice—but because God is perfect, his justice represents fairness, not revenge.

Jewish Symbols

- Mezuzah—a box containing a piece of parchment on which is written the Shema Yisrael. According to the Torah, Jews are to place a mezuzah on every doorframe of their homes in order to fulfill the mitzvah to inscribe the Shema "on the doorposts of your house."
- Menorah—a seven-pillared candelabrum and symbol of the Jewish people. It was originally used in the Temple and is closely associated with Chanukah, the festival of lights.
- Tefillin—a pair of black leather boxes containing verses from the Bible, attached to the head and arm during prayers in order to fulfill several of the mitzvoth given to Jews.
- Shofar—a small ceremonial trumpet made from a ram's horn.
- Kipah—a skullcap worn in synagogues and, more often, by Orthodox Jews. It symbolizes the missionary aspect of Judaism as well as the awareness of God above oneself at all times. Also called a yarmulke.
- Magen David—the Star of David, the symbol of Judaism. Legend says that it is modeled after the shield the young warrior David wore into battle.

Seven Laws of Noah

According to Jewish tradition, when God commanded Noah to build an ark to save his family from the flood, he also gave him seven additional commandments that were to be binding for all people:

1. Not to commit idolatry
2. Not to commit blasphemy
3. Not to commit murder
4. Not to have forbidden sexual relations
5. Not to commit theft
6. Not to eat flesh cut from a living animal
7. To establish courts of justice to punish violators of the other six laws

These commandments are binding not only for Jews but for others as well; any non-Jews who observe these commandments are assured of a place in the world to come. It is here that the Jewish God offers "an eye for an eye" justice in response to human murder.

Maimonides and the Thirteen Articles of Faith

Maimonides was the most important medieval Jewish thinker. He was a Spanish rabbi, physician, and philosopher best known for developing a continuation of Aristotelian thought. His major doctrine is that it is impossible for the truths revealed by human intelligence to contradict the truths of God. Maimonides wrote a manifesto of thirteen articles of faith summarizing what he took to be the minimum requirements of Jewish faith. The thirteen articles of faith are:

1. God exists.
2. God is one and unique.

3. God is incorporeal.
4. God is eternal.
5. Worship and prayer are to be to God only.
6. The prophets spoke truth from God.
7. Moses was the greatest of the prophets.
8. The Written and Oral Torah were given by God to Moses.
9. There will be no other Torah.
10. God knows the thoughts and deeds of men.
11. God will reward the good and punish the wicked.
12. The Messiah will come.
13. The dead will be resurrected.

613 Mitzvot

The 613 mitzvot are commandments found in the Torah. There have been several attempts to compile them, but the standard list comes from Maimonides. The list contains a mixture of positive commandments (that it is required of a Jew to do) and negative ones (that a Jew is forbidden from doing). Some apply to particular kinds of people (e.g., only men or only people within the state of Israel) or only at a particular time (e.g., during particular holidays). Some only apply to the destroyed Second Temple. All commandments may be broken in order to save a life, with the exception of three categories:

- Murder
- Idolatry
- Forbidden sexual behavior

It is considered better to die than to break any of the commandments that fall under these categories. Life is considered so important to Jews, however, that is it forbidden to do a mitzvah if it endangers a life (for example, doctors may make calls on Shabbat, even though it technically breaks a commandment, because not to would endanger others' lives).

Shema Yisrael and the Many Names of God

The most important prayer in Judaism is the Shema Yisrael, whose words, when translated, are: "Hear, O Israel: the LORD our God, the LORD is one." The recitation of this prayer is a mitzvah (commandment) for Jews, illustrating the importance of the Jewish belief of one and only one god. In the Hebrew Bible, God has many names, but only one personal one, YHWH (known as the holy tetragrammaton). The other names, such as Elohim, Adonai, and El simply illustrate aspects of God. God is so holy to Jews that writing the name YHWH in Hebrew is forbidden. In ancient practice, to know the secret name of something was to have power over it, and the practice of using a euphemism for YHWH is common. Often, God will be referred to as Adonai, meaning "my Lord," by Jews in order to avoid saying the true name of God.

Christianity

Jesus's Birth

Sometime between 7 and 2 B.C., Jesus of Nazareth was born. According to the Christian Bible, he is the Son of God whose only human parent was a virgin, Mary. She gives birth to him in a manger in a stable while traveling with her husband, Joseph, to Bethlehem in Judea for the Roman census. An angel then appears to shepherds in a field, announcing the birth of the Messiah, and they come to worship the child. According to one gospel, Magi or wise men come to see the child later, bearing gifts to him in a house. Upon hearing of the child's birth, King Herod announces that all children under the age of two in Bethlehem will be killed, whereupon the family flees to Egypt. After this point, the Gospel of Luke mentions Jesus having a religious discussion in the temple at the age of 12, but otherwise no more is heard of him until the beginning of his ministry as an adult.

Jesus was born in to a Hebrew society racked with political difficulty. It had been colonized, along with the entire Mediterranean region, by the Roman Empire, with Augustus Caesar on the throne. The reign was brutal but stable, and the entire empire shared a Greco-Roman intellectual culture, a common functional language, and Roman infrastructure, from building styles to roads. Roman religion was on the wane and provoked little interest; meanwhile, Judaism was recruiting converts in Israel. Mystery religions, like the cult of the Egyptian god Osiris, were attracting followers; because they tended to be democratic in membership, allowing slaves (of which there were many in the Roman Empire) to join, they were popular. Jewish interest in the Messiah was on the rise; many Jews hoped for a prophesied military ruler to defeat Rome. There was a general anxiety about what many perceived as the imminent end of the world. Jesus began his ministry in a violent, anxious land fraught with political tension and convinced the end of the world would occur at any moment.

Enemies Created by Jesus's Ministry

Jesus's ministry had created many enemies; to himself and his disciples, he was the incarnation of God, a belief that was heretical to many. Other enemies included the Pharisees (of which he may have himself been a member, and of which some of his disciples certainly were), the Sadducees, and especially the Zealots, violent revolutionaries who hoped for a Messiah who would use his power against the Romans.

Crucifixion of Jesus

Around 33 A.D., Jesus was crucified in Jerusalem, condemned to death by the Roman governor Pontius Pilate. According to the Bible, a week before his execution, Jesus warned his disciples that he would soon be killed by the authorities. During the next week's Passover festival in Jerusalem, Jesus entered the city on a donkey and was greeted enthusiastically. He spent time preaching and held a Passover meal with his disciples. That night, his disciple Judas Iscariot betrayed him to the Jewish leadership who turned him over to the Romans for a show trial, after which he was brutally beaten and executed by hanging from a cross. He was entombed that day, but women coming to tend the tomb three days later found it empty. Over the next forty days Jesus appeared bodily to various people, then was witnessed ascending to heaven. This miracle is the central act of Christianity. According to Christian tradition, Jesus's self-sacrifice redeems mankind from their sins.

Paul

Paul is known as the second founder of Christianity. He did not meet Jesus during his earthly ministry. The New Testament Book of Acts, however, describes Paul's vision of Jesus on the road to Damascus—one that changed him from being a persecutor of Christians to a champion of the faith.

Paul's significance is as a missionary of Christianity; he put forth the doctrine that Jesus' execution redeemed mankind from their sins. Paul was by no means the most active missionary of the early Jerusalem Church, but his story is documented by the New Testament. He was a Pharisee from Tarsus in Asia Minor. After his conversion to Christianity, he made three missionary journeys across Asia Minor and Greece. Eventually he was arrested by Roman authorities in Jerusalem and presumed executed. He began preaching first to Jews and then to Gentiles, making Christianity appealing by abolishing the requirement for them to adhere to Jewish law. He converted them with a baptism ritual and celebrated the Eucharist. By abolishing the need to follow Jewish law, Paul set in motion Christianity's missionary thrust and separated it permanently from Judaism.

Consolidation of the New Testament

Many Christians expected Jesus's imminent return to earth after his death; therefore, they did not necessarily take much care to document his life. It was converted Christians who came later who made a systematic attempt to compile the information they had. The four gospels, telling the story of Jesus, were written between 50 and 70 A.D. Other books circulated by Christians included histories and epistles (letters, mostly written by Paul, to congregations offering advice and encouragement in their faith). While the books may have been generally recognized as a fixed canon, they were not universally declared to be so until the fourth century, when the Council of Laodicea authorized 26 of the 27 books that currently comprise the New Testament, Revelation being omitted at that time.

Apocrypha of Christianity

Many texts were ultimately excluded from the official New Testament, either because they were of questionable value, their authorship was uncertain, they contained theological or other errors, or they contradicted other canonical texts. To this day, there are various versions of the New Testament in use by different sects that regard different books as canonical and apocryphal, though all the major Christian groups—all Protestant denominations, as well as the Roman Catholic and Eastern Orthodox churches—agree on the classification of the New Testament. (They do, however, disagree on a few Old Testament books' canonicity.) These apocryphal writings include the Gnostic Gospels, writings from the Gnostic sect of Christianity that recount Jesus's supposed sayings after his resurrection. (These writings date from the period of Jesus but were not discovered until the modern era.) In addition, the Gospel of the Hebrews was in circulation for some time but eventually determined to be apocryphal. There are several Infancy Gospels addressing the early life of Jesus, in addition to gospels according to different disciples of Jesus, books of acts concerning various apostles, noncanonical epistles, and books concerning the life of Mary.

Gnostic Christians

The first major controversy of early Christianity concerned the Gnostic Christians, a mystical sect whose beliefs are unclear at this point, but who seemed to agree on the principle of a "divine spark" in all people, and that matter, of which the world was composed, was a hindrance to this divine spark and therefore evil. Because of this, the world must be redeemed by a messiah. They may have been a Jewish sect that predated Christ. Gnostics also believed in esoteric, private revelations which only their own members could access. The Gnostic belief that matter was evil tended towards one of two extremes: believing that all bodily impulses ought to be subdued for one's spiritual benefit (asceticism), or believing that all bodily impulses were able to be indulged freely, because the spirit is all that mattered (hedonism).

Jesus's Relationship to Prophecy of Jewish Messiah

Jesus was an extremely controversial figure in the Israel of his day. He attracted many followers; simultaneously, many Jews were concerned that support for any messianic movements would expose them to punishment by the Romans. Followers of Jesus argued that he was the Messiah for the following reasons, among others:

- He was born of a virgin.
- He was born in Bethlehem.
- He was a descendent of David.
- He was crucified.
- He was the prophesyd Suffering Servant of Isaiah.
- He fulfilled Isaiah's prophecy about God.

Jews not convinced of this counter-argued that the idea of God becoming a man was insulting to God, that Jesus was likely born in Nazareth, and that the Suffering Servant stood for Israel the nation, not an individual. Theologically, Jesus was not the Messiah Jews had expected. Under foreign occupation, Jews hoped the Messiah would be a military ruler who would literally free Israel from its oppression, but this was not among Jesus's priorities. Some Christians say that Jesus will do this for Israel at the second coming, which Jews argue is not mentioned in the Old Testament.

Eschatology

Some scholars define Jesus's central message as an eschatological one, a warning about the imminent end of the world. The Israel of his day was especially concerned about this, as evidenced in the Book of Revelation, and Christians throughout history have been concerned that they were living in the "end times." Christians believe that Jesus will return once more to make a final judgment of humanity before ending the world. Christians have historically been focused primarily on the world to come, a focus which, perhaps paradoxically, has motivated some great achievements to the benefit of mankind in the present world. Christians are unique among major religions for this focus on the end times, although it is a focus by no means shared by all Christians. Protestants are especially concerned with it. Some interpret the eschatological language in Revelation literally, while others, known as "amillennialists," believe the passages metaphorically describe the whole age between Christ's first and second comings and hence do not provide clues by which Christians can interpret current events as harbingers of the end. All major Christian groups, however, believe in an eventual return of Jesus in final judgment.

Christianity in the Roman Empire

Christianity began under the Roman Empire, a regime that tolerated local religions for the most part but was especially threatened by Christianity. Belief in Roman deities was on the decline, but a certain amount of respect for them was expected of Rome's conquered peoples. Because Christianity was considered by some to be a secretive religion, with violent-sounding rites (eating the body of God, for instance), Romans were suspicious of Christians and thought of them as less than loyal subjects. Under various emperors, crackdowns on Christians were intermittent but occasionally very violent; persecution that existed was a product of local governors rather than a statewide policy. Christians suffered especially under Nero in the first century A.D. and were publicly executed, including being fed to lions in the Coliseum and made into human torches. The fourth-century emperor Constantine, however, received a religious vision on the battlefield and converted to Christianity. His 313 Edict of Milan made toleration of Christianity the law of Rome, and by 380 Theodosius I had made Christianity the official religion of the empire.

Christian Monasticism

The monastic tradition of Christianity began in Egypt in the third century A.D., although there is no Jewish tradition of monasticism. Originally, monks were ascetics, and engaged in acts of self-torture and deprivation to prove their faith, in imitation of Jesus's forty days in the desert. This tradition gradually died away and was replaced by a tradition of communal living, celibacy (although not in the eastern tradition), poverty, and obedience. Western monasteries are headed by abbots and are guided in their purpose by the Rule of St. Benedict, St. Augustine, or St. Basil, depending on the order. There are many orders of monks and nuns, but all share the common purpose of pursuing an active and contemplative life in service to God. The original western mendicant orders (orders relying on the community for their financial support) are the Franciscans, Carmelites, Dominicans, Servites, and Augustinians. In medieval times, monasteries were important sources of education, translation, and scholarly work. Today they exist to share the Christian faith and serve the poor.

Early Christian Church

Initially, Christian life centered on Jerusalem, but Alexandria and Antioch became later capitals. Jesus had designated the apostles to lead the church after his death, and Simon Peter became the bishop of Rome. Although each large city in the empire had a bishop, a major church leader, the bishop of the Church of Rome eventually solidified his role as the primary leader. In 330 A.D., the emperor Constantine, a Christian convert, moved his capital to Byzantium, leaving a political vacuum in Rome that was soon filled by religious leaders. Compounded by political controversies in eastern churches, the church soon established that the Roman bishop stood for Christian orthodoxy. Eventually, the bishops of Rome would be known as popes.

Simon Peter, James, and Stephen

Simon Peter was appointed bishop of Rome after the death of Jesus, but he soon moved on to other communities to do missionary work. According to Roman Catholics, Jesus specifically appointed him as the human head of the church before his death, telling him, "On this rock I will build my church." The popes that followed Simon Peter are then presumed to have this universal authority passed down to them. (Protestants disagree with this interpretation, generally holding that the "rock" of Matthew 16:18 is Peter's faith or confession.) James was a brother of some sort of Jesus, although different Christian sects take issue with the idea of Mary bearing children naturally. (For instance, Roman Catholics and Eastern Orthodox hold that Mary was a virgin her entire life.) Although he was not a follower of Christ until after the crucifixion, James converted and assumed the leadership of the early church in Jerusalem after Simon Peter left for Rome. He was the first bishop of Jerusalem and the author of the Epistle of James. Stephen was a disciple of Jesus who preached in the streets of Jerusalem after Jesus's death. He was tried for blasphemy and executed after speaking against the temple and the law, thus making him Christianity's first martyr.

Conversion of Paul to Christianity

The figure of the apostle Paul begins as a persecutor of Christians, although scholars are not sure in what capacity. By Paul's own account described in his letters, he traveled to Damascus to arrest Christians. On the road there, however, he experienced a divine vision in which Jesus himself appeared personally to Paul, revealing the truth of his resurrection, and Paul was struck blind. Jesus then appeared to the disciple Ananias and instructed him to find Paul and cure his blindness, which Ananias was able to do. Paul converted to Christianity immediately, was baptized, and began his ministry.

Early Christian Church Leadership

The leaders of the church were disorganized immediately following Christ's death. Many Christians expected Jesus to return at any moment, and their concern was not for creating a long-lasting church hierarchy, nor for recording the events they had witnessed. As years passed and he had not returned, however, there grew a need for organization to serve the growing number of followers. Simon Peter, disciple of Jesus, was the first bishop of Rome. Bishops were placed in charge of the Christian community in particular geographical areas, and many of them had different notions about Christian doctrines. Paul's letters indicate that he spent a great deal of energy correcting errant doctrine and practices in other churches. The church had several offices, starting with the twelve apostles who were appointed by Christ. These apostles then appointed other officers in the churches, such as pastors, teachers, deacons, and evangelists. The first deacons were appointed in Jerusalem by apostles to help with the congregation's material welfare, whereas the other offices focused more on teaching doctrine. As the imperial powers began to lose stability around 400 A.D., the power of the church increased to fill the vacuum, strengthening Christianity in Europe.

Apostles' Creed

In the early Christian church, several movements arose, offering a different interpretation of the significance of Jesus and the role of God in human affairs. In order to establish an orthodox faith for the church, the early church leaders created the Apostles' Creed, a statement of faith for the church around 340 A.D.:

> "I believe in God the Father Almighty, Maker of Heaven and earth.
>
> And in Jesus Christ, his only Son, our Lord, who was conceived by the Holy Ghost, born of the Virgin Mary, suffered under Pontius Pilate, was crucified, dead, and buried: He descended into hell; the third day He rose again from the dead; he ascended into heaven, and sitteth on the right hand of God the Father Almighty; from thence He shall come to judge the quick and the dead.
>
> I believe in the Holy Ghost, the holy catholic* church, the communion of saints, the forgiveness of sins, the resurrection of the body, and the life everlasting. Amen."

*The word catholic means "universal" and does not refer to the Roman Catholic church.

These words were carefully scripted to refute particular points of doctrinal dispute the church fathers had with heretical sects. This creed, or a variation of it, became the basic statement of faith in the eastern and western Christian churches.

First Council of Nicaea and the Nicene Creed

In the fourth century A.D., Arius, a Christian preacher in Libya, argued that Jesus was an eminently high and powerful creature, but not divine like the Father. To the church fathers, this was heresy, and to refute this statement, the First Council of Nicaea was held in 325. A new statement of faith was adopted for the church, and over many decades, was revised to counter additional heresies. The eventual wording, besides restating certain aspects of the Apostles' Creed, emphasized that Jesus was of the same substance or essence as the Father, being begotten but not created. A major controversy of the council was whether to use the term for "same substance" (*homoousios*) or "similar substance" (*homoiousios*), where the terms differed only by one letter, specifically one iota; to preserve the unity of Christ and the Father, the term for "same substance" was used in the creed. This Nicene Creed remains an official statement of faith for Western and Eastern Christians.

Christian Crusades

The Latin kingdom of Palestine eventually succumbed to Arab conquest beginning in the seventh century. From the eleventh to the thirteenth centuries, Christian armies attempted to retake Palestine from its Muslim rulers, stop Muslim expansion into the Byzantine Empire, and expand Christian territory through nine major and several other minor military campaigns. The church sponsored nearly all the crusades, with most crusaders being subjects of the Holy Roman Empire or the Franks in France. In addition to forays into the Middle East, crusades were also fought against Christian heresy and Islamic forces in Spain and Italy. Most crusades failed, though there were intermittent victories, including European control of Jerusalem for a century beginning in 1099. In the end, European crusaders retreated, but not before sacking the eastern Christian city of Constantinople, creating a permanent rift between the eastern and western branches of the church. In addition, contact with the Muslim world introduced Europeans to advances in medicine, science, and architecture.

Spanish Inquisition

Catholic Spain, which had been ruled by Islamic governments for centuries, drove the Muslims out and reinstated a Catholic monarchy in the middle ages. In the fifteenth century, King Ferdinand II and Queen Isabella I began tribunals in cooperation with the church, to ensure a Catholic orthodoxy in Spain. Jews were forced to convert or face expulsion, and the tribunals investigated their sincerity. Protestants were persecuted as well, though there were not many present in Spain. Muslims were forced to flee. Among the crimes pursued were witchcraft, sodomy, blasphemy, and heresy. The tribunals sometimes employed torture to secure false confessions and burned at the stake those found guilty.

Martin Luther and Ulrich Zwingli

Martin Luther was the most outstanding figure of the Protestant Reformation. After being nearly struck by lightning, Luther became a monk and noted scholar. Outraged by the rampant corruption within the church, he nailed a text with 95 theses to the church door at Wittenberg in 1517. His particular objections were to abuses by the laity, especially simony, nepotism, and the sale of indulgences. Luther's aim was to instigate reform, but he was eventually excommunicated and banned from writing. He continued writing in secret, aided by the new invention of the printing press, and was supported by political leaders. By 1522, the Protestant Reformation was underway, and Luther organized the Protestant church in Germany. Influenced by Luther, the Swiss reformer Ulrich Zwingli agitated for reforms of Catholicism as well, including an end to the celibate priesthood, the veneration of statues and icons, and the worship of saints. Zwingli and Luther, however, were divided on their doctrine of the Lord's Supper—Luther believing that Christ was physically present, and Zwingli denying this—which prevented their followers from holding a unified Protestant front.

Social Conditions That Allowed the Protestant Reformation

The Protestant Reformation was a social movement with roots in the immediate past. The relatively recent invention of the printing press by Johannes Gutenberg allowed for two important developments that aided the Reformation: the highly efficient distribution of written ideas and the translation of the Bible into the local vernacular. Peasants unable to read Latin could see for themselves what the Bible contained. In addition, there was an upsurge of nationalism after the medieval period, a general clamoring for national rulers with whom Rome did not interfere. For rulers, the Reformation was something to capitalize on as a means to political independence. Henry VIII of Britain withdrew from the Catholic Church and founded the Church of England, partly as a way to obtain a divorce, but primarily to assert his independence from Rome. Luther attracted great support from German rulers, who saw the Reformation as a way to control church property, in addition to a general fondness for his doctrine of "the priesthood of the believer."

Schism of the Medieval Christian Church

When Constantine moved the political capital of the Roman Empire from Rome to Constantinople, the eastern and western branches of the Catholic Church began to drift further and further apart. Without effective political leaders in Rome, church leaders took on a larger role, while the more powerful rulers of Constantinople created no such power vacuum. The causes of the schism were linguistic, cultural, political, and theological. The main theological issue was the role of the papacy, which Eastern Church patriarchs did not accept as divine. In addition, the "*filioque*" clause of the Nicene Creed, which is Latin for "and the son," changed the creed to say that the Holy Spirit "proceeds from the Father and the Son." This was unacceptable to the Eastern Church, as it had been added to a long-established creed and violated their understanding of the Trinity. The final blow came in the middle ages. In 1054, Pope Leo IX excommunicated the eastern patriarch Cerularius, and in 1204, western crusaders sacked Constantinople, rendering the breach unfixable.

European Wars of Religion of 1562-1648

The period following the Protestant Reformation was marked by religious wars across Europe. The Thirty Years' War began in 1618 in the Holy Roman Empire, after Luther-supporting leaders refused to accept the new Catholic emperor. The war caused massive famine, disease, and death in the empire, ultimately losing 30% of its population before eventually dissolving as an empire. The Eighty Years' War (1568–1648) began with a rebellion of the Protestant Netherlands against their rulers, the Spanish Empire. The French Wars of Religion (1562–1598) were fought between the Calvinist Huguenots and the Catholic majority. The Edict of Nantes (1598) guaranteed all French subjects freedom of worship, basically ending the war. (Some conflict continued afterward.) Later, in 1685, the edict was rejected. Most French Protestants eventually left France. The Peace of Westphalia ended both the Thirty Years' War and the Eighty Years' War; it declared that state sovereignty took precedence over religious leadership, recognized the Peace of Augsburg of 1554 (which had declared that the religion of a region's leader was the official religion of its people), and guaranteed freedom of worship for believers in minority religions.

Missionary Movement of Christianity

One advantage Christianity has among religions is its adaptability, that it is not tied to a particular cultural expression. With the advent of the Christian church outside of Israel, specific cultural customs are not strictly essential to the practice of the faith. This makes Christianity more accessible to people without access to Christian cultural history. The doctrine of salvation has historically motivated a missionary impulse in Christianity. From the very early days of the faith, beginning with Paul (and, it is said, Thomas in India), Christians have traveled far to preach about their religion and gain converts. Spanish missionaries attached themselves to explorers in the western hemisphere in order to convert any people they encountered. Perhaps paradoxically, Protestants, influenced by Calvinism, experienced a resurgence in missionary energies from their doctrine of predestination. Their belief was that, as God was sovereign over all affairs, He could also bless the missionaries with favorable reaction to their preaching. By the twentieth century, nationalist movements in colonized territories grew to resent missionary work, believing it to be a tool of "racism" and imperialism. In some newly independent nations, conversion became a crime for both the missionary and the convert.

Development of Catholic Doctrine

Between the Council of Trent and the Second Vatican Council, Catholic theology remained more or less unchanged. A few doctrines, however, were established during this period:

- Papal infallibility. The major product of the first Vatican Council (1869), papal infallibility declares that when a Pope speaks officially ("from the chair," or *ex cathedra*) on issues of faith and morality, God grants him a special gift of infallibility.
- The Immaculate Conception. In 1854, Pope Pius IX confirmed as dogma what had been in common belief previously, that Mary, Jesus's mother, had not only conceived a child as a virgin but had also been born without original sin herself. (So, the Immaculate Conception does *not* refer to Jesus's conception.)

- The bodily assumption of Mary. In 1950, Pope Pius XII made official Catholic dogma that Mary was assumed body and soul directly into heaven at the end of her earthly life. The dogma leaves unsettled whether Mary died prior to being assumed.

Development of the Pope

In the early centuries of Christianity, power was gradually concentrated in the person of the bishop of Rome, who became known as the pope, from the Latin *papa*, meaning "father." According to Roman Catholic belief, the pope in Rome had supremacy over the church from the beginning, starting with Peter the apostle. As the papacy grew in power, the Roman Empire fell, being invaded by Christian conquerors that spared the church while destroying the institutions of the state. At the Council of Chalcedon in 451, the Bishop of Constantinople was declared to have powers similar to those of the Roman bishop, and gradually the eastern churches split from the western ones, though this did not become official for several centuries.

Protestant Fundamentalist Movement

The Protestant Fundamentalist movement was a largely American phenomenon, a response to liberalism and modernity in the United States. The effects of the scientific revolution and the Enlightenment were clearly felt by the end of the nineteenth century, and they threatened prevailing Protestant beliefs about the nature of the world. Those who believed that the Bible's claims could be historically criticized as erroneous became known as Modernists; those who believed Scripture was infallible were known as Fundamentalists. Fundamentalism in Christianity seeks to reaffirm orthodox Christianity. Fundamentalists believe that the Bible is inerrant, and seek to apply its teachings not only to spiritual life, but also to secular areas, whenever the Bible makes claims in such areas. Fundamentalists believe that the Bible, in addition to being a moral text, touches upon scientific and other matters as well. Fundamentalist Christians tend to oppose any act in secular society that contradicts biblical principles. For example, they often oppose the teaching of evolution in public schools, feminism, and homosexuality.

Changes in Christianity Since World War II

The postmodern and existential philosophical movements of the twentieth century had a tremendous secularizing effect on western societies. Church attendance among traditionally Christian Europeans has fallen to as little as 2% in some countries, while in the United States attendance numbers have remained mostly the same (and much higher than in Europe). The Roman Catholic Church in particular has struggled for clergy in the past decades, and has debated eliminating the celibacy requirement for clergy and nuns in an effort to improve recruitment. The missionary movement, however, has increased the numbers of Christians in traditionally non-Christian parts of the world, like Asia and Africa. The number of Korean Christians has grown tremendously in the twentieth century. The adaptability of Christianity has led to a non-Western version of Christianity in many places, using local symbols and mythology to illustrate Christian principles, and what had traditionally been an imported religion from Europe has taken on more authentic local flavor in many parts of the world.

Second Vatican Council

The biggest changes in the Catholic Church since the Council of Trent took place during the Second Vatican Council of 1962–1965. In response to declining numbers of Catholic adherents, church leaders made sweeping modernizing reforms of Catholic doctrine in order to make it more accessible to the laity, many of whom felt increasingly alienated from the church. Some of the most important doctrinal changes included:

- Allowing the local language to be used in place of Latin in many parts of the Mass
- Abolishing the traditional Index of Prohibited Books
- Allowing more community participation in worship
- Embracing more ecumenical principles, including the doctrine that salvation is a mystery known only to God
- Acknowledging that non-Catholics can also be considered true Christians
- Condemning anti-Semitism and officially no longer holding Jews responsible for Jesus's death
- Allowing music in religious services in nonstandard ways
- Simplifying religious rites generally

Religious Conversion and Ministry of Jesus

The documented adult life of Jesus begins with his baptism in the river Jordan by John the Baptist, a popular and charismatic figure who used the rite as a symbolic act of penitence. After this, Jesus went into the desert for forty days and nights, fasting, where he was tempted by Satan with easy glory, but refuted him with Scripture. Jesus then returned to Galilee to begin to preach, which he did for 1-3 years (the gospels are unclear on the length of his ministry). He selected between four and twelve disciples and traveled as a rabbi, teacher, and healer, preaching in a charismatic style. There is no central theme of Jesus' ministry. He preached on the kingdom of God, the importance of repentance, and the implications of his divinity. Morally, he emphasized inner purity over against the Pharisees' merely external "righteousness," showing that they, not he, were the true breakers of the Mosaic law. Part of Jesus's ministry involved miracles, including turning water to wine, healing the sick, blind, and lame, raising the dead, and walking on water.

Council of Trent and the Catholic Counter-Reformation

The Protestant Reformation swept European society into chaos, and the Catholic response was the Council of Trent, a conference of church leaders held periodically from 1545 to 1563. Feelings were highly divided: while some leaders' aim was reconciliation with Protestants, most aimed to state Catholic doctrine so explicitly as to prevent any possibility of reconciliation, and it was this that was accomplished. Some of the doctrinal points stated as a result of the Council included:

- A reaffirmation of Catholic Tradition as equal in authority to the Bible.
- A declaration that the Latin Vulgate Bible was the one true sacred canon.
- A declaration of the church's sole authority in interpreting Scripture.
- A reaffirmation of the veneration of saints and sacred images.

Like the Protestant Reformation, the Catholic Counter-Reformation sought to purify the church of corruption, but from within. Some of the reforms included modifying the system of indulgences, founding seminaries for the proper training of clergy, and establishing new monastic orders aimed at outreach to communities alienated from the church.

Twentieth Century Ecumenical Movement in Christianity

The general decline in church attendance by Christians after World War II, as well as the problems created by inter-denominational conflicts, led to the twentieth century ecumenical movement. The movement's aim was Christian unity, and it was officially begun in Amsterdam in 1948 at the World Council of Churches. Protestant ecumenical movements had been in place for over a century, but this movement moved in the twentieth century toward a goal of unity for all Christians. The ecumenical movement, however, has made little progress in reconciling Christians. Some Protestant denominations with relatively small theological differences have united, especially those that originally split over now-moot social issues (for example, slavery in the United States). Meanwhile, schisms in the Presbyterian and Anglican churches have resulted from new social issues, such as the ordination of female or homosexual clergy. Ultimately, the Orthodox, Catholic, and Protestant churches remain deeply divided.

Christian Evangelical Movement

The Christian religion has always been one of evangelism, i.e. the recruitment of non-Christians for the purpose of conversion. In the twentieth century, however, many Christian churches, especially American Protestant congregations, grew increasingly interested in evangelizing nonbelievers and believers of other faiths to Christianity. Their efforts to do so have become increasingly organized in recent decades, and take many forms, from traditional missionary work overseas to street preaching. Their message is generally to be born again, placing one's faith in Christ for the forgiveness of sins. The evangelical population overlaps somewhat with the fundamentalist population, and tends to be Bible-focused, often literally so, emphasizing Jesus's death and resurrection as the means to salvation. A trend in American churches has been evangelizing nonreligious Americans living in suburban isolation through the "megachurch," a church serving an enormous population, and providing many social services, from matchmaking to daycare.

Avignon Papacy and the Issue of Antipopes

During the medieval age, the Catholic Church became increasingly powerful and increasingly corrupt. Kings and church leaders fought for power, and the church, vastly wealthy, behaved almost as a state itself, with standing armies. Selling church offices for money became commonplace. In 1309, Pope Clement V, a Frenchman, moved the papacy to Avignon, where it spent nearly seventy years under the thumb of the French king. This was the "Avignon papacy." Almost all the church leaders during this period were French, and these changes cost the church support in nations that were enemies of France. In 1378, Pope Urban VI was elected, and he restored the papacy to Rome, but the church cardinals voided the election, choosing a different pope instead. The Council of Pisa was convened in 1409 to settle the issue of papal authority, but chose a third pope instead. Since there could only be one pope, the other claimants were "antipopes," even though there was confusion in identifying them. The Council of Constance, held 1414–1418, restored the papacy officially to Rome, producing unity in the church but not an end to church abuses. That would be addressed during the Counter-Reformation.

Protestant Reformation and Previous Reformers

Martin Luther did not act in isolation in rejecting the corruption of the Catholic Church. For two centuries, various reformers had raised similar objections to the church's practice of indulgences, atonement for sins through payments to the church, and simony, or the sale of church positions. By the sixteenth century, there were widespread calls for reform, of which Luther's was simply the loudest. John Wycliffe, a fourteenth century Oxford scholar, wrote about many of the ideas later represented in the Protestant Reformation. He translated the Latin Bible to English, and organized a band of wandering preachers called Lollards. Wycliffe was condemned posthumously at the Council of Constance in 1415, then unearthed and burned. Around the same time, John Hus in Bohemia gained great support in Prague by speaking out against the papacy. He was condemned at Constance and burned at the stake. Savonarola, a fifteenth-century Dominican monk, advocated a strict personal moral reform, arguing that Florence was subject to God's wrath because of its moral failings. He gained the support of many Florentines, then was excommunicated and hanged.

John Calvin

John Calvin was a sixteenth-century French reformer whose thought was influential in the Reformed tradition of Christianity as well as in Puritanism. In 1536, Calvin wrote the *Institutes of the Christian Religion*, in which he outright rejected the authority of the Roman Catholic Church, arguing that the Bible was the sole source of extant special revelation intended for the church. Influenced by Augustine, two of Calvin's major contributions to Christian doctrine were predestination and justification by faith (which Martin Luther also taught). Predestination argued that God, without any consideration of the goodness or wickedness of a person (that is, unconditionally), elected a portion of mankind to salvation, leaving the rest to damnation. The doctrine's motivation was to emphasize God's total sovereignty over all things and the all-sufficiency of grace (not human works) in salvation.

Justification by faith (also called "justification by faith alone") is the doctrine that only through faith can men be free from the penalty for their sin (damnation). Yet while he held that works are worthless in obtaining justification, Calvin believed that Christians should work hard and live simply and virtuously, out of gratefulness for their free justification.

Christian Monasteries in Medieval Western European Life

Christian monasteries have historically played a critical role in intellectual life. The flowering of urban intellectual life associated with thirteenth-century Europe is centered on the monastery. Before printing presses, the transcription of books was done primarily by monks, and their libraries were among the most impressive in Europe. They hosted visiting clergy, held religious debates, and cared for pilgrims traveling through the area. In addition, monks fed the poor and cared for the sick, especially during the Black Death. Monasteries were the center of educational life as well. Gradually, their role came to encompass education generally, and Catholic schools became commonplace across Christian Europe.

Cult of Mithras

The main competition of Christianity in the early centuries was the Cult of Mithras. This secretive religion was an initiatory society, with secretive knowledge passed from individual to individual. Because it was not a text-based religion, Mithraism's theology varied widely by location. In some locations, the cult was all male; in others, women were allowed a limited role. Mithraists seem to have practiced baptism and met in caves or subterranean spaces. Some of its iconography seems to have survived in the rites of Freemasonry. The cult died out after Theodosius I made Christianity the official Roman religion and outlawed paganism.

Social Gospel Movement

Beginning in the late nineteenth century, the Social Gospel was a liberal Protestant intellectual movement in the United States that viewed the gospel fundamentally as a means to correct contemporary social problems, downplaying the doctrine of sin and the necessity of individual conversion. Inspired by the belief known as postmillennialism, which states that Jesus would return to earth only after progressively instituting a prosperous and peaceful "millennium" age upon the earth, Social Gospel adherents opposed individualism and argued for a more socially aware theology, with increased power vested in the state. Some of the problems they addressed were poverty, alcoholism, racism, slums, child labor, war, and the rights of workers. The Social Gospel emphasized the goodness of human nature and the humanity of Jesus. After 1950, the movement declined somewhat, but its influence was felt a decade later in the civil rights movement, as well as the continuing interest of many liberal Protestant sects in pacifism and social justice issues.

VIRGIN MARY

Mary, the mother of Jesus, is held in high regard by all three major Christian traditions. In Protestantism, she is an example of a very highly regarded woman, receptive to God's word and obedient to his commands. In Orthodox Christianity and Catholicism, she is one of the very highest saints. Catholics and Orthodox Christians venerate Mary but do not worship her; she is human, not a deity. Some Catholics use prayer beads known as a rosary to direct prayers to Mary, who can intercede on their behalf. The Catholic and Orthodox doctrine of Mary's perpetual virginity states that Mary was a virgin her entire life, and rejects the notion of James as Jesus's full brother. (Protestants originally affirmed this idea as well, but not as a dogma of faith; modern Protestants generally deny her perpetual virginity.) In addition, Catholics believe in Mary's *immaculate conception* (that Mary was free of sin from the moment of her conception) as well as her bodily assumption into heaven.

MAJOR DIVISIONS OF CHRISTIANITY

Roman Catholicism: Catholics believe in the divinely-given infallible authority of the Magisterium, i.e. the teaching authority of the Church, comprised of the Pope and the bishops. They believe that a body of unwritten special revelation, called Tradition, is also available alongside Scripture for the Church's benefit, and that the Magisterium alone can authoritatively interpret both. Catholics adhere to many set rites and sacraments, which they view as critical to salvation. Protestantism: While classical Protestants revere church authority and see the teaching offices (elders and pastors) as valuable, they deny that such offices can be infallible, thereby affirming a right of private interpretation for all individuals. Protestants affirm Scripture alone as the extant source of special revelation for the church, and emphasize that faith alone is needed for individuals to be justified before God. Eastern Orthodoxy: While sharing many traditions with Catholicism, Eastern Orthodox Christians believe the ultimate goal of human faith is a close union with God, through both faith and works, making believers themselves more and more divine in a process called "theosis." Orthodox Christians also differ on their doctrine of the Trinity, denying the *filioque* clause, and they deny the supremacy of the Pope.

GOD

Christianity believes in one God who is the Creator of the universe. He is omnipotent, omniscient, perfectly good, holy, eternal, immutable, infinite, and incorporeal. God has a personality and cares about and connects with people individually. God is spoken of in Scripture in male terms, though he is not strictly male. The Christian doctrine of the Trinity says that while there is one divine nature, three Persons exist as fully God: the Father, Son, and Holy Spirit. The Father is Ruler over all and planned out salvation, the Son became incarnate in Christ to accomplish salvation on the cross, and the Holy Spirit applies salvation to believers, including indwelling them.

SATAN

Satan, alternatively called Lucifer or the Devil, is the prime figure of evil in Christianity. He began as an angel, but he rebelled against God and was banished from heaven. He is identified in the Bible as the serpent who tempts Eve with the fruit from the forbidden tree. He tempts Jesus when he is fasting in the desert. According to Christian eschatology, when Jesus returns to earth, Satan will be cast into hell. Some Christians argue that Satan is a metaphor for evil rather than an actual spirit and express problems with the idea of Satan having free will if God is omnipotent. Popular Christianity depicts people being possessed by Satan, and he is generally thought to be one of the main forces that tempts people into sin, the other two being the world and the flesh.

Marcionism to Christianity

Marcion was the son of the Bishop of Pontus. In 140 A.D., he arrived in Rome hoping for a job with the church. He represented a point of view with its roots in Gnosticism, though he may not have been a Gnostic himself. He believed in the Gnostic concept of two gods: one of vengeful justice, the creator of the world, and the other a god of pure goodness, who begat Jesus. Jesus came to earth to save man from matter and from their old god of justice; therefore Christians have no need for the Old Testament in their sacred literature. Marcion was excommunicated for this heresy, but the point of view that the Old Testament depicts an angry and vengeful God while the New Testament's God is one of love is still prevalent in some Christian thought.

Montanism

In the second century A.D., Montanus brought the first charismatic strain of Christianity to the church. He contended that the Holy Spirit of the Trinity eluded dogma, and could cause Christians to prophesy and speak in tongues. He also preached that the second coming of Christ and the end of the world were nigh. The movement persisted in small numbers into the eighth century, despite its being labeled heresy. This strain of zealotry has recurred in Christianity, most notably in modern charismatic strains like Pentecostalism (sometimes known as neo-Montanism).

The Trinity

The Trinity is the central doctrine of Christianity and unique among religions. God is understood to be three "mutually indwelling" persons in one godhead, interrelated and distinguishable but having one identical nature. The three figures are:

- God the Father: the creator of the universe, entirely unoriginated
- God the Son: eternally begotten of the Father, became incarnate as Jesus Christ, sacrificed to redeem mankind
- God the Holy Spirit (or Holy Ghost): the spirit of God present in the world and in individuals. The Holy Spirit is said to bestow supernatural powers on people under its possession.

The paradox of God being simultaneously three entities and one is the central mystery of Christianity, proof that the ways of God are beyond, though not against, human reason. A few modern denominations of Christianity are "nontrinitarian"; that is, they do not believe in the Trinity, or they believe it is a metaphor for three aspects of God rather than three separate persons (also known as modalism, or Sabellianism). Some Christians, along with Muslim and Jewish critics, argue that belief in a Trinity is tantamount to polytheism.

Doctrinal Differences Between Eastern and Western Christianity

When considering Western Christianity as encompassing both Catholicism and Protestantism, certain distinctive doctrines of the Catholic Church (e.g. papal supremacy or the Marian dogmas) would not distinguish all Western Christianity from the East, though they would distinguish Roman Catholicism from Eastern Orthodoxy. The Western and Eastern conception of God differs in two ways. First, the West tends to consider God first by contemplating the one divine nature (e.g. expounding upon the attributes of God), and afterward considering the three personal distinctions within the Godhead. By contrast the East tends to start with the three divine Persons and then consider how they are unified. Second, the West tends to view God as simple/unified, whereas the East makes a distinction between His "essence" and "energies"; we cannot access the former, but we can access the latter. The West and East also differ in their doctrines of salvation. The West tends to emphasize the judicial and forensic aspects, discussing the guilt of sin, while the East focuses more on mystical transformation. This is clear in their doctrines of original sin.

The West tends to favor the incorporation of Greek philosophy and scholasticism, while the East has a lesser emphasis upon systematic theology.

BRANCHES OF PROTESTANT CHRISTIANITY

There are technically thousands of denominations of Christianity, but generally speaking, Protestant branches can be grouped under four main categories, each of which has important doctrinal differences with the others. They are:

- Lutheran: The original Protestant sect, founded by Martin Luther, prominent in northern Germany and Scandinavia. Lutherans emphasize justification by faith, a traditional liturgy, and a mild form of baptismal regeneration (i.e. that one is born again through baptism).
- Church of England/Anglican: This branch has its origins in England and emphasizes the social responsibility of Christians in addition to their faith in God. Also has traditional liturgy. Methodism is an offshoot of this.
- Anabaptist: The most distinctive tenet of this set is adult baptism. Many Anabaptists rejected prevailing social structures; some embraced greater state control over the realm, while others emphasized complete pacifism. Many also claimed to depend upon private revelations from the Spirit.
- Reformed/Presbyterian: This branch, prominent both in the UK and in continental Europe, was heavily influenced by the theology of John Calvin and has predestination as a distinctive tenet. Arminian churches (founded by Jacob Arminius) are an offshoot of this tradition, even though they deny predestination.

LUTHERAN BRANCH

Lutheranism is the original Protestant sect. Its original, and still main, difference with Catholicism concerns the issue of justification. Lutherans believe that faith in Christ is necessary and sufficient to remove one's penalty for sin. There are no works, they argue, that could sufficiently please God when all humans are inherently sinful; hence we depend on Christ's merits, unified with us by faith. Lutherans do continue to follow Catholic practice in many areas, mostly in their liturgy, but do not subscribe to the seven sacraments of Rome; they only practice baptism and communion. They subscribe to the doctrine of consubstantiation. While transubstantiation teaches that the bread and wine in communion are literally transformed into the body and blood of Christ, consubstantiation teaches that Christ's body and blood are physically present "in, around, and under" the elements, though the elements remain as bread and wine. Lutherans believe that every word of the Bible is true, and that every word is the immediate and direct word of God, through verbal inspiration to its writers. Scripture is the highest authority for the church. Lutherans subscribe to the doctrine of original sin—that humans were created perfect and sinless but suffer today from original sin, which they have inherited from Adam and Eve.

ANGLICAN AND METHODIST BRANCH

The Church of England (also known as the Episcopal Church or Anglican Church outside of England) was founded by Henry VIII in a political dispute with the Pope. It traditionally follows Protestant doctrine while having Catholic rituals (proposing itself as a middle way between Catholicism and radical Protestantism), but it does not accept the authority of the Catholic Church. It utilizes the Book of Common Prayer for its liturgy. Its ecclesiastical head is the Archbishop of Canterbury, but, in what distinguishes the Anglican Church most, the monarch of England is considered head of the church. Anglicans subscribe to the Apostles' Creed and accept the two sacraments of communion and baptism. John Wesley founded Methodism in the eighteenth century, as a sub-branch of the Church of England addressing the needs of the urban working classes, but as differences emerged it gradually became accepted as a sect in its own right. It emphasizes evangelism and the responsibility incumbent on Christians to improve society. It places great value on reasoned interpretation of the Bible, and accepts the value of church tradition in addition to Scripture. Its largest number of adherents is in the United States.

Pentecostal Branch

Pentecostalism is an umbrella term for an evangelical group of Christian churches, particularly in the United States, that believe the Bible is literally true and inerrant, and that the Holy Spirit of the Trinity speaks through people through spiritual gifts. These gifts may include faith healing, prophecy, or glossolalia, "speaking in tongues," which involves speech-like vocalizations under the influence of the Holy Spirit. Pentecostalism arose in the late nineteenth and early twentieth centuries in America, though there have been charismatic movements throughout Christianity. Salvation in Pentecostalism comes through the grace of God alone through faith, and not through good works, but the ordinance of adult baptism is necessary to confirm salvation, as is speaking in tongues in some sects. Roles for women are typically restricted to traditional ones, and congregations are often relatively multicultural. Two of the major Pentecostal denominations are the Assemblies of God and Church of God in Christ.

Anabaptist Branch

The Reformation can be divided generally into two branches, the Magisterial Reformation (Lutheran, Anglican, Reformed) and the Radical Reformation (Anabaptist). While the three branches of the Magisterial Reformation embraced the abiding authority of both church and state, recognizing the existent hierarchies while also affirming the right of private interpretation, the Radical Reformers tended to be more revolutionary and egalitarian in their societal outlook. Modern Anabaptist sects sometimes reject elements of the modern world, like technology, for this reason. The most distinctive doctrine of Anabaptism is adult baptism; rather than being baptized as infants, no one is baptized until he can consciously profess faith in Christ. Many Anabaptists are pacifists, interpreting the Sermon on the Mount to mean that one should never strike another. After historical persecution in Europe, most Anabaptists immigrated to the Americas. They have also believed historically in separating themselves from nonbelievers. Modern branches of Anabaptism include Mennonites and the Amish. The Amish eschew technology and live in isolated communities, while the Mennonites abstain from public office and the military and are concerned with peace and social justice.

Reformed and Presbyterian Branch

Presbyterianism and the Reformed churches are the branch of Christianity most influenced by John Calvin. The doctrine of predestination is key in this branch; Reformed Christians and Presbyterians believe that because God is sovereign, he has selected those people who will be given salvation. Sinners will be unredeemed unless God chooses to change their hearts. All people are equally at God's mercy, and God chooses some to save and some to condemn. Reformed thought was developed and systematized in the seventeenth-century Synod of Dort, which asserted what are today called the five point of Calvinism, summarized in the acrostic TULIP:

- **T**otal depravity: without grace, no man can turn to God
- **U**nconditional election: God elects some without any consideration of their merits or good works
- **L**imited atonement: Christ's death was intended only to save the elect
- **I**rresistible grace: the elect are necessarily converted at the appointed time
- **P**erseverance of the saints: those who are born again will necessarily continue in that state until their deaths

Society of Friends, Unitarian Universalism, and Jehovah's Witnesses

Society of Friends: Also known as the Quakers, this sect has no clergy, advocating instead the complete equality of all people and the existence within all of an "inner light" of God. Worship services are frequently held in silence until God calls someone to speak. Quakers have roots in Anabaptism and are traditionally pacifists.

Unitarian Universalism: This modern sect is nontrinitarian and has no set dogma. It does not believe in the inerrancy of the Bible, nor does it believe that Christianity is the exclusive way to salvation. Rather, it seeks to incorporate elements of all religions and worldviews, including atheism and agnosticism.

Jehovah's Witnesses: This sect, begun in American in the nineteenth century, is also nontrinitarian, and believes that God's kingdom on earth is imminent. Jehovah's Witnesses believe in biblical primacy on all matters, both religious and secular. They do not accept blood transfusions, vote, serve in the military, salute national flags, or celebrate birthdays or Christian holidays.

Seventh Day Adventists and Christian Science

Seventh Day Adventists: This sect, founded in nineteenth-century America, emphasizes the imminent second coming of Christ. It celebrates the Sabbath on Saturday, advocates a healthy diet, and does not believe in the human soul. It believes that the mind and body are one, that death is "soul sleep," and that the wicked dead are destroyed, not punished eternally, at the second coming.
Christian Science: This is a nineteenth-century American sect founded by Mary Baker Eddy. Its chief doctrine is that the material world and evil are an illusion. It also believes that physical illness is a product of fear, ignorance, or sin, and that prayer and Bible study can heal illness. Christian Scientists typically do not receive medical care, though their teachings do not strictly forbid them.

Seven Deadly Sins and Seven Cardinal Virtues

The seven deadly sins and seven cardinal virtues are the classification used by the Catholic Church to explain and instruct followers about moral behavior. The list was formally compiled by Pope Gregory I in 590 A.D., and is derived from one created by the monk Evagrius Ponticus in the fourth century. The seven deadly sins are:

1. Lust (originally "extravagance"): excessive or unhealthy sexual appetites
2. Gluttony: overconsumption, particularly of food or drink, or wastefulness
3. Greed: in particular, the accumulation of wealth and the associated betrayals or advantage-taking of others
4. Sloth (a substitution for the original "despair"): laziness or, more specifically, failure to take advantage of one's gifts and privileges
5. Wrath: anger and violence, including self-hatred
6. Envy: the desire to rid others of their advantages
7. Pride: self-importance, and in general the putting of oneself first before God. This is the most serious of the seven sins

The corresponding seven cardinal virtues are:

1. Chastity
2. Temperance
3. Charity
4. Diligence
5. Patience
6. Kindness

7. Humility

Major Tenets of Roman Catholicism

Catholic doctrine states that the Catholic Church is the infallible, authoritative interpreter and custodian of the divine revelation from God, which includes both a written form (Scripture) and an unwritten form (Tradition), passed on since the time of the apostles. The apostles were Jesus's representatives on earth, and they passed on their authority and teachings through the Catholic Church. God, who exists as a Trinity, takes a personal interest in humans, and can be reached by them through prayer. Moreover, prayers can be made to various saints and to Mary for their intercession. The human soul is immortal, and God grants salvation and eternal life to the souls of those people who are sufficiently obedient to his will. Humans have free will in gaining salvation from God. All men are in either a state of sin or a state of grace. If one is in a state of sin when he dies, he will suffer eternal hell, but if one is in a state of grace, he will either suffer purgatory (if he has remaining venial sins which need punished) or enter heaven. Venial sins are sins which oppose but do not destroy love (charity or agape) in the sinner's soul, whereas mortal sins necessarily destroy love, and hence place the sinner back into a state of sin. The seven sacraments are the primary means by which one enters into and maintains oneself in a state of grace: e.g., baptism begins spiritual life, the Eucharist nourishes it, and penance/confession restores it.

Sunday Catholic Mass

A Sunday Catholic mass is conducted according to a particular script, and although since the Second Vatican Council mass may be held in local languages, its form remains constant in every congregation. There are four parts to a mass:

1. Introductory rites: The priest enters with a deacon, if the congregation has one, and altar boys. He welcomes and blesses the congregation.
2. Liturgy of the Word: The priest gives three readings from Scripture. He or another church leader gives a homily, a sermon that illustrates the readings. The congregation recites the Nicene Creed or the Apostles' Creed, and then "Prayers of the Faithful" are spoken by a church leader, with the congregation responding with "Lord, hear our prayer."
3. Liturgy of the Eucharist: The Eucharistic Prayer, a call and response section, follows, then the Lord's Prayer. Members of the congregation give one another the "Sign of Peace." The priest gives Communion to the congregation.
4. Concluding rites: The priest offers a blessing to the congregation and a recessional song may be sung.

Major Tenets of the Orthodox Eastern Church

Orthodox Christians believe in the Trinity, although they focus first on the three divine Persons prior to explaining their unity in the single divine nature. (Thus they tend towards, but do not fall into, tritheism, whereas the West tends towards modalism.) Eastern Orthodoxy liturgy is emphatically Trinitarian. Unlike Roman Catholicism, there is no infallible Magisterium for the Orthodox Church, but they still see the tradition of the church fathers as an important guide. The church as a whole (not just the higher offices) is led by the Spirit, and thus infallible in this corporate sense, in its interpretation of Scripture. As regards original sin, unlike the West, they deny that others share in Adam's guilt, preferring to limit it to the inclination to sin found in Adam's descendants. Through this sin and moral weakness, man becomes separated from God, but Jesus heals this gap by assuming and purifying human nature. Thus by participating in Christ through the Church, and by becoming more like him (theosis), Christians can attain salvation. Hell is not a separate place of punishment where retributive justice is meted out. Instead, both heaven and hell are the same place, where the righteous will love God and so experience pleasure, while the wicked will hate God and so experience torment.

Five Solas

Protestantism can be summed up in the "five solas" of the Reformation, especially #1 and #3:

1. Sola Scriptura ("Scripture alone"): the Bible is the church's sole source of special revelation. There is no unwritten source (Tradition), nor is there a Church authority (Magisterium) which can infallibly interpret the Bible.
2. Sola Gratia ("grace alone"): man can do nothing to merit God's favor; God must bestow it purely of grace
3. Sola Fide ("faith alone"): faith, not works, justifies a sinner before God (i.e. removes his liability to punishment)
4. Solus Christus ("Christ alone"): Christ alone is the mediator between God and man; there is no need for a human priesthood
5. Soli Deo Gloria ("glory to God alone"): because salvation is entirely of God, He alone is to receive glory

Jesuits in Christian History

Just before the Catholic Counter-Reformation, Ignatius Loyola, a Spanish soldier who made a vow to become a "soldier for Christ," studied theology at the University of Paris, and together with other students formed an order of men devoted to Christian missionary work. They organized themselves in military fashion and took vows of poverty and celibacy. They gained permission from the Pope to found the Society of Jesus, also known as the Jesuits. These Catholic men were missionaries and educators, known for their intellectual accomplishment and their commitment to educating the young. Jesuits founded universities as a means of missionary work. Jesuits are one of the largest Catholic religious orders today. They operate on six continents, converting nonbelievers and doing educational work. Jesuits vow absolute obedience to the Pope and to the head of the order.

Predestination

The Reformed and Presbyterian churches' doctrine of predestination teaches that, because God knows all things and is sovereign over all things, he ordains who will receive salvation and who will not. This decree is then carried out in history, so that the elect will be the ones who receive salvation (by placing faith in Jesus), and all the nonelect will culpably fail to do so, thus being guilty of punishment. This doctrine is not fatalism, for it does not teach that one's actions are meaningless or irrelevant to one's eternal state, for it remains true that all who repent and believe will attain salvation. One's actions still determine one's future, even if all one's actions are predetermined. This is the starkest doctrine of predestination. Other (arguably weaker) forms contend that God, on the basis of foreknowing who would receive him, then chooses to elect those people to salvation. A still different form of the doctrine teaches that God directs or orients all men toward salvation (as an arrow toward a target), even though all men can freely veer off that path to their detriment.

Christian Calendar

Though the exact days vary between Eastern and Western Christianity, the Christian calendar begins with the season of Advent, the Wednesday nearest November 30. Advent is traditionally associated with fasting and repentance. Christmas, the Feast of the Nativity, is celebrated on December 25. It celebrates Christ's birth. January 6 is the Epiphany, marking the visit of the Wise Men to the infant Jesus. Ash Wednesday, the start of the Easter season, symbolizes human mortality by marking Christians' foreheads with ashes. Ash Wednesday marks the beginning of Lent, a 40-day symbolic abstention rite. Palm Sunday is the week before Easter, and commemorates

Jesus being welcomed to Jerusalem. Thursday is Maundy Thursday, the date of the Last Supper, followed by Good Friday, a day of mourning, fasting, and repentance commemorating Jesus's execution. Easter Sunday is the holiest day for Christians, marking the central symbol of Christ's resurrection from the dead. Pentecost, the most important holiday after Easter, commemorates the gift of the Holy Spirit conferred on the disciples by the resurrected Christ and the birth of the church.

Gospels

The four canonical gospels of the Bible, written by Matthew, Mark, Luke, and John, all of whom were writing after the death of Jesus, describe the birth, life, ministry, death, and resurrection of Jesus. Other gospels exist but are not part of the official canon of the church. The major events described in the gospels are:

- Jesus's genealogy: He is a descendent of David
- Jesus's miraculous birth to a virgin mother
- Jesus's baptism, time spent fasting in the wilderness, and temptation by Satan
- Jesus's ministry
- Jesus's arrest, trial for blasphemy, and execution
- Jesus's miraculous resurrection from the dead and ascension to heaven

The three synoptic gospels (Matthew, Mark, and Luke) portray Jesus as the Son of God, and recount his teachings and reception by society. John envisions Jesus as the incarnation of Logos, the "word" present at the beginning of creation.

Four Christian Gospels

The gospels of Matthew, Mark, and Luke, known as the synoptic ("one view") gospels, are largely similar in details about the life of Jesus. The gospel of John, likely written later, is notably different in focus. It concentrates on Jesus as the physical incarnation of the Word of God, rather than as the Son of God. It also specifically focuses on Jesus's relationship with several women, which is why it is known as "the women's gospel." Unlike the synoptic gospels, John describes Jesus's ministry as lasting for at least three Passovers and focused in Jerusalem rather than Galilee. John also fails to describe an ascension to heaven, while the synoptics include it. The Books of Matthew and Luke are incredibly similar, suggesting that they had a common, earlier source, known as the "Q gospel." Matthew focuses most clearly on Jesus as the Jewish Messiah, while Mark describes him as a man of action. Luke emphasizes his compassion and miracle work.

Sermon on the Mount to Christianity

The Sermon on the Mount is depicted in the gospel of Matthew as one in a compilation of five of Jesus's teachings. It is a commentary on the Ten Commandments and Mosaic Law, in which Jesus declares that he is the fulfillment of the law and the new covenant. The Beatitudes open the sermon; in these, Jesus describes the blessed people of the heavenly kingdom (describing them as poor, hungry, and merciful, among other qualities). Jesus offers an example of how to pray, a text now known as the Lord's Prayer in Christianity. In this sermon Jesus largely corrects the false interpretations of the Mosaic law made by the Pharisees, teaching how they failed to live according to its precepts, especially by restricting it merely to outward actions. For example, against the teaching that the prohibition on adultery merely forbade intimate relations with a neighbor's wife, Jesus taught that it also forbade any lust for her in one's heart. Some interpretations of the sermon see Jesus as abrogating the Mosaic law and placing a new law in its place, such as advocating pacifism when Jesus instructs his followers to "turn the other cheek."

CRUCIFIXION OF JESUS

The crucifixion is the central event in Christianity. Believing that humans are born with the taint of original sin and are unworthy of a happy afterlife without God's grace, Christians believe that humans deserve to be punished eternally for their wickedness. Rather than doing this, however, God, ever-merciful, sends his son to earth to suffer and die as a sacrifice for all people. Without this sacrifice, known as "substitutionary atonement," humans would be incapable of entering heaven. Different Christian sects view this slightly differently. Catholics emphasize the payment of Jesus's life to God as reparation for the sins of mankind. Eastern Orthodox Christians argue that God sent Jesus to defeat Satan through self-sacrifice in a spiritual battle, and that Jesus purified human nature by assuming it and undergoing all the stages of its existence. Protestants most vividly affirm that Christ substituted himself to take on the penalty due to sinners.

WAYS CHRISTIANITY BROKE WITH JEWISH TRADITION

From the time of Jesus, Christianity moved away from Jewish tradition in important ways. Christianity emphasized the importance of self-restraint and nonviolence in ways that Judaism, whose adherents had a long history of battling their geographical neighbors, had not. Importantly, Jesus told his followers that Christianity represented a new covenant with God, and did not require its adherents to obey Jewish laws regarding diet and the Sabbath; Christians maintained the tradition of the Sabbath, but moved it to Sunday in remembrance of Jesus's resurrection. The doctrine of the Trinity is another important difference; Jews tend to view the Christian Trinity as akin to polytheism and, therefore, blasphemous. Importantly, Christians view their religion as a universal one, not one confined to a particular people. As a result, Christians recruit converts from other religions in a way that is unknown in Judaism.

RITE OF THE EUCHARIST

The ritual of the Eucharist, also known as the Lord's Supper or communion, is the most important ritual in Christianity. It is modeled after the Last Supper, the meal (a Passover) held by Jesus and his disciples the night before his execution. It reminds Christians of their community and their commitment to their religion, and in many traditions, it also confers grace to proper recipients. Bread and wine (in some sects, grape juice) are passed through the congregation; in Catholicism and some Protestant sects, the priest blesses them and gives them individually to the worshippers. The main conflict in Christian doctrine regarding the Eucharist is the issue of transubstantiation and consubstantiation. Catholics believe in transubstantiation, which states that, in accordance with Jesus's statement to his disciples, "This is my body; this is my blood," the bread and wine are literally transformed into the body and blood of Christ. Lutherans believe in consubstantiation, that Christ's body is physically present "in, around, and under" the bread and wine, which themselves remain as bread and wine. But most Protestant branches maintain that the rite is symbolic of Christ's sacrifice and that the Holy Spirit is present during the rite, but that the bread and wine do not change their physical character.

EASTER

Easter is the most important holiday in the Christian calendar. It celebrates Jesus's resurrection from the dead and self-sacrifice on behalf of humanity. Churches use festive flowers, particularly lilies, and elaborate music. In the Catholic Church, an Easter mass is celebrated, with readings from the Old Testament, followed by readings from the gospels. Easter is a traditional time for converted Christians to be baptized, and those who have already been baptized often symbolically renew their baptismal vows at Easter. In the Catholic Church, confirmations are also done at this time. Protestant churches sometimes have a "sunrise service," reflecting the women of the gospel to whom Jesus appeared early in the morning. Easter is celebrated on a different Sunday in the

Orthodox Church from the other two main Christian sects. Orthodox Christians traditionally prepare for Easter, or Pascha, with a forty-day period of fasting and austerity. They hold a midnight Easter service in which a flame is symbolically lit in total darkness, then the congregation parades with the cross around the church. A communal meal is shared very late at night.

Christmas

Christmas is by no means the most important Christian holiday, but it is the most widely celebrated Christian holiday, and is widely celebrated in secular society. Christmas celebrates the birth of Jesus. It is a feast marked by merriment, including elaborate meals, gift-giving, charity, and song. Churches are decorated with holly, ivy, and poinsettia, and in a tradition borrowed from European pagans, Christians decorate ceremonial evergreen trees in their homes. Church services are held on Christmas Day, regardless of the day of the week. Catholics hold a midnight mass and churches of all denominations hold pageants, often centered on children. Decorations include depictions of the nativity scene, including the infant Jesus, Mary, and the three magi who came to pay homage with gifts. Children may also act out the nativity scene in church productions.

Baptism and Confirmation

Baptism: Baptism is the rite of admission into the church. It involves water in a symbolic "rebirth" of a person into the religion. In some sects, the church leader sprinkles or pours water upon the new Christian, while in others, the believer is immersed in a pool of water. In some churches, infants are baptized soon after birth, while in certain Protestant sects the doctrine is to baptize only adults who have made a conscious choice. Baptism was begun by Paul to mark believers' conversion from pagan to Christian. Later it became a symbolic washing away of sin. Confirmation: In the Catholic and Orthodox Churches, as well as some Protestant sects, confirmation is a ritual marking a believer's full membership in the church. Catholic confirmation takes place at the age of reason, traditionally around ten. Orthodox confirmation takes place immediately after baptism. Anglican confirmation takes place in the teenage years. In some traditions, the person being confirmed takes the "confirmation name" of a saint as a totem.

Rituals Surrounding Marriage and Death

A Christian marriage ceremony usually takes place in a church, and is conducted by a church leader. The wedding ceremony includes vows by both parties to honor God in their relationship. The congregation acts as witnesses, vowing to support the couple's relationship. In the Catholic Church, marriage is one of the seven sacraments, and the wedding is part of a larger ritual mass.

In Catholicism, one of the seven sacraments is the anointment of the dying with oil and the hearing of the last confession. After death, a wake is held the evening before the funeral, with eulogies and personal remembrances of the deceased. A funeral ceremony is held in a church, and in Catholic practice it is part of a larger ritual mass. A shorter service is held graveside before burial. In Orthodox tradition, there are five different kinds of funeral service, depending on the deceased. A Christian death is typically followed by a burial, as in Jewish tradition, but Christians also view the practice as honoring Jesus, who was buried.

Saint Augustine

After Jesus and Paul, Saint Augustine is the most important contributor to Christian theology. Augustine is the source of Christians' understanding of human nature and the need for the church to redeem their souls. Augustine, a Christian convert born in the fourth century in North Africa, wrote two important Christian classics: *Confessions* and *City of God*. Augustine's theology concerns what he sees as the inherent moral weakness of humans, inherited from Adam and Eve, who sinned against God. This sinful nature was the curse of all mankind from that point. Human beings are sinners and none deserve salvation, but God, who is merciful, sent his Son to die as an atonement. Moreover, God predestined those who would be saved by such means. Calvinists later took up his themes on predestination and developed them more rigorously. Augustine struggled with lust himself and wrote at length of it, going so far as to deem sexual desire sinful. He also created the doctrine of "just war," teaching that defensive wars can be fought for the sake of preventing a greater evil.

Saint Thomas Aquinas

The thirteenth-century Dominican priest and scholastic Saint Thomas Aquinas is possibly the most important Christian intellectual and a deeply influential figure in Western philosophy generally. Influenced by the writings of classical Greece, which had been preserved by Arab scholars and were recently available in Europe, Aquinas devoted his work to the study of faith and reason. His work *Summa Contra Gentiles* was a defense of the Christian faith against others, and his *Summa Theologiae* became the standard theological platform of the Catholic Church. Aquinas integrated Aristotelianism with Christian theology in his work and argued that not only faith but also reason were necessary to explain the world fully. His use of natural theology offered rational arguments for the existence of God.

His teachings on ethics have been greatly influential in Catholicism, including his "doctrine of double effect," which teaches that an action with an evil consequence can be permissibly (non-sinfully) performed, so long as (1) the action itself is not intrinsically evil, (2) the evil effect is not proportionately graver than the good effect of the action, and (3) the evil effect is not intended, either as an end in itself or as a means unto the good effect of the action. His teachings on natural law have also been enormously influential, not only in Catholic sexual ethics but in philosophy at large.

Seven Sacraments of Catholicism

- Baptism: Baptism is necessary to wash away original sin, entering a sinner into a state of grace by infusing supernatural virtues (faith, hope, and love). Performed on children, sometimes laity, and even non-Catholics, can perform these in emergencies.
- Confirmation: Confirmation is an extension of baptism in which young Catholics confirm, at the age of reason, their commitment to the faith. They are anointed with oil and receive special graces of the Holy Spirit, strengthening what was received in baptism.
- Penance: Penance involves confessing all the mortal sins of which one is aware in order to move oneself from a state of sin to a state of grace. One must intend to perform the acts of penance prescribed by the priest in order to receive the absolution.
- Eucharist: The Eucharist, or communion, is a required rite of Catholics, in which they eat bread and drink wine that has literally become, under the priest's blessing, the body and blood of Christ.
- Extreme Unction: Dying Catholics should be anointed with oil by a priest and confess for the last time, in order to strengthen them to remain in a state of grace. Now called the Anointing of the Sick.
- Matrimony: Catholic marriage is a sacred and unbreakable symbol of Christ's relationship with the church. Christ elevated this from a natural institution to a sacrament when he was on earth.
- Holy Orders: For those who enter the clergy instead of marrying, holy orders are the spiritual equivalent of marriage and are considered sacred.

Saints

Catholicism lists more than ten thousand saints, who are identified as particularly exemplary in their Catholic faith. There is a formal process of canonization for saints after their deaths. Saints are holy individuals, though not deities, and examples for others to emulate. Saints can intercede on a believer's behalf with God if prayers are directed through them; consequently, in folk Catholicism prayers to saints are often directed through candles and shrines. The Eastern Orthodox tradition is similar to Roman Catholicism in this regard, except that it lacks a formal and uniform process of canonization, instead deferring to local customs and traditions. Most Protestant denominations do not recognize the special category of saints, believing the veneration of saints to be a practice not unlike idol worship. Anglicans do recognize saints, however, as those who have been recognized by believers and who serve as inspiration for believers. Other Protestants use the term "saint" more generally to refer to all Christians; the existence of an individual's relationship with Jesus Christ is enough to make that person a saint, since he is then set apart as holy by his faith.

Afterlife

Christians believe in an afterlife of heaven and hell to which all people will be assigned eternally. Most Protestants hold that all those who are believers at their deaths will go to heaven, everyone else being consigned to hell, but some Protestants hold to a form of "once saved, always saved," where someone can believe at one point in his life, fall away, and still go to heaven when he dies. The Catholic view is that those in a "state of grace" when they die will go to heaven or purgatory, while those in a "state of sin" (that is, everyone not in a state of grace) will go to hell. What determines whether someone in a state of grace goes to purgatory or not is whether he has unpardoned venial sins which need purging. Indulgences help to reduce the time required in purgatory. While a few sects believe that the wicked will be annihilated, most hold that hell is a place of eternal damnation. Some describe the pains of hell as literal hellfire while others take a more metaphorical approach and emphasize the absence of God's blessings rather than the presence of his wrath. The Eastern Orthodox view also denies that hell is a separate place, but instead sees it as one place which the righteous and the wicked will experience differently, according to whether they love or hate God.

Role of Women

Christianity has traditionally been led by men, since the Bible attributes headship to husbands and to men in the church. Paul's epistles especially have themes of female submission, comparing husband and wife to Christ and the church; he even goes so far as forbidding women to teach men in the church. Paul also emphasizes a certain spiritual equality between man and woman, stating that "there is neither male nor female" in Christ, though for him this does not remove male headship. Roman Catholicism venerates Mary and includes some female saints and figures, but by and large women are not among the major names in church history. The roles of women have changed somewhat in the modern era in response to feminism, although Catholicism and Eastern Orthodoxy remain faithful to traditional gender roles. In certain Protestant sects, leadership roles are more open to women, although not in the more conservative denominations. In some, it is traditional for women to lead the church only in partnership with their husbands.

Role of Homosexuals

Traditionally, Christianity has condemned homosexuality as a sin. Christians who agree with the condemnation of homosexuality point to passages in both the Old Testament and New Testament that appear to support them, while other Christians deny that these texts refer to loving, monogamous homosexual relationships. Though there was no disagreement on this subject until modern times, the biblical witness on homosexuality has become a subject of fierce debate. In most sects, homosexual behavior is condemned, though in some homosexual identity can be accepted so long as gay Christians adopt lives of celibacy. In a minority of denominations, homosexuality is embraced. In recent years, the blessing of homosexual marriages has caused schisms in some churches, including liberal Presbyterianism (e.g. the PCUSA) and American Episcopalianism.

Sacred Texts

Christians accept the Old Testament and the books of the New Testament as the authoritative word of God, but the composition of the Old Testament varies by denomination. The Catholic and Orthodox Old Testament includes additional books, known as the Deuterocanonical texts, not present in the usual Protestant canon: Tobit, Judith, Additions to Esther, Wisdom of Solomon, Sirach, Baruch, Additions to Daniel, 1 Maccabees, and 2 Maccabees. The Eastern Orthodox do not have a formal canonical list, though they often have additional canonical books as well, such as 3 & 4 Maccabees.

The books of the New Testament are:

- 4 Gospels (Matthew, Mark, Luke, John)
- Act of the Apostles
- 13 Epistles from Paul to Christian churches
- Epistle to the Hebrews
- Epistle of James
- 2 Epistles of Peter
- 3 Epistles of John
- Epistle of Jude
- Revelation

Christian Symbolism

- Crucifix: A symbolic rendering of Christ's suffering on the cross during his execution. Often worn as a necklace by Catholics. The term usually refers only to crosses on which Christ is depicted.
- Fish: Also known as the *ichthus*, the Greek word for fish, whose letters stand for various aspects of Jesus's character. Used as a symbol by Christians during the Roman Empire, when Christians met in secret.
- Flames: Flames are a symbol of the Holy Spirit, especially as he was manifested at Pentecost, and appear often in Christian art.
- Halo: A symbol of holiness in Christian art, the halo appears as a glow around the head of holy people.

Relationship of Individuals to the Human Body

Jesus himself did not appear to be an ascetic. He appeared to accept the mind and body as one unit that was not inherently foul. He did, however, teach that the body could be used as an instrument for sin and that the body could generate temptations. Paul also acknowledged the flesh to be the source of many temptations, and even encouraged celibacy under certain circumstances for those who had the gift of self-restraint. Saint Augustine, himself confessedly prone to lustful temptation, held that the human body was a great source of sin and temptation, arguing that both nonprocreative sex and sexual excitement were sinful. Monastic Christianity from the very beginning stressed personal physical deprivation as a means of focusing the spirit on worship of God. Although much of this self-torture gradually fell away, the spirit of austerity has been a constant theme in Christianity.

IMPORTANT TERMS

Apostle—Generally, a representative and a messenger. In Christianity, the term specifically refers to the twelve contemporary followers and supporters of Christ, responsible for preaching the gospel and appointing other leaders to establish the church.

Christ— "Anointed one," referencing the practice of anointing the heads of kings with oil. The name given to kings in Israel, as applied to Jesus as an honorific. Known in Hebrew as "Messiah."

Disciple—A follower. The twelve apostles were also Christ's disciples, and after Christ's death, they, in turn, had disciples of their own.

Absolution—The removal of an individual's liability to be punished for his sin.

Apologetics—The defense of one's faith.

Original sin—The doctrine that all humans have inherited a disposition to sin (called a "sinful nature" by Protestants) from Adam and Eve, as well as a penalty of guilt for that sin.

Justification—The process or act by which one becomes or is declared righteous before God. Protestants emphasize that this is an act by which one is declared righteous (even though internally sinful), but Catholics emphasize that this is a process by which one becomes and remains truly, internally righteous.

Sanctification—Literally, being set apart, or made holy. The Bible treats this morally, so that believers are progressively set apart by becoming more upright.

Total depravity—a Reformed doctrine which holds that man, without divine grace, is utterly unable to save himself by turning to God in genuine repentance and faith.

Grace—Either the disposition of favor within God, motivating him to act for the benefit of man, or the gifts which God gives as a result of such a disposition. (Thus we can speak of God, motivated by grace, as bestowing many "graces" upon his people.)

Islam

MUHAMMAD

Because Islam is the youngest of the major world religions, details on its founder's life are widely available. Muhammad was born in 570 A.D., and raised by his uncle in Mecca, an important town on the trade routes in Arabia. He belonged to the Quraish tribe, which controlled the Ka'ba, a black meteoric stone revered by local tribes. Muhammad was illiterate but made a living working on the trade caravans, becoming exposed to people of many religious backgrounds. Muhammad married a wealthy widow, Khadija, and had six children, of whom only his daughter Fatima survived him. Muhammad pursued religious questions after his marriage and become convinced that the end of the world might be near. During meditation, Muhammad was visited by the angel Gabriel, who dictated to him God's word. Muhammad converted to monotheism and began preaching what he had learned. He converted others to his prophetic vision but faced opposition from Meccans. He migrated to Medina and became a successful political and religious leader, but died without leaving a successor.

Muhammad is revered as a religious leader and the last and greatest of the prophets. Muslims believe that he was sent directly by God as a man to warn people about how to live in a way that would please God. Most Muslims believe that Muhammad is an example of humanity at its best; his hadiths, or words, and his sunna, for example, are the sources of the greatest authority and wisdom after the Qur'an itself. The Qur'an does not dwell on Muhammad's biography, and it is not especially interesting to Muslims, as he was not himself a divine figure. He is revered as a devoted prophet and a source of great knowledge and dedication to transmitting God's word and starting the faith, but he himself was fully human.

ENCOUNTERS WITH GABRIEL

Muhammad, on his spiritual quest, took to meditating periodically in a cave near Mount Hira for days at a time. On one of these sojourns, Muhammad was visited by the angel Gabriel, who announced his presence with the word "Recite!" This began Muhammad's first vision, which became Sura 96 of the Qur'an. Muhammad had additional encounters with Gabriel over the next 23 years, in which he received prophecies from Allah in a trancelike state, memorized them, and later taught them to his literate companions, who recorded them. Muhammad worried for his sanity initially, feeling that his visions may have been the product of a jinn. His wife and friends, however, believed in the spiritual importance of his visions, and Muhammad gradually became convinced that Allah was using him as a voice and that he was the last of the prophets, with the complete and final revelation of God's word.

HISTORICAL CONTEXT IN WHICH ISLAM AROSE

By the seventh century, the tribal Arabian peninsula had been exposed to and influenced by many religions for thousands of years, including Judaism, Zoroastrianism, and Christianity. Some western tribes were Jewish, possibly the lost tribes of Israel, but most were polytheistic animists, worshipping a pantheon of gods, though the details are lost to history. There were local deities as well as the supreme god, Allah. Angels, fairies, ghouls, and demons interacted freely with human lives. There was a focus on sensual pleasures and on the immediate present; time was synonymous with death. The town of Mecca was wealthy and situated on a major trading route. Its economy was bolstered by animistic pilgrims coming to worship the Ka'ba, the black meteoric stone enclosed by a structure filled with art and said to have been built by Adam. There were clan disputes over its control.

Early Spread of Islam

During Muhammad's life, his message was ridiculed initially, then embraced by some and received with hostility by others. Muhammad's message of a united monotheistic faith was politically and religiously threatening; Mecca's economy was helped greatly by animistic pilgrims, and political leaders feared he wanted to usurp their power. Muhammad's message of social justice was threatening to the interests of the wealthy. In addition, his rejection of tribal beliefs was seen as shameful to the clan ancestors. Muhammad's wife Khadija, his sons Zayd and Ali, and his wealthy friend Abu-Bakr were Muhammad's first converts, who proselytized for Islam. After Khadija's death, Muhammad married other women in politically advantageous matches that helped his missionary movement. In addition, after his tribe was banished to a small quarter of Mecca and he feared for his safety, Muhammad and his supporters fled to Medina and Abyssinia, where they sent messages to neighboring nations and Bedouins, asking them to join their religion.

Hijrah

Muhammad's message of monotheism was threatening to the political interests of Mecca. In 620 A.D., after receiving death threats, Muhammad solicited the help of the leaders of Yathrib, a town 300 miles and an eleven-day journey away. Yathrib was a multicultural town with deeply ingrained tribal conflicts, and it needed a powerful leader who would settle disputes impartially. Muhammad's leadership impressed them, and they arranged for him to become the judge of Yathrib. Some Jews there also had thoughts that he might be the Messiah. In 622 A.D., after word of Muhammad's planned journey reached the Meccan leaders, they planned to attack Muhammad quickly, but he escaped on September 24 with Abu-Bakr before they were able, making the journey in eight days. This journey became known as the Hijrah, and its date marks the beginning of Muslim calendars. Yathrib became the first true Muslim community and was eventually renamed Medina, which means "City of the Prophet."

Violence After Muhammad's Journey to Medina

Muhammad's political troubles did not end after the Hijrah. After his move to Medina, the preexisting rivalry between Mecca and Medina intensified. What Muhammad began as a series of raids on the other city's caravans, intended to rebuild Medina's treasury, eventually became military campaigns against the enemies of his Medinan theocracy.

At first, Muhammad was an effective judge in Medina; the Medina Charter guaranteed freedom of religion to all of its citizens, which included other "People of the Book," such as Jews, Christians, and Muslims. Eventually, however, Medinan Jews had abandoned the idea that Muhammad might be the Messiah, and a division between Muslims and Jews arose, with Muhammad becoming increasingly hostile toward Medinan Jews, and Medinan Jews, in turn, supporting Meccans in their campaign against Muhammad. The Jewish matron Zainab poisoned Muhammad at a dinner she held for him, an act whose physical consequences remained with Muhammad for the rest of his life. In 627 A.D., the Meccans invaded Medina but failed, resulting in a great victory for Muhammad. By 629, Muhammad's forces were so strong that they took a pilgrimage to Mecca and were not hindered. The next year, Muhammad repeated the journey and destroyed the idols of Ka'ba; with this act, Muhammad became the sole leader of the Arabians.

Worldwide Spread of Islam

Muhammad died after completing a pilgrimage to Mecca; within a hundred years, Islam had reached every corner of the Arabian peninsula and had traveled across North Africa to Spain, where Muslims ruled Spain for seven centuries. Part of the reason for Islam's appeal was that it did not recognize national boundaries; with one statement of faith, anyone could become a Muslim. As a religion, Islam was not difficult to practice, requiring no conversion rituals or genetic lineage, no formal study and no esoteric meditation practices. The Byzantine and Persian empires had struggled for control of Palestine in the preceding centuries, and both empires were overstretched. Arab peoples lacked a strong leader, and into this vacuum Islam stepped. Muslim conquerors were not resisted by their conquered peoples, many of whom were grateful for new leadership. By the eleventh century, Islam reached India and western China, by the fifteenth it was dominant in Indonesia and Malaysia, and in the nineteenth it was traveling south through Africa.

Muhammad's Night Journey

One of the most important and illustrative stories of Islam concerns Muhammad's night journey. While living in Mecca, Gabriel came to Muhammad during the night, purified him, and took him on a journey on a winged horse through the seven heavens. Muhammad spoke with the previous prophets and the important religious figures on this journey: Adam, John the Baptist, Jesus, Joseph, Enoch, Aaron, Moses, and Abraham. Then Gabriel put Muhammad on a flying carpet, where he ascended alone to speak personally with Allah. To Muhammad, Allah said, "I am speaking to you just as I spoke face to face with Moses," illustrating Muhammad's status as at least as great as that of other prophets. Muslims worldwide celebrate the anniversary of this journey today, and this story is critical in Islam for illustrating Muhammad's special relationship with God, although Muhammad remains fully human and not divine.

Caliph

A caliph is a representative of God through the Islamic religion on earth. The caliphate and its associated controversies result from Muhammad's lack of a plan for the religious leadership of Islam after his death. Only one of Muhammad's children, Fatima, survived his death, and he did not explicitly designate her as leader. He did appoint, during his life, his friend Abu-Bakr to lead prayers in Medina, which led to arguments after Muhammad's death about the proper leadership of the faith. The caliphate is the only organized office of Islam; unlike most other major religions, Islam is not hierarchical and individuals can fulfill most of their religious duties on their own.

The first four ("Rightly-Guided") caliphates of Islam are:

- Abu-Bakr: A friend and father-in-law of Muhammad's, Abu-Bakr served as caliph from 632 A.D. until his death in 634 A.D. He suppressed Bedouin rebellions, thereby uniting the Arabian Peninsula under Islam, and began missionary movements to neighboring empires, declaring a jihad against the Christians of the Byzantine Empire.
- Umar: Another father-in-law of Muhammad's, Umar served as caliph from 634–644. Umar conducted a series of successful military campaigns, capturing Damascus, Jerusalem, Babylon, and Alexandria, and instituted an official policy of religious tolerance. Umar was assassinated by a Persian Christian.
- Uthman: Uthman was a member of the powerful Umayyad family, and served from 644–656. He expanded the empire to Persia and Cyprus, but appointed family members to important positions and compiled a definitive text of the Qur'an, resulting in controversy. A group of Egyptians assassinated Uthman, resulting in a civil war.
- Ali: Ali, Fatima's husband, declared himself caliph amid great controversy, challenged by a rival claim by Uthman's cousin Mu'awiya. Ali served from 656–661 but was ultimately assassinated.

Schism Between Ali and Mu'awiya

Ali declared himself caliph unilaterally, a claim challenged by Uthman's cousin Mu'awiya. A civil war erupted immediately. The two men agreed to submit their rival claims to a council, which asked both to abandon their claims. Ali refused to do so. The Kharijites, a group angry that Ali had submitted his claim to human decisions, turned on him, appointed its own caliph, and made plans to assassinate both Mu'awiya and Ali. In 660, Mu'awiya, supported by Egypt, Syria, and the Kharijite faction, declared himself the official caliph. The Kharijites assassinated Ali, but before they could assassinate Mu'awiya as well he consolidated his power, ended the civil war, and began the first hereditary Muslim dynasty.

Umayyad Dynasty of Islam

Begun by Mu'awiya, the Umayyad Dynasty lasted for nearly a century, overseeing the spread of Islam to North Africa as far as Spain, as well as India. The Umayyad Dynasty was a far greater political than religious empire. Its capital was Damascus, and its chief imperial goal was the elimination of the Byzantine Empire. The Umayyad Dynasty had an official policy of religious tolerance for its conquered people, but a host of reasons including lower tax rates led to a high rate of conversion to Islam. Christian opposition to the Umayyads in the Byzantine Empire was fierce, and in 750, a rival family, the Abbasids, used this instability to their advantage, overthrowing the Umayyads and establishing a new dynasty.

Abbasid Dynasty of Islam

The Abbasid Dynasty was marked by far more peace and stability than had characterized the previous Islamic rulers. From 750 to 1258, the Sunni Abbasid family presided over an intellectually flourishing but decadent Islamic golden age. Its claim to power was based on genetic descent from one of Muhammad's uncles. Under Abbasid power, Muslim and non-Muslim intellectuals in the empire translated and transmitted the knowledge of classical Greece and India, as well as Arabic mathematics, to the West. The dynasty was eventually defeated by its own creation, the Mamluk army in Turkey, which persisted at greatly reduced levels of power for several hundred years. After World War I and the defeat of the Ottoman Empire, the caliphate officially came to an end. Pan-Arab nationalist movements have persisted for centuries, periodically agitating for a new caliphate. Most attempt to use peaceful persuasion to restore the caliphate, while others, such as al-Qaeda, argue that the caliphate is the only legitimate Muslim government and that the destruction of the nation-state system cannot be accomplished nonviolently.

Schism Between Sunni and Shi'ite Muslims

The Sunni-Shi'ite schism began with the controversy over the caliphs Mu'awiya and Ali. Shi'ite Muslims (from "Shi'ite Ali", the "party of Ali") do not consider Mu'awiya one of the "rightly guided caliphs," and believe that Ali, Muhammad's son-in-law and cousin, was meant to be Muhammad's direct successor from the beginning. After Ali was assassinated in 661, his son Husayn challenged Mu'awiya and the Umayyad dynasty but was defeated militarily. Husayn and many members of his family were killed in the battle. Shi'ite Muslims have allegiance to Ali and his descendents, and focus generally on the hereditary leadership of Islam. Shi'ites also focus strongly on the tragic history of Islam and martyrdom, viewing Husayn and Ali as the original martyrs of the faith.

Results of World War I and Modern Oil-Based Economy

During World War I, the Ottoman Empire was allied with Germany and Austria. After its defeat, it was broken up by the Allied Powers into nations whose borders were unrelated to cultural or geographical reality. Tribal membership was split across national borders and rival tribes and religious factions were forced together into nation-states. In the mid-twentieth century it was discovered that Middle Eastern nations contained the world's largest supply of crude oil. Immediately this discovery increased their wealth and international political power exponentially. Later, the Muslim nation of Indonesia was discovered to have a large petroleum reserve as well. Some internal reform movements, including Islamic feminism, have arisen in Islamic nations in response to increased exposure to western nations. More often than not, however, this increased power has meant that western nations ignore human rights abuses because of their dependence on oil produced by nations administered by repressive regimes. In the post-colonial world, Islam has become an increasingly attractive religion to Africans, who view it as having associations with social justice and self-determination without the baggage of European imperialism.

Influence of Shi'ite Islam on the Iranian Islamic Revolution of 1979

In 1953, the democratically elected Iranian Prime Minister was overthrown and replaced with Shah Mohammed Reza, widely viewed in Iran as an Anglo-American mouthpiece. In 1979, student radicals took American embassy workers hostage, the Ayatollah Khomeini returned from exile in Paris, and a (rigged) national referendum installed an Islamic national government based on pure Twelver Shi'ite Islam. The reasons for this course of events are complex, but lie strongly in Shi'ite Islam and its long history in Iran. Islam has long had serious reservations about secular civil authority. In addition, from the time of Ali's assassination, Shi'ite Islam has been interested in imagery of martyrdom and bloodshed, as well as in the return of the imam Mahdi, who cannot return without the proper government, run on Islamic principles, to receive him. In accordance with beliefs about Ali's intentions for an Islamic government, the Iranian government has a committee of five ayatollahs who oversee legislation and ensure its conformance with Islam. Religious leaders called mullahs oversee public education, and the Supreme Leader, a grand ayatollah, must confirm all prospective presidential candidates.

Development of the Qur'an

Allah revealed the Qur'an through the angel Gabriel directly to the prophet Muhammad over a period of twenty-three years. Because Muhammad was illiterate, he memorized the messages from Gabriel and passed them to others, who memorized them as well. As the Qur'an was the direct word of Allah, it was considered a blessing to commit passages to memory, but at some point, fearing that those who knew it by heart were in danger of dying in battle, literate companions committed the messages to writing. Uthman, the third caliph, acting in concert with others, developed an authoritative version from the various versions that had gradually come into existence after the prophet's death.

Sunni Islam

Sunni Islam, practiced by 85% of Muslims, is considered by its practitioners the orthodox and traditional path of Islam. ("Sunni" means "principle" or "path.") The sources of Islamic wisdom for Sunnis include the Qur'an and hadith, traditions about the words and acts of the prophet Muhammad. Sunnis believe that the first four caliphs of Islam were the legitimate successors to Muhammad, that they were chosen by men, and that this choice was as legitimate as any, as God did not specify particular successors. Shi'ite Islam is believed to have taken too many liberties with legitimate Islam and to have corrupted its practice. Specifically, Sunnis object to Shi'ite ideas about the caliphate and the hidden imamate. For answers to questions not found in the Qur'an or the hadith, there are four equally valid legal traditions in Sunni Islam, and whichever appeals most to a particular believer is a legitimate choice. Sunni Islam is a majority religion in most Muslim countries; Iraq is about half Sunni, and Iran it is a minority sect.

Shi'ite Islam

Shi'ite Islam represents about the beliefs of about 15% of all Muslims, but it is a majority religion in Iran and represents about half of Iraqi Islam. Although it broke from Sunni Islam initially over leadership disputes, theological differences have since evolved. In Shi'ite Islam, the imam, or hereditary religious leader, is divinely inspired and selected by God through Muhammad. Different Shi'ite sects believe in a different number of total imams, but all believe that Ali was the rightful successor to the prophet and that some imams have not actually died but are in hiding on Earth.

The imam Mahdi, the "guided one," is a messiah figure that will return to lead the world into an era of peace and justice. Because of the assassinations of Husayn and Ali, bloodshed and martyrdom are important themes in Shi'ite Islam. Shi'ites also revere imams as examples of saintliness for humans to emulate. Because of the divine nature of the imam, clergy can re-interpret the Qur'an as necessary, and Shi'ite Islam generally supports the idea of theocracy, as religious leaders are the best qualified to provide leadership.

Veneration of Ali and Husayn

The focus on martyrdom in Shi'ite Islam, as well as the divinely ordained nature of religious leaders, has evolved into a focus on the person of the holy figure. Husayn's assassination is reenacted by Shi'ite Muslims every year in a passion play, in a series of events known as the Muharram. The sites of his martyrdom and important life events, along with those of the twelve imams (or seven, in some sects) are the objects of pilgrimage for Shi'ites. Shi'ite holidays include commemorations of the life events of these holy figures. Shi'ite Muslims believe that a pilgrim to the shrines of these holy figures and their relatives has access to these holy figures, who can intercede on their behalf with Allah.

Sects

There are three main branches of Shi'ite Islam:

- Zaidites: This is the most traditional Shi'ite sect, and the one most closely aligned with Sunni Islam. Unlike other Shi'ites, who curse the names of Abu-Bakr and Umar at Friday services, Zaidites do believe that God chose these imams. They believe that Zayd is the fifth imam. Zaidites have had a continuous but not powerful dynasty in Yemen since the ninth century, as well as periodic leadership elsewhere.
- Ithna'ashari (Twelver Shi'ites): the majority of Shi'ite Islam. Twelvers believe that the twelfth and last imam is Muhammad al-Muntazar, who disappeared in 878 into a cave at the Samarra mosque at age five, but did not die. Twelvers believe that he will return as the Mahdi, as predicted by Muhammad in a hadith. He is known as the "concealed imam," who selects representatives on earth to provide guidance on his behalf.
- Ismailites (Sevener Shi'ites): This sect, mostly active in India, Pakistan, and Africa, believes that Isma'il, the first son of the sixth imam, will soon return as the imam Mahdi.

Sufi Tradition of Islam

Sufism, the mystical branch of Islam, grew in response to the materialism and decadence of Muslim rulers around the ninth century. Influenced by Christians in the Middle East as well as mystical Hinduism in India, Sufis have a long tradition of asceticism. Sufis are based in orthodox Islam and take the Qur'an as their central text, but believe also in the possibility of knowledge of God through mystical experience. Sufis believe that their belief system is true to the original spirit of early Islam. Sufis approach God through trance dancing, poverty, abstention from worldly pleasure, and feats of extremism, such as coal-walking. Sufis place great emphasis on love for humanity and beauty, and are known for their poetry. Sufis hold two main principles: tawakkul, absolute trust in God, and tawhid, the belief that there is no deity but God. Some Sufis interpret this second principle as meaning that nothing exists outside God, as Hindus believe. Other Muslims criticize this belief as being pantheistic or insufficiently humble before God.

Ahmadiyya Islam

Ahmadiyya Islam is a nineteenth century movement of Indian Islam. Its founder, Mirza Ghulam Ahmad, claimed to be the Messiah and an incarnation of both Jesus and Muhammad. Ahmadiyya Muslims believe that Jesus was not, as the Qur'an states, crucified, but that he faked his execution and lived out his life in India. After Ahmad's death in 1914, Ahmadiyya Islam split into two camps: the Qadiani, who believe he was a prophet, and the Lahore, who believe that he was an Islamic reformer. Ahmadiyya Islam has some theological crossover with Sufism. Ahmadiyya Islam is popular in Pakistan, and numbers around 170 million adherents. It has a much stronger missionary aspect than other branches of Islam. Most Muslims, who believe that Muhammad is the last and greatest prophet, denounce Ahmadiyya Islam as heretical.

Wahhabi Movement

Wahhabism is a traditionalist reform movement of Islam. It was begun in 1744 by Muhammad ibn-Abd al-Wahhab, and was opposed to all religious innovations, which it viewed as straying too far from a strict understanding of Islam. It argued against any schools of thought that did not originate in Medina around the time of Muhammad's life. Wahhabists are also known as Wuwahiddun, "defenders of unity." Early in its development, Wahhabism attached itself to the House of Saud, and became the state doctrine of Saudi Arabia as that family rose to power. It has historically been especially opposed to Sufism, which it views as heretical, but has simultaneously adopted many Sufi practices, such as architectural austerity (Wahhabi mosques are plain white, with no minarets), the veneration and intercessionary abilities of saints, pilgrimage, and the importance of personal religious experience. Wahhabis have had a strong missionary tradition, and the wealth of the House of Saud has facilitated Wahhabism's influence on Islam worldwide. Wahhabism has been particularly influential on the Taliban regime in Afghanistan and the caliphate-restoration movement of Osama bin Laden.

Druze and Alawites

Two minority syncretic traditions within Islam are the Druze and the Alawites. Traditional Islam considers both heretical. The Druze are a syncretic blend of Christianity, Judaism, and Islam that arose in the Lebanese mountains in the eleventh century. The Druze religion began as an eschatological movement that predicted the imminent end of the world; their holy figure, al-Darazi, is an Egyptian caliph whom they consider to be the last and greatest incarnation of God and whose return is expected at any point. They are a purely inherited tradition that does not accept converts. Their traditions are esoteric and they practice many secret rituals. They advocate the spiritual superiority of women. The Alawites were founded by Muhammad ibn Nusayr in the border area of Turkey and Syria in the ninth century. Alawites believe that Ali was not simply an imam but an incarnation of God. Their rituals incorporate traditions of both Islam and Christianity, including wine rituals, the celebration of Easter and Christmas, and reincarnation.

Imam

The word "imam" has different meanings in Shi'ite and Sunni Islam. In Sunni Islam, the imam is the prayer leader. During Friday services the imam leads the assembly in prayer. He is always male and has religious training, but has no divine qualities. In Shi'ite Islam, the imam is one of twelve (or, in the case of Ismailite Islam, seven) divinely ordained historical figures who continue to guide humans through their representatives on Earth. They are infallible, sin-free examples for humans to emulate. These "mujtahids" are Shi'ite clergy, not divine figures. The Shi'ite imam Mahdi is a messiah figure whose coming will usher in an age of peace.

Predestination

In Islam, Allah is omniscient and omnipotent, and the role of humans is to submit to His will. No act occurs without Allah's consent. In Islam, humans can choose from a variety of available paths in life, all of which are created by God. Most Muslims agree that human beings, not God, are responsible for their choices to sin and that ultimately God decides human fate but that humans must still choose good, especially the common good. Shi'ite Islam places more emphasis on the human ability to make choices, and the day of judgment of human behavior that will accompany the arrival of the imam Mahdi. Although it can seem contradictory, Allah has foreknowledge of human choices and yet humans have the freedom to choose their path. Because Allah has created all that happens in the universe and Allah is all good, nothing happens that is truly evil. Everything that Allah allows is ultimately wise, even if difficult for mere humans to understand.

Hadith Canons

The Hadith Canons are thousands of texts recounting Islamic traditions dating from various caliphates. They recount Muhammad's sayings and acts during his lifetime, including some things that were done in Medina but clearly had Muhammad's tacit approval. Because there is no record of his objections to these activities, they are now part of an accepted tradition of Muslim behavior. The hadiths are not without controversy; they are not divine, but rather memories of the prophet passed down through his companions and told to a chain of people, eventually being written down. The trustworthiness of the sources determines the authenticity of the hadiths they wrote, and there are varying opinions about which are considered canonical. Six separate hadith canons exist; the most highly regarded is the ninth century *Book of al-Bukhari*.

Sharia and Fiqh

Sharia, or Islamic jurisprudence, developed in response to the rapid spread of Islam worldwide. Because the sunna (Muhammad's behavior) and the Qur'an did not necessarily apply directly in every environment and situation, a broader understanding of how to apply Islamic principles to Muslim life around the world needed to be developed. This was Sharia, meaning "the way," or the true path of religion. In order of authority, Islamic principles derive from the following sources:

- The Qur'an
- The hadiths
- Ijma, or the consensus of the Islamic community in Median near the time of Muhammad's life (for Sunnis only)
- Qiyas, or analogies, based on the principles found in the Qur'an (for Sunnis only)
- 'aql, or dialectical reasoning (for Shi'ites only)

Fiqh, meaning "understanding," is the art of applying Sharia on matters on which the Qur'an is silent. Fiqh is a process by which Sharia is interpreted and a set of principles that are not sacred, as they are developed by men. There is little distinction in Islam between law and religion, particularly for Sunnis.

Five Pillars of Islam

The Five Pillars of Islam are described as follows:

- Shahadah: repetition of the creed. This confession of faith in front of two Muslim witnesses is the membership requirement of the Muslim faith.
- Salaht: daily prayer. Five ritual prayers are required of adult Muslims, and their sequence is carefully scripted.
- Zakaht: almsgiving. One or more taxes are assessed on Muslims' property, and the proceeds used for Islamic institutions and to aid the poor. In addition, Muslims are expected to be generous with those less fortunate.
- Sawm: fasting during Ramadan. Every year, during the holy month of Ramadan, Muslims are expected to obey a sunrise to sundown fast.
- Hajj: pilgrimage. At least once during a Muslim's life, if they are financially able, he is expected to undertake a pilgrimage to the Ka'ba in Mecca.

SHAHADAH

The Shahadah is the Muslim confession of faith. Spoken in Arabic, the creed is "La ilaha illa Allah; Muhammad rasul Allah." ("There is no God but Allah; Muhammad is the messenger of Allah.") It is the most common sentence spoken in a Muslim's life, often said many times a day. When a child is born into a Muslim family, these words are whispered into his or her ear, and faithful Muslims try to make these words their last as well. The muezzin's call to prayer includes the Shahadah, as do the daily prayers. Unlike other religions, which have more complicated membership requirements, Islam requires only this confession (in front of two Muslim witnesses) for an individual to become a Muslim. This creed cannot be undertaken lightly, however. Seven conditions must be in place before the Shahadah is meaningful:

- Knowledge of its meaning
- Confidence in it
- Sincerity
- Truth
- Love of the Shahadah
- Submission to its requirements
- Love for it and those who submit to it

SALAHT

Salaht consists of five required daily prayers. In accordance with Muhammad's designation of the Ka'ba as the most sacred site for Muslims, Muslims pray toward Mecca (specifically towards the Ka'ba). The prayers take place at dawn, noon, midafternoon, sunset, and nightfall.) In Muslim-majority communities, the muezzin calls Muslims to prayer from the minaret of the local mosque; in non-Muslim-majority communities, the call to prayer is done at the mosque entrance. Prayer can be done at the mosque or on one's own, with the exception of Friday prayers, where mosque attendance is obligatory. In order to pray, Muslims must perform ritual ablutions, washing their bodies in a clean environment. In the mosque, worshippers are segregated by sex; in some mosques, women are not allowed. The prayer sequence consists of thirteen parts, which must be performed in Arabic in the proper sequence. Each Muslim has his or her own prayer rug on which they perform a series of standing, kneeling, and prostrate prayers. These ritual prayers glorify Allah and reaffirm a Muslim's submission to Him rather than petitioning for aid.

ZAKAHT

Muslims are expected to behave charitably and share their possessions with orphans, widows, and the poor. To give alms is obligatory if a person is financially able; in Muslim countries zakaht has often collected as a tax (although now it is only done in Saudi Arabia), representing between 2.5 and 10% of the value of a person's possessions. This money is used to support religious institutions, schools, and students. In addition to the zakaht, Muslims are expected to give voluntarily to the needy. Shi'ite Islam collects an additional 20% to support the hidden imam and his earthly representatives. The money is used to aid the imams as well as the poor and traveling people.

SAWM

During the holy month of Ramadan, Muslims follow a ritual fast known as sawm. During daylight, they must abstain from not only food, but also drinking, smoking, and sexual intercourse. This is an act of repentance for Muslims; Allah is understood to pardon those who obey the Ramadan fast. The fast lasts all day, during the times when it is possible to distinguish a white thread from a black one. Because the Muslim calendar is lunar rather than solar, the month of Ramadan is not during the same season from year to year. Since abstaining from water can be especially difficult during the summer, especially in desert nations, sawm is an act of dedication as well as penitence. Nursing mothers, small children, and those who are ill or traveling are not obligated to participate in sawm.

Hajj

All Muslims, if they are financially able, are expected to undertake a pilgrimage to the Ka'ba in Mecca at least once in their lifetime. The pilgrimage dates from pre-Islamic times but has been adapted as part of Muslim practice. A Muslim who has fulfilled this religious obligation is granted the venerated title of "haji" to affix to his or her name. During their trip, pilgrims fast as though for Ramadan, and are not allowed to cut their hair or nails. They wear no head covering, simple shoes, and white, symbolizing both their unity as Muslims and their equality in Islam; there is to be no clothing that would indicate a wearer's wealth. The ritual is highly scripted; from outside of Mecca, pilgrims must walk to the Ka'ba. There, they circle the stone seven times and kiss it. On the tenth day, pilgrims sacrifice a sheep or goat.

Ramadan

The ninth month of the Islamic lunar calendar, Ramadan, is a holy month. It is a month of fasting, penitence, and religious reflection, followed by a three-day feast. Ramadan commemorates both Muhammad's victory at Badr, and his receipt of the first revelations of the Qur'an. While Ramadan has a penitent aspect, it is a larger symbol of Muslims' obedience to God's commandments rather than an act of atonement. Muslims abstain from food, drink, sex, and evil thoughts and actions during daylight hours during Ramadan. At the end of the month, Muslims celebrate with a festival, 'Id al-Fitr, in which they exchange gifts, pay respects to the dead, and send holiday cards.

Islam's Relationship with Judaism

Islam, Christianity, and Judaism all trace their ancestry to Abraham, and Muslims accordingly revere the leaders of Judaism and Christianity. Abraham, Moses, and Jesus, among others, are considered prophets in Islam. Muslims believe that it was Abraham who placed the first religious shrine in the Mecca Valley, the holiest place in Islam. Like Judaism, Islam believes in an omniscient, omnipotent God who takes a personal interest in human beings and has, on occasion, communicated with them. Tensions between Jews and Muslims have existed from the early centuries of Islam, as Jews have labeled Muhammad a false prophet and even a madman. Both religions, however, stress the importance of obedience to God's commandments, though they differ on the content of those commandments.

Islam's Relationship with Christianity

Since Muslims claim that Islam is a purer and more complete form of the religion of Abraham, Muslims will claim a great deal of common theology with Christianity. The Qur'an explicitly states that the God of the Hebrew and Christian Bibles is the same God as Allah, and that Islam is the more progressively-revealed form of Christianity, although the person and character of this God are described differently. However, Islam also firmly believes that Jews and Christians have over time allowed errors to creep into their religions, whereas the Qur'an, dictated directly from God to Muhammad, is infallible. It reveres the Jewish and Christian prophets, but believes that Muhammad was the "last and greatest of these." Muslims reject the doctrine of the Trinity as polytheistic, although the Qur'an inaccurately construes the Trinity as involving the Father, Jesus, and Mary. They also reject the idea of a human Messiah, arguing that humans cannot be raised to the level of God. The Muslim messiah figure, the Mahdi, or Twelfth Imam, is not universally accepted among Islamic sects. Islam teaches that Jesus was a prophet, like Muhammad, and was born of a virgin mother. They do not, however, believe he was crucified, but instead hold that he ascended directly to heaven. The Qur'an states that Jews and Christians can enter into heaven despite their false religion, so long as they believe in God and perform sufficient good works.

Six Articles of Muslim Faith

The six articles of Muslim faith summarize Muslim doctrine. They are:

- The belief in one God. Allah is omniscient, omnipotent, merciful, and compassionate.
- The belief in God's angels, pure and obedient divine beings who worship God and act as His messengers. The angels include Gabriel, who conveyed the Qur'an to Muhammad, the angel of death, and the angel who guards Paradise, among others.
- The belief in God's books, particularly the Qur'an, but also including the Torah, the Psalms, and the Gospel.
- The belief in God's prophets, who have been appointed by God to impart wisdom to mankind. Prophets mentioned in the Qur'an include Adam, Noah, Abraham, Lot, Ishmael, Isaac, Jacob, Joseph, Moses, Aaron, David, Solomon, Elijah, Job, Jonah, Zachariah, John the Baptist, and Jesus.
- The belief in the Day of Judgment. All human beings will be resurrected from the dead and judged when the world ends, and they will be resigned to either Heaven or Hell.
- The belief in predestination. God knows all that has happened and will ever happen.

Muslim Conception of God

Muslims believe that God is omnipotent, omniscient (of everything that has happened or will come to pass), merciful, and compassionate. He is the creator of the universe and the personal deity of all people. God is the supreme power of the universe, indivisible, and eternal. (Of all the major religions, only Islam and Judaism believe in this level of undiluted monotheism.) There is no greater sin in Islam than to put someone or something else on par with Allah ("shirking"). Allah ("the god") has ninety-nine names in Islam, but is only one God; the 99 names simply illustrate God's many qualities. Islam states that God has revealed his will through messengers and prophets throughout history. Prophets convey God's message for a particular place and people. Muhammad is one of many prophets, but he is the final and greatest prophet. Muhammad illustrates Allah's quality of mercy; Allah sent Muhammad to save mankind by warning them about proper behavior. The Qur'an is the undiluted word of God. Its messages are the final authority on all issues.

Qur'an

The Qur'an, meaning "reading" or "recitation," is the holiest book in Islam and the central object of its theology, more important than any person. It consists of 114 suras, or chapters, organized by length. For Muslims, the Qur'an is eternal, sacred, and literally true. As it was revealed in Arabic, it is only truly sacred in Arabic, and is otherwise known as a translation of the Qur'an, not the Qur'an itself. Muhammad is the final prophet, according to Islamic belief, and so the Qur'an is the undistorted, final word of God. Unlike other religious books, such as the Hebrew and Christian Bibles, which have become corrupted over hundreds of years, the Qur'an remains pure. Because the Qur'an reproduces God's exact words, reading or reciting it is a blessing, and committing it to memory is an act of piety. The Qur'an is one of three ways Allah guides humans, the others being through the example of Muhammad and through the angels.

Minor Heavenly Figures

In addition to Allah, Muslims believe in semidivine figures that aid in human affairs or hinder them. The main categories are:

- Angels: Angels are benevolent attendants of Allah in seventh heaven, where they serve as His messengers to humans, as the angel Gabriel did with Muhammad. Angels are one of three ways in which Allah guides human beings, the others being through Muhammad and the Qur'an.

- Jinn: Jinn are mortal spirits, created from fire, whose existence was a belief of pre-Islamic Arabia. Jinn have a nature between human and angelic. Some are friendly and some malevolent. They possess free will and can make themselves visible to humans at will.
- Iblis, or Shaytan: the devil. Iblis is a fallen angel, cast out of heaven due to his pride. He is the leader of the jinn. Iblis has a certain range of power allowed by Allah, but is not wholly evil, as he is Allah's creation. Rather than an evil god, Iblis is a tempter of mankind and responsible for the fall of Adam.

Death and Afterlife

The afterlife as conceived by Islam is dualistic, containing an eternal paradise for the righteous and eternal damnation for the wicked. The Qur'an is particularly focused on the aesthetics of the afterlife that would be affecting to those living in desert societies: lush gardens in paradise, harsh winds in hell. In Islam, two angels are appointed to each human being beginning at puberty to keep a record of that person's deeds in life. After death, her soul sleeps until the day of judgment, when bodies rejoin their souls, the books of deeds are opened, and Allah judges humans' merit, assigning them to a level of heaven or hell for eternity. It is necessary both to have faith and to live a life of good deeds to be saved from hell. Those who sin but sincerely repent can be saved as well. The Qur'an specifies two unique doctrines regarding the afterlife:

- Those who die fighting for God are immediately sent to God's presence.
- The "enemies of Islam" are immediately sent to hell upon their deaths.

Mosque

Mosques are the religious centers of Muslim life, but they do not hold the place of reverence that religious buildings do in other religions, as is perhaps appropriate for a religion that originated with nomadic people. In Islam, the place one worships is not particularly important; almost all religious duties, with the exception of Friday prayers, can be performed elsewhere. Mosques host the five daily prayers, as well as Friday prayers, funeral services, and prayer services on two holidays, Eid ul-Fitr and Eid ul-Adha. Mosques also act as centers for the collection and distribution of zakaht. The imam of a mosque is the leader of prayer. During Friday prayer services, the imam leads the community in prayer and gives a sermon, either in Arabic or in the vernacular of the area. In addition, mosques are often associated with religious schools called madrassas, some of which have become important institutions of higher learning.

Rites of Passage

Children

At birth, Muslim infants are welcomed into the Ummah with the call to prayer. Seven days after birth, a naming ceremony takes place. The infant's head is shaved and the weight of the hair in gold or silver is given to charity in a ceremony known as Aqiqah. Boys are circumcised either at this time, or, less commonly, any time up to puberty. The Bismillah ceremony, at age four, marks the start of religious education. At puberty, boys and girls are expected to take up their assigned gender roles and participate fully in the Muslim community. Female genital mutilation is practiced in some, but by no means all, Islamic countries. Some Sunni hadiths argue for the practice, but it is not mentioned in the Qur'an.

Marriage and Death

Arranged marriages are common in the Muslim world. The husband's family pays a dowry to the wife's, which she may keep in the event of a divorce. Men are usually allowed by shar'ia to marry up to four wives, provided they can treat them all equally, but this is a privilege usually reserved for the wealthy. Marriage ceremonies may take place at the mosque or at home, but they are led by the imam and include a marriage contract agreed to by both parties. It is considered desirable in Islam for a dying Muslim's last words to be the Shahadah. After death, the body is washed three times, anointed with spices, and wrapped in white cloth. Muslims are always buried facing toward Mecca; they are never cremated. A simple funeral is held at a mosque or the burial site. It is considered a show of faith in God's power to have a short grieving period, traditionally three days. The graves of loved ones are visited at holidays.

ROLE OF WOMEN

It is difficult to separate the status of women in Islamic nations from the status of women in developing nations generally, which is a category into which most Islamic nations fall. Muslim women enjoy a higher social status than pre-Islamic Arabian women did, but it is undeniable that the status of women in Islam as it is practiced is significantly lower than that of men. Women are expected to be subordinate to their husbands, fathers, and male relatives. Proving a rape case is nearly impossible under shar'ia, since a woman is required to provide four male witnesses to prove her claim. Afterwards, male relatives may sometimes kill the victim in order to redeem family honor. In most Islamic nations, there are laws governing female modesty in dress, ranging from a headcovering to a burqa, which covers all but the hands and feet. This practice is most conservative in the Middle East.

Polygyny is legal under most Islamic governments, although the Qur'an stipulates that the practice is only allowed if a husband can treat his wives equally. Women under most Islamic governments do enjoy some important rights, including divorce. Mothers belong to a particularly revered class in Islam.

ROLE OF HOMOSEXUALS

The status of homosexuals in Islam is universally poor. The Qur'an condemns both male and female homosexuality, as do all schools of shar'ia. All humans are assumed to be naturally heterosexual. Lesbianism is considered a sin of the same caliber as adultery, while, as in the Hebrew and Christian traditions, male homosexuality is considered a grave sin. Seven nations currently allow the execution of male homosexuals; all are Islamic governments run on shar'ia principles. There is, however, a tradition in the Islamic world of accepting a certain degree of attraction between older and younger men as natural, even expected.

ISLAMIC TABOOS

The Qur'an and the hadiths of Muhammad set explicit rules for daily life as it should be practiced by Muslims. In a tradition not dissimilar to that of Judaism, Islam divides animals into the categories of halal (allowed) and haram (forbidden) for eating purposes. Animals that can be eaten must be slaughtered by cutting their throats, and Allah's name must be invoked while doing so. Pigs, animals of prey, and mules are all haram. Dogs are considered haram as well and may not be kept as pets; their only acceptable use is as herders. Alcohol is haram as well, but halal if not used for intoxicating purposes. Gambling and charging interest are forbidden in Islam as well.

JIHAD

Jihad is an Arabic word meaning "struggle." It has a host of secondary meanings, from building mosques or performing missionary work to armed struggle. Usually, however, it is used in an internal sense, to describe a Muslim's attempt to live in a way that pleases Allah, a struggle of the heart that Allah will reward. "Jihad" can be used to mean "holy war" as well, but the Qur'an recognizes only defensive war as legitimate in Islam. Muslim scholars argue over the exact implications of "defensive war"; while clearly the Christian Crusades were a legitimate jihad for Muslims in the Middle East, the armed struggles of the twentieth century are less clear. In addition, while many Muslims are opposed to Zionism, other Muslims see the conflict with Israel as a political struggle rather than a religious one. The Muslim terrorist groups of the early 21st century argue that a global "jihad" against Western and Muslim governments is legitimate, but this is a minority opinion; most Muslims agree that waging war against noncombatants is an explicit violation of the Qur'an.

Islamic Calendar and Muslim Holidays

There are two festivals in mainstream Islam. They are:

- 'Id al-Adha, the feast of sacrifice. This feast commemorates Abraham's willingness to sacrifice Ishmael to please God. (In Judaism it is Isaac he sacrifices; in Islam he sacrifices Ishmael at the Ka'ba.) Each household sacrifices an animal while reciting a ritual prayer, and shares the meat with the needy. Gifts are often exchanged as well.
- 'Id Al-Fitr, the breaking of the Ramadan fast. After the month of Ramadan has finished, Muslims celebrate with communal meals, gift-giving, and visiting friends and relatives.

In addition, Muslims celebrate three minor holidays:

- Al-Hijra, the New Year, also known as Muharram.
- Ashura, a day of atonement and fasting that traditionally commemorated Noah's departure from the ark as well as Moses' exodus. This period is especially important to Shi'ites, who commemorate the death of Husayn in a festival that consists of ten days of mourning and a passion play.
- Lailat al-Miraj, the festival of the prophet's night journey. Mosques and minarets are lit, and hadiths concerning the event are read.

Islamic Symbols

The Muslim faith is associated with a handful of well-known symbols, but often it takes pride in the beauty of Arabic script, choosing to decorate flags and architectural features with beautifully rendered calligraphy of Qur'anic passages. The star and crescent is a famous Islamic symbol, though it was appropriated from the Ottoman Empire, and is featured on several national flags. Shi'ite Islam often features sword iconography, representing the martyrdom of Shi'ite leaders. White, black, green, and red are colors associated with Islam. Green has sacred connotations in Islam; representing Muhammad as well as the lush gardens of paradise.

Beliefs About Human Nature

While Muslims take as sacred the story of Adam and Eve in the Garden of Eden, they do not interpret the doctrine of original sin as Christians do. In the Muslim version, Adam and Eve are punished with mortality for their failings, but they are repentant and Allah forgives them. Because of this mercy, humans are born with sin, not inherently guilty but in a state of gratitude to God, for which they must submit to his will. Human beings are Allah's finest creation, expressly made in order to worship God. Their task on Earth is to avoid the trap of pride and humble themselves before Allah.

Important Terms

Islam—"Submission." The practice of Islam is a continuous process of submission to the will of an omnipotent, omniscient God.

Muslim— "One who submits." To be a Muslim is an active process of submitting to the will of God and reasserting one's intention to do so.

Ummah— "Community." Ummah can refer to either the worldwide community of Muslims or the worldwide community as a whole.

Allah— "The god." Believed by Muslims to be the same god worshipped by Jews and Christians, as well as by pre-Islamic Arab religions (but conceived by them as a distant creator deity).

Din— "Religion," with the specific connotations of "duty" and "practice."

Iman—The articles of faith of Islam.

Ihsan—Right conduct.

Ibadat— Religious duty.

*Iman, ihsan, and ibadat are the three levels of faith in Islam.

Religious Movements

Jainism

Jainism is the religion of extreme asceticism. Jainism holds that only through the defeat of bodily desires can enlightenment be achieved. The universe, for Jains, is composed of only soul and matter. The goal of life is to release one' soul from the confines of matter. Because both soul and matter are eternal, there is no beginning or end to the universe, and no need for external gods; like Theravada Buddhism, Jainism does not believe in the importance of external deities. All living things have an eternal soul; therefore, Jains practice near-absolute nonviolence toward all creatures. Intentional harm to any living creatures is absolutely forbidden, and while lay Jains can defend themselves from violence, Jain monks may not do even that. There are two camps of Jainism. Svetambara is the more liberal of the two, and accepts women into monasteries. Svetambara monks wear white robes. Digambara is a deeply conservative sect; it views women as the source of temptation and evil in life, and has such a strong commitment to asceticism that Digambara monks live their lives mostly naked.

Monastic Vows

Jain monks take five vows when they enter the monastery. They are:

- Practicing ahimsa, or noninjury to life. Jain monks are vegetarian, sweep paths before them with a broom to avoid the accidental injury of an insect, and avoid any occupation that might cause harm to a living creature (e.g. agriculture).
- Always speaking the truth. Jain monks speak only after sincere deliberation, and speak plainly to avoid accidental offense, including the avoidance of jokes.
- A refusal to take anything not given freely. This is a commitment not simply to nonstealing, but to refusing anything not expressly offered.
- Renunciation of sexual pleasure. Jains believe that the pleasures of the flesh are evil and a source of distraction from one's path.
- Renunciation of all attachments, including love for other people, as attachments are a distraction from one's commitment to enlightenment.

All Jains try to keep first three duties. Monks are committed to all five.

Duties

In addition to their commitment to three of the Jain monastic vows, all Jains view their lives as consisting of six basic daily duties:

- To pray and meditate.
- To serve their elders. Parents are viewed by Jains as the most important gurus.
- To study spiritual literature.
- To maintain self-control, over one's body and one's temptation by sensual pleasures.
- Austerity. Jains renounce certain foods and activities, and demonstrate their commitment to enlightenment by putting themselves through stressful rituals and feats of endurance, like fasting and enduring extreme temperatures.
- Performing works of charity.

Relationship to Hinduism and Buddhism

Jainism and Buddhism arose in the sixth century A.D. as a reaction to Hinduism. Both reject the Hindu caste system and its enormous number of deities. Jainism's founder, Mahavira, like the Buddha, founded the sect while on a quest for personal enlightenment. Unlike the Buddha, however, Mahavira advocated extreme asceticism, viewing the pleasures of the world as a hindrance to enlightenment. Naked, Mahavira begged for food, sleeping in different locations to avoid attachments. Buddhism and Jainism reject Hinduism as abstract, a collection of rituals that are insufficient to help individuals in existential pain. In addition, both reject Hinduism's monism. Jainism believes that both the physical world and the world of souls are real. Like Hinduism and Buddhism, Jainism believes in the cycle of karma and rebirth. In Jainism, the goal of life is to avoid accumulating any karma, so in many ways Jainism is a religion of nonaction. The monastic life is idealized, but few Jains can afford to become monks. Unlike Buddhism, Jainism has only ever been popular in India.

Hare Krishna Movement

The International Society for Krishna Consciousness, or the Hare Krishna movement, was founded in 1966 in New York City by A.C. Bhaktivedanta Swami Prabhupada, who continues to fill the role of spiritual leader even after his death. It is a sect of Hinduism but explicitly rejects "the pantheism, polytheism, and caste consciousness that pervades modern Hinduism." The Bhagavad Gita is the central text in the movement, which members study in a guru/disciple structure. Krishna has a higher status than in traditional Hinduism, and is equated with God. Its seven official goals include bhakti yoga, the propagation of knowledge and the encouragement of "Krishna consciousness," peace via chanting the names of God (the "Hare Krishna" chant, meant to induce a state of total awareness), and the promotion of a simple lifestyle. Hare Krishna members are vegetarian, nondrinking, egalitarian, antisectarian, and take a great interest in the work of peacemaking.

Mormonism

The Church of Jesus Christ of Latter-day Saints, known as Mormonism, is a fundamentalist Christian sect devoted to restoring what it sees as original, pure Christianity. Mormonism was founded in the United States in the nineteenth century, by Joseph Smith. Smith received a series of visions from God, Jesus, John the Baptist, Peter, James, John, and an angel, Moroni. He was advised of the location of two golden tablets, written by a branch of the ancient Israelites who migrated to the Americas. Smith was miraculously granted the ability to translate them; this text was published as the Book of Mormon. The Book of Mormon describes the Biblical history of America, including Jesus's visit during his ascension to heaven.

Basic Beliefs

The basis of the Mormon Church lies in Christianity, though many of its tenets are rejected soundly by other Christians. Its understanding of the afterlife, the nature of God, and biblical history is at odds with most Christian beliefs. Mormons believe in two deities known as "Our Father in Heaven" and "Our Mother in Heaven," who are gods but have physical bodies and earthly children. Mormon marriage, if performed in a temple, is eternal, and families remain together forever in an afterlife in which humans can become divine. Mormons believe that Christianity has become corrupt through the loss of much of its teachings over the centuries, and that Joseph Smith's revelation marks the beginning of a restoration of true Christianity. Church leaders are prophets who continue to receive divine revelations, and Mormons proselytize heavily worldwide through their mission work.

Nineteenth and Twentieth Century Efforts to Reform Hinduism

Contact with European colonialists led to movements to reform Hinduism in the nineteenth and twentieth centuries. Missionaries in India in the nineteenth century, along with the reformer Ram

Mohan Roy, known as the "Father of Modern India," pressured the British colonial government to reform practices that had become associated with Hinduism. These groups particularly objected to the practice of suttee, or bride-burning, and child marriage. Suttee is a practice where a widow, either as a show of piety or by compulsion, throws herself onto her deceased husband's funeral pyre. Mohandas K. Gandhi, an Indian-born, British-trained lawyer, was Hindu but influenced strongly by the Jain doctrine of ahimsa, or absolute nonviolence. Gandhi led the Indian anticolonialist movement through a campaign of nonviolent resistance, including fasts and civil disobedience. Gandhi agitated as well for the reform of the caste system, particularly the treatment of Dalits, or "Untouchables," in India. The 1948 Constitution of India, as a result of these efforts, officially forbids discrimination against Dalits.

Sikhism

Sikhism is the fifth-largest religion in the world. It was founded in India in the fifteenth century by Guru Nanak Dev, who was born Hindu but disturbed by the distance and discord between Islam and Hinduism. Its chief object of veneration is the name and message of God, known as "the true name," a formless, impersonal God identified with the universe itself. Sikhs do not claim a monopoly on a pathway to God and stress the equality of all people. Sikh theology includes doctrines of karma and reincarnation, but rejects elaborate rituals. Sikhs are expected to engage with the world, work for a living, and not blindly follow traditions or be ascetics. Sikhs do follow a daily ritual of a purifying bath and the reading of hymns and prayers. Sikhs follow holy scripture as well as the teachings of ten historical gurus. There are five traditional Sikh dress rituals: uncut hair, a steel bracelet, a wooden comb, a ceremonial dagger, and long cotton underwear: all objects associated with the Sikhs' past as honored warriors.

Baha'i Faith

The Baha'i faith was founded in nineteenth century Persia, by the prophet Baha'u'llah, a Shi'ite Muslim who in 1852 received a vision from God in which humanity was a single race, speaking a single language. The remaining forty years of his life were devoted to writing scripture outlining his vision of peace. Since then, the sect has focused on peacemaking, emphasizing the unity of all religions. It works toward a world government with a single language, the elimination of prejudice, and universal education. Baha'is are guided by basic rules of conduct: not to kill, thieve, misbehave sexually, gamble, become intoxicated, or gossip. Baha'is accept the divinity of all previous prophets but are themselves considered apostasic by older Abrahamic religions. Baha'i practitioners are expected to pray and perform service daily, as well as periodically fasting. This emphasis on peace and the interconnectedness of all religions is evident in Baha'i architecture, where nine doorways and a domed roof are symbolic of the many possible paths to God.

New Age Movement

The New Age movement is a twentieth-century Western spiritual movement that is decentralized in structure and in beliefs. New Age honors the individual's connection with the universe in whatever way they see fit, but is often characterized by a reverence for nature, a belief in the unity of mind and body, and a rejection of rigid dogma. New Age practice can include elements of meditation, divination, and communal living, but may include none of those. Some New Age practices include traditions from one or more of the major religions, particularly Eastern religions, while others are entirely between the individual and the universe. God is generally understood as an abstraction, but there may be lesser deities (angels, fairies, spirit guides) who intervene in human lives. Life is generally understood to have some sort of common purpose that may be unknown to people, and the qualities of synchronicity and intuition are valued. Some people may be blessed with psychic or healing gifts, which may not be explicable by science.

Voodoo

Voodoo is a syncretic tradition that began with African slaves in Haiti, with origins in West African, Native Caribbean, and Catholic traditions. Voodoo is a polytheistic religion with multiple deities, who are used as intermediaries to worship the high god (Bondyè). African deities are worshipped alongside Catholic saints. Voodoo adherents practice religious ancestor worship, as in West Africa, as well as witchcraft, trance dancing, and animal sacrifice. Voodoo practitioners are notable for their belief in zombies, the dead who have been revived. Voodoo incorporates charms, amulets, and herbs to cast magic spells, but also uses elements of Catholic practice, including holy water, crucifixes, and Catholic prayers. Haitian Voodoo has spread and transformed with Haitian immigration to other places, notably Louisiana.

Umbanda

Umbanda is a syncretic religion with origins among African slaves in Brazil. Like other syncretic religions originating in colonial nations, it incorporates elements of Catholicism, as well as West African beliefs. From Catholicism, Umbanda takes its belief in monotheism and its reverence for the Christian Gospels. From African religion it takes its minor deities, spirits call Orixas who are the manifestations of God in the world. Ancestors can be contacted and petitioned for aid, and some individuals have psychic abilities allowing them to convey spiritual messages. Umbanda also believes in reincarnation, divination using snail shells, and its musical rituals.

Santería

Santería is a syncretic religion from the Caribbean, originating with Cuban slaves. It combines Catholicism with traditional Yoruba beliefs from West Africa. Under the Catholic authority of Cuba, slaves practicing traditional beliefs had to disguise their deities under the names of Catholic saints. Eventually, this evolved into a blended religion, in which figures from each belief system appear under two names, in a Catholic version and an African version. For example, Catholic saints have a Yoruba equivalent in the figure of the orisha, or spirit. Many Cubans consider themselves both practitioners of Santería and Catholicism. As in many nations with a native religion and an imported one (for example, Japan), Santería believers often divide their spiritual lives into two parts: one, governed by Santería, focuses on the here and now, and the other, governed by Catholicism, focuses on the afterlife.

Effects of Scientific Revolution on Organized Religion

The scientific revolution of the second millennium A.D. had profound effects. The triumph of reason and the development of the scientific method put matters of knowledge to a new, more rigorous analysis. The received wisdom of holy books, particularly in Roman Catholicism, was made questionable or outright doubtful as a result of the discoveries made by scientific inquiry. The origin and structure of the universe, previously thought to be the direct creation of a personal God was now, for many, subject to rational analysis. For others however, scientific inquiry had been, for quite some time, another means of understanding God and glorying in what He had made—as in the case of Newton and Boyle. Some European scientists, most of whom were self-declared Christians, found a way to reconcile their religious beliefs with the empirical knowledge brought by science. This was Deism, an eighteenth-century belief in a God who had created the universe and no longer had any direct impact on the world, leaving it instead to run on scientific principles. Ultimately, however, the scientific method of rational inquiry created a rift in society between traditionalists who continued to maintain that God's revealed word was authoritative, and rationalists, who argued that the holy books had to be considered in light of modern discoveries.

Nation of Islam

The Nation of Islam is an American religion founded by Wallace Fard Muhammad in 1930s Detroit. Wallace received a prophetic vision from Allah, in which it was revealed that Islam is the only possible religion for African-Americans. Its explicit mission is the betterment of black American life, spiritually, economically, and socially, and it advocates black pride and black separatism, piety and self-determination. Many of its leaders have been charismatic, in the tradition of African-American Christian churches. Though based loosely in Islam, the religion is not considered Islamic by mainstream Islam. It differs in its beliefs about race, God, creation, and prophecy. Mr. Muhammad is thought to be both the Christian Messiah and the Mahdi of Islam. Nation of Islam theology is often accused of hatred toward white people and anti-Semitism; traditional Islam teaches that all races are equal. In addition, the Nation of Islam advocates an eventual world Islamic government. The Nation of Islam is famous for having taken great steps toward easing the lives of American inner city residents, especially through drug rehabilitation programs.

Liberation Theology

Liberation theology is a twentieth-century Christian movement that seeks to make Christianity more accessible and relevant to the world's poor. A conference of Catholic bishops was convened at Medellin, Colombia, in 1968, where they laid the platform for this new understanding; based on passages in the New Testament about poverty, liberation theologians read the Bible through the lens of the world's poor and oppressed. They argue that poverty is the product of sin, the sin being exploitive capitalism, and seek to address these sins by applying Christianity to modern social problems. This is seen as a fulfillment of the church's mission in two ways: it puts into practice Jesus's love for the oppressed and Catholics' obligations to serve the poor, and makes the church more accessible to those whose lives are consumed by poverty. To its opponents, liberation theology is akin to Marxism, since it emphasizes greater state control to redistribute wealth on behalf of the poor. The Catholic Church has specifically denounced any alliance of Catholics with Marxists. Liberation theology, while still predominantly Catholic, has influenced Protestant theology as well, and has resulted in increased efforts to cultivatve "social justice" among Christians generally.

Rastafari Movement

The Rastafari movement is a Jamaican religion with its origins in 1930s black consciousness. Influenced by the black separatist preaching of Marcus Garvey, Rastas interpreted the crowning of emperor Haile Selassie of Ethiopia as the literal fulfillment of a Biblical prophecy about a black messiah. The movement is named for Selassie, whose former name was Ras Tafari. Selassie is considered the incarnation of the Christian Trinity and the reincarnation of Jesus Christ. Rastafari takes the Bible as a central text, with a particular focus on the prophecies of the Book of Revelation. It advocates the divinity of Jesus Christ but claims that the West has corrupted the Biblical message. It emphasizes black self-sufficiency, solidarity, and purity. Rastas eat a strict diet of raw vegetarian food and abstain from alcohol and milk. They do, however, use a potent form of marijuana in religious rituals, citing its reference in the Bible. Rastas believe in the second coming of Selassie, wherein he will create a paradise on earth in the highlands of Ethiopia. Over sixty percent of all Jamaicans are connected with the Rastafari movement.

Cargo Cult

A cargo cult is a social movement, usually in the South Pacific, that results when an isolated society suddenly comes in contact with Western technology. Cargo cults were common after World War II, when societies whose islands were used briefly by Western military forces and then suddenly abandoned. The "cargo" left by these Westerners, in terms of both material goods and new metaphysical questions, was significant. Often, the islanders' encounter with new technology led them to believe that these visitors had been some sort of deity or messiah, or that these foreign cultures had stolen their goods from the islanders' ancestors. New religious doctrines developed as a result. In some cultures, reproductions of World War II-era military rituals are staged in the hopes that they will summon the military they encountered during the war, who will bring more cargo. In others, they have begun to pray to their ancestors, to bestow cargo upon them as well. Due to the often-syncretistic nature of religion in these regions, cargo cults sometimes are associated with a doctrine of Christian apocalyptic expectation.

WICCA

Wicca is a nature-based religion with unclear origins that was popularized in the 1950s. Wiccan practitioners themselves claim that their religion has ancient origins; whether this is true is unclear. Wicca has general similarities to the mythology of pre-Christian Britain. Wicca practitioners, or witches, worship a goddess and/or a god, which are seen as part of a greater godhead and representing opposite aspects of the universe. These deities may be manifested in other minor deities as well. Wiccan beliefs include a Buddhist-like understanding of reincarnation and an Otherworld, or Summerland, where the dead rest between lives. Witches cast magic spells according to set rituals, honor seasonal changes, and may practice divination. Ultimately, beliefs in the afterlife are not important to Wicca; it focuses on the here and now. Seasonal festivals are a holy time of nature reverence for Wiccans, and their practice of solstice celebrations has its origins in Celtic and other European pagan traditions.

DSST Practice Test

Want to take this practice test in an online interactive format?
Check out the online resources page, which includes interactive practice questions and much more: **mometrix.com/resources719/dsstintrowr**

1. The term basic religion generally applies to:

a. Religions that are ultimately concerned with release from the cycle of life, death, and rebirth
b. Religions that believe in the divine judgment of the world.
c. Missionary religions, such as Christianity and Islam.
d. Religions of contemporary people whose religious ideas are not preserved in written form.

2. In Western cultures, religion is typically defined in terms of:

a. Collective and social identities on the basis of spiritual criteria
b. Set of beliefs having to do with a god or gods, through which people are taught a moral system
c. The number of followers it has
d. The way people deliver themselves from their plight without the help of a god or gods

3. Social scientists began to propose a number of different theories about the origins of religion during the ____________.

a. Middle Ages
b. Eighteenth century
c. Neolithic Age
d. Nineteenth century

4. Mana, a Melanesian term considered by some to be the basis of religion, is defined as:

a. An unseen force believed to inhabit extraordinary persons, objects, or phenomena
b. The recognition of a special relationship between a human and a species of animals, plants, or inanimate objects
c. The veneration and use of natural or prepared material objects with special potency for the purpose of averting evil or attaining powers
d. A way of dealing with the spirit world through an individual recognized as spirit-possessed and gifted in dealing with supernatural forces

5. Using the list provided, which of the following shows the correct pairing of a scholar with his theory about the origin of religion?

I. Wilhelm Schmidt—Original monotheism
II. Ludwig Feuerbach—A projection of human needs
III. Sir James George Frazer—Nature worship
IV. Edward Burnett Taylor—Animism

a. I, II, and III
b. II, III, and IV
c. I, II, and IV
d. I, II, III, and IV

6. Which of the following is NOT one of the three basic types of religious violence?

a. Acts of violence that are inherently religious
b. Acts intended as punishment for people believed to be evil
c. Violence directed toward government leaders
d. Violent clashes between religious communities

7. Commonly found in indigenous religions of Native North America, South America, and Africa, the belief that trees, rocks, rivers, plants, and animals are spiritually alive is known as __________.

a. Creationism
b. Animism
c. Traducianism
d. Speciesism

8. Native North American religions can best be described as all of the following EXCEPT __________.

a. Polytheistic
b. Monistic
c. Monotheistic
d. Monastic

9. Among the Incas of Peru and the Aztecs of Mexico, human sacrifice was:

a. Forbidden by the gods of the hunt
b. Performed only in times of drought
c. Routine and extremely important to the cultures
d. Considered an abomination against the sanctity of human life

10. In many indigenous African religions, including the Yoruba of West Africa, the High God appears as a creator who:

a. Withdrew from active participation in the world after creating it
b. Demanded yearly human sacrifices in his honor
c. Punished those who betrayed him by cursing their children
d. Lived on earth in human form before ascending to the heavens

11. The youngest major world religion is __________.

a. Christianity
b. Hinduism
c. Islam
d. Judaism

12. The most rapidly growing religion in North America and Europe is __________.

a. Christianity
b. Hinduism
c. Islam
d. Judaism

13. State Shinto was instituted in 1889 to:

a. Prevent citizens from worshipping the kami-dana in the privacy of their homes.
b. Keep the people faithful to the spirit of ancient Japan by encouraging patriotism and support for the nation's interaction with the rest of the world
c. Emphasize the Shinto traditions that remained following the takeover of shrines, for political purposes, by the rulers of Japan during the Meiji era
d. Establish the Bushido warrior code

14. Aryans who did not migrate into India became the founders of the ancient Persian religion of ____________.

a. Zoroastrianism
b. Hinduism
c. Jainism
d. Sikhism

15. The universal goddess of fertility, a woman warrior and the queen of heaven and the stars, who was worshipped in cultures throughout Mesopotamia and beyond, is known as __________.

a. Ceres
b. Hera
c. Itzamna
d. Ishtar

16. Polytheism helped the Greek and Roman cultures of classical times attempt to:

a. Oppress the lower classes
b. Understand phenomena in the natural world
c. Curtail the creation of a pantheon
d. All of the above

17. Throughout history, religion has been marked by the interweaving of ideas and rituals between religious groups; also known as ___________.

a. Altruism
b. Syncretism
c. Reciprocity
d. Cooperation

18. What is one way Christianity differs from Judaism and Islam?

a. Judaism and Islam deny that God is everywhere at once (omnipresent).
b. Jews and Muslims hold that Jesus was merely a prophet, while Christians see him as the Son of God.
c. Judaism and Islam are both intended to be confined to one people-group, not universal.
d. Judaism and Islam are unitarian, while Christianity is trinitarian.

19. Hinduism can trace the origins of some of its religious themes and forms to:

a. The I Ching
b. The sixth century B.C.
c. The third millennium B.C.
d. Stonehenge

20. The Vedas are comprised of:

I. A collection of hymns to the Aryan gods
II. The Avesta
III. The Upanishads
IV. The Brahmanas

a. I and II only
b. I, II, and III only
c. I, III, and IV only
d. III and IV only

21. In the Bhagavad Gita (Song of the Blessed Lord), one of the greatest classics of religious literature, Lord Krishna emphasizes the importance of bhakti, which may be defined as:

a. The cycle of rebirth and death that afflicts every living being until moksha
b. The illusion-creating power of the cosmic mind
c. Ardent devotion to a deity in grateful recognition of aid received or promised
d. A system that sees the universe as a dualism of the forces of spirit and matter

22. The Law of Manu provides the outline for:

a. India's caste system
b. Proper rites for sacrifice
c. Soft secularism
d. Hard secularism

23. Hinduism has been the source of what three religions?

a. Judaism, Baha'i, and Christianity
b. Jainism, Sikhism, and Buddhism
c. Buddhism, Taoism, and Confucianism
d. Zoroastrianism, Baha'i, and Sikhism

24. Upanishads are:

a. Practices of self-denial for the attainment of spiritual enlightenment
b. The three major gods of modern Hinduism
c. Philosophical writings from the classical teachers of Hinduism
d. Evil spirits believed to cause sickness

25. Vishnu appears in Hinduism in many forms known as:

a. Gopis
b. Sati
c. Bhakti
d. Avatars

26. Dharma can best be described as

a. Spirit
b. Duty
c. Fertility
d. Soul

27. Shiva is the Hindu god of:

a. Creation
b. Good fortune and prosperity
c. Death, disease, and destruction
d. Love, benevolence, and forgiveness

28. Linked with the Law of Karma, India's caste system acquired a kind of moral justification. Which statement best illustrates this line of thinking?

I. If a man was born a Shudra, it was because he had sinned in a previous life
II. A Brahmin had every right to exalt his social position; his good deeds in a previous life earned him the privileges he enjoyed in his present life
III. The class with the best record of spiritual attainment should be the one at the top of the caste system
IV. Anyone who did not attempt to address the inequalities of society was considered impious and morally reprehensible

a. I and II only
b. II, III, and IV only
c. I and III only
d. I, II, and III only

29. Which of the following is NOT true about Buddhism?

a. It was the world's first missionary religion
b. Its place as a major world religion was secured by Asoka, the emperor of India from 268 to 232 B.C.
c. It was founded by Siddhartha Gautama according to the principles of the caste system
d. Its most basic teachings are those of the Four Noble Truths

30. Before his enlightenment, the Buddha lived as a _____________.

a. Prince
b. Shiva
c. Mahavira
d. Monk

31. According to the Buddha, humanity is kept bound to the endless cycle of birth and death by _____________.

a. Upaya
b. Tantra
c. Karuna
d. Tanah

32. Buddhism teaches that the way to end suffering and find enlightenment is to follow:

a. The Kalpa Sutra
b. The Eightfold Path
c. The Doctrine of the Mean
d. The Chain of Causation (also called Dependent Origination)

33. Which of the following principles are essential to eliminate anatta in one's daily life?

I. Do nothing to satisfy one's own desires
II. Love everyone but not anyone
III. Protect one's family from the "Three Intoxications"
IV. Strive for attainment of the skandhas

a. I, II, and III only
b. I and IV only
c. II and IV only
d. I and II only

34. Prominent in Sri Lanka, Thailand, and Burma; Theravada Buddhism adheres to:

a. The way of the elders
b. The expansive way
c. The path of mysticism
d. The Vehicle of Mantras

35. Who founded an aggressive, nationalistic Japanese sect of Buddhism based on the Lotus Sutra?

a. Siddhartha Gautama
b. Bashō
c. Nichiren
d. Nanak

36. According to the Bodhisattva Doctrine of Mahayana Buddhism, one who is destined for enlightenment:

a. Achieves salvation through disciplined meditation during years of monastic isolation
b. Postpones his attainment of nirvana in order to help alleviate the suffering of as many people as possible
c. Must bear witness to a miracle recognized by dharmic prophecy and transcribe the event as it pertains to the Eightfold Path
d. Reaches divine liberation, or nirvana, through strict moral and spiritual devotion to the original tenets of the elders

37. A sacred circle visualization chart used in Tantric Buddhism is known as:

a. A lama
b. A stupa
c. Mudra
d. A mandala

38. Nirvana can best be described as:

a. Life after death
b. Liberation
c. Meditation that transcends ordinary consciousness
d. A heavenly state of bliss

39. Which of the following is characteristic of China during the lifetime of Confucius?

I. It was the Warring States Period
II. The feudal system had begun to break down
III. China's moral and social order was corrupt
IV. Individual self-interest began to replace the concept of group responsibility

a. I and II only
b. I, II, and III only
c. II, III, and IV only
d. None of the above

40. Confucianism ascribes to a doctrine of ethical relationships between individuals that is very similar to:

a. The "Golden Rule" in Christianity
b. The "Forty-Seven Ronin" in Shintoism
c. The Kabbalah in Judaism
d. The "Five Pillars" of Islam

41. Confucianism calls the fundamental virtue of goodness and benevolence _______.

a. Li
b. Jen
c. Analects
d. Xiao

42. The Confucian principle that human relationships must conform to their ideal meanings is known as:

a. Li
b. Jen
c. The rectification of names
d. The Doctrine of the Mean

43. The Confucian term Chun-tzu is translated as:

a. The Golden Mean
b. Filial piety
c. The Superior Man
d. Flowing vital energy

44. In the 500 years after death of Confucius, the principles of Confucianism became an integral part of Chinese culture, religion, and government due to all of the following EXCEPT:

a. Disciples who earned government positions training and advising leaders
b. The Book of Mencius
c. Hsün tzu
d. Fa-jia (the Legalists)

45. Some scholars believe that the Tao Te Ching was originally written to be a guide for princes and the governing elite, encouraging:

a. Expansionism as the one way (Tao) to peace and freedom
b. Warfare against dissenting nations
c. Government noninterference in the lives of people
d. Polytheism as the path to end political chaos

46. Which of the following themes does Taoism support?

I. Life itself is the greatest of all possessions
II. Unity of the universe comes from a mysterious and indefinable force
III. Life should be lived simply according to the path of nature
IV. Fame, pride, and glory bring discord to society

a. I, II, and III only
b. II and IV only
c. I, III, and IV only
d. I, II, III, and IV

47. One of the major contributing factors to the growth of Taoism as a philosophy-religion was:

a. Confucianism
b. The development of yin and yang
c. The decline of the feudal system in China
d. The White Cloud Abbey of Beijing

48. Followers of Taoist magic sought immortality through all of the following methods EXCEPT __________.

a. Celibacy
b. Breath control
c. Alchemy
d. Diet

49. Judaism is considered:

a. A mystical religion
b. A historical religion
c. A polytheistic religion
d. All of the above

50. The man who led the Hebrew people out of slavery in Egypt was __________.

a. Abraham
b. Isaac
c. Jesus
d. Moses

51. The sacred language of Judaism is __________.

a. Israeli
b. Urdu
c. Hebrew
d. Arabic

52. Which of the following is a theme that has dominated the course of Jewish religion?

a. A single, righteous God is at work in the social and natural order of the Jewish people
b. God forms a covenant with redeemed individuals
c. Jews are God's chosen people and have a special mission to in history to spread God's word throughout the world
d. All of the above

53. Judaism recognizes all of the following names for God EXCEPT ___________.

a. Elohim
b. El-Shaddai
c. Yahweh
d. Asherah

54. The term Kabbalah refers to:

a. The Bible
b. The occult
c. The Talmud
d. Religious deference

55. The scattering of Jews from their homeland after years of conquest is the ________.

a. Talmud
b. Diaspora
c. Midrash
d. Mishnah

56. The largest group within Judaism is that of ______________________.

a. Orthodox Jews
b. Reformist Jews
c. Conservative Jews
d. Reconstructionist Jews

57. Which of the following statements is NOT true about the Ark of the Covenant?

a. It was the most sacred possession of the Israelites
b. It contained the sacred relics of the Exodus
c. It served as a portable shrine
d. It described the rituals of Ramadan

58. Obedience to God and decent behavior toward members of the community are specifically addressed in:

a. The Talmud
b. The Qur'an
c. The Ten Commandments
d. The New Testament

59. The holiest of all Jewish holidays is:

a. Rosh Hashanah
b. Yom Kippur
c. Passover
d. Hanukkah

60. The movement dedicated to the establishment of a Jewish national homeland is known as _____________.

a. Zionism
b. Hasidism
c. Gnosticism
d. Marcionism

61. The founding of the state of Israel in the twentieth century was a major response to:

a. World War I
b. Atheism
c. The Holocaust
d. Islam

62. The day of rest and worship observed by Jews is __________.

a. Sunday
b. Sabbath
c. Holi
d. Shavout

63. Which of the following are characteristics of Orthodox Judaism?

I. Men and women are separated in the synagogue
II. It stresses the view that the divine revelation in the Torah is complete
III. Women can be ordained as rabbis
IV. Food must be prepared according to Kosher standards
V. Rabbis conduct the Sabbath service in the vernacular

a. I, III, and V only
b. II and IV only
c. I, II, IV, and V only
d. I, II, and IV only

64. The teachers or religious leaders in Judaism are known as __________.

a. Priests
b. Scribes
c. Zealots
d. Rabbis

65. The earliest converts to the Christian church were:

a. Jews
b. The Roman emperor Constantine
c. The Roman upper class
d. Jainists

66. The man frequently called the "Second Founder of Christianity" is __________.

a. Jesus
b. Simon Peter
c. James
d. Paul

67. Which of the following groups did NOT oppose the teachings of Jesus?

a. Pharisees
b. Zealots
c. Apostles
d. Sadducees

68. Biographical information about Jesus's birth and childhood is found in the:

a. Gospels of Mark and John
b. Old Testament
c. Epistle of Jude
d. Gospels of Matthew and Luke

69. Christians were persecuted by the Roman Empire during the period between 64 and 330 A.D. because:

a. They refused to accept the official Roman gods
b. They were accused of performing secret rituals that included eating human flesh
c. They refused to give allegiance to the emperor
d. All of the above

70. According to the New Testament, two basic rituals associated with early Christianity were:

a. Baptism and animal sacrifice
b. Baptism and Eucharist
c. Eucharist and communion
d. Yasht and communion

71. The expansion of the Christian canon during the second century reflects:

a. The invention of the printing press
b. The founding of Rome's first state-funded university
c. Increasing concerns about Christian unity
d. The division between Eastern and Western Christianity

72. Which of the following is NOT part of Augustine's religious doctrine?

a. In his infinite mercy, God sent his son to die for the sins of those who had been predestined for salvation
b. Adam and Eve had willfully chosen to sin against God and thus had passed an original sinful nature on to future generations
c. In the Trinity of the Father, Son, and Holy Spirit, there is no subordination of one entity to another
d. Because sacraments are instituted by human beings, those performed by unworthy priests are ineffectual

73. In an attempt to preserve its integrity, the ancient Catholic Church endeavored to develop:

a. A policy of selling indulgences that allowed Christians to have their sins pardoned
b. An ecclesiastical canon separating belief and ritual
c. A system of doctrine that was clarified and purged of error
d. A pragmatic policy of orthodoxy

74. Jesus's ministry included all of the following aspects EXCEPT:

a. Miracles
b. Liberalism
c. Parables
d. Eschatology

75. Christianity became the official religion of the Roman Empire in the:

a. Fourth century
b. Middle Ages
c. Second century
d. Lifetime of Christ

76. The Christian movement that believes the Bible should be interpreted as a scientific and historical work, as well as a moral and religious text, is _____________.

a. Liberation Theology
b. Mormonism
c. Evangelical
d. Fundamentalism

77. The main issue dividing Eastern and Western Christians during the Middle Ages was the:

a. Erection of cathedrals
b. Monastic movement
c. Papacy
d. All of the above

78. The Christian scholar Thomas Aquinas used the writings of ancient Greek philosopher Aristotle to argue that:

a. The Roman persecution of early Christians was ethically justifiable
b. Both reason and revelation were necessary for Christian belief
c. The Protestant Reformation should be suppressed
d. Latin should be the official language of the Eastern Orthodox Church

79. Who, of the following, was NOT a leader in the Protestant Reformation?

a. Martin Luther
b. Ulrich Zwingli
c. John Calvin
d. Ignatius Loyola

80. Major factors leading to the Protestant Reformation include:

a. The ascension of a new pope, the selling of indulgences, and the assassination of Martin Luther
b. German expansionism, the invention of the printing press, and the destruction of Luther's Ninety-five Theses
c. The decline of the papacy, the rise of European nationalism, and the new learning of the Renaissance
d. None of the above

81. The modern ecumenical movement in Christianity seeks:

a. A reunion between the Eastern and Western churches
b. Expansion of Catholic missionary work in undeveloped countries
c. Official recognition of a feminine theology
d. Funding for the causes championed by the religious right

82. When the Catholic Church began to see large numbers of Christians leaving the Church for Protestant denominations, it responded by:

a. Establishing a new set of dogma
b. Convening the Council of Trent
c. Issuing a revised version of the Bible
d. Calling the Second Vatican Council

83. The oldest and most widely accepted holiday in the Christian calendar is ________.

a. Pentecost
b. Christmas
c. Easter
d. Advent

84. The word "Muslim" means:

a. Allah.
b. One who submits
c. The chosen one
d. The clear path

85. The holiest city in Islam is ________.

a. Bethlehem
b. Jerusalem
c. Mecca
d. Baghdad

86. The religion of pre-Islamic Arabia was primarily ___________.

a. Judaism
b. Monotheistic
c. Zoroastrian
d. Polytheistic

87. Islam originated with the Arabian desert people in:

a. Iraq
b. The seventh century
c. The time of Jesus
d. The 1100s

88. The Ka'ba is:

a. The clear path, or right way of life, set forth for mankind in the Qur'an
b. The alms-tax charitable obligation set forth in the "Five Pillars" of Islamic duty
c. An incantation of worship for Allah
d. A black stone structure that is the focal point of prayer orientation and pilgrimage

89. Muslims consider the founding event of the Islamic faith to be:

a. The Hijrah
b. The birth of Sufism
c. Muhammad's first vision
d. The Jews assimilation into Arabic tribes

90. Muslims believe that the Qur'an was:

a. Written by Mohammad
b. Revealed to Mohammad by the angel Iblis
c. Revealed to Mohammad by the angel Gabriel
d. Discovered in Mecca by Mohammad

91. An imam is:

a. A priest
b. A community leader
c. A figurine of Muhammad
d. A holy spirit

92. For Muslims, Friday is:

a. The Feast of Sacrifice when the head of the household kills an animal and provides a feast
b. A day of rest
c. The Feast of Fast-Breaking when they exchange gifts, visit friends and relatives, and pay respect to the dead
d. The day when they are required to pray at a mosque with other Muslims

93. The word "jihad" refers to:

a. War against other Muslims deemed too Westernized
b. Holy warfare
c. The duty to spread Islam by arms
d. All of the above

94. Shi'ite Muslims believe that:

a. The descendants of Ali-Zain should be the leaders of the faith
b. Martyrdom is a sin
c. The festivals of the Sunnis should not be observed
d. The figure of imam is a myth

95. The Five Pillars of Faith in Islam include all of the following EXCEPT:

a. Charity
b. The afterlife
c. Pilgrimage
d. Ramadan

96. The most important declaration in the Muslim faith is:

a. "There is no god but Allah"
b. "Allah guides whom he will, and lets whom he will go astray"
c. "Allah does not guide the wicked"
d. "Fight them, till there is no persecution and the religion is God's"

97. The Mutazilah school of Muslim thought:

a. Maintained that Allah grants individuals free reason through which they are capable of both distinguishing good from evil and choosing between them
b. Taught that humans are solely subject to the will of Allah
c. Declared that the Qur'an was eternal and uncreated by human hands
d. Believed in the anthropomorphism inherent in the literal interpretation of the Qur'an

98. Sufis are:

a. Expert scholars in the application of reasoning to interpret Islamic law
b. Spirits capable of assuming human and animal shapes either to help or hinder mankind
c. Members of the mystical sect of Islam
d. Religious endowments for work that is pleasing to Allah

99. Which of the following is true about the "Black Muslim" movement in the United States?

I. It appealed primarily to poor African Americans in large cities
II. Its leaders from its conception to the present day have included Malcolm X; Martin Luther King, Jr.; and Minister Louis Farrakhan
III. It has been associated with anti-white and anti-Semitic ideas
IV. It has rejected integration

a. I and II only
b. III and IV only
c. I, II, and IV only
d. I, III, and IV only

100. The collection of tradition relating to the actions and sayings of Muhammad is the __________.

a. Qur'an
b. Hadith
c. Imam Mahdi
d. Pancasila

Answer Key and Explanations

1. D: Religious systems that are alive today are grouped into four categories: basic religions, religions originating in India, religions originating in China and Japan, and religions originating in the Middle East. In addition to referring to the religions of prehistoric people, basic religions are those of contemporary people whose religious ideas are not preserved in written form. A—Religions that are ultimately concerned with release from the cycle of life, death, and rebirth are characteristics of those from India. B & C—Religions that believe in the divine judgment of the world, including such missionary religions as Christianity and Islam, are characteristic of those religions that originated in the Middle East.

2. B: Western cultures tend to define religion in terms of a set of beliefs having to do with the gods, through which people are taught a moral system. A—In Africa, the Middle East, and much of Asia, collective and social identities are defined on the basis of spiritual criteria. C—Religion is not defined by the number of followers a certain religion has. D—How people deliver themselves from their plight without the help of gods is a characteristic of some Eastern religions but is not a definition of religion in Western cultures.

3. D: In the nineteenth century, the social sciences were being developed and anthropologists were first beginning to investigate primitive cultures. It was during this time that various theories about the origin of religion were proposed.

4. A: Mana is defined as an unseen force believed to inhabit extraordinary persons, objects, or phenomena. B—The recognition of a special relationship between humans and a species of animals, plants, or inanimate objects is totemism. C—The veneration and use of natural or prepared material objects with special potency for the purpose of averting evil or attaining powers is fetishism. D—A way of dealing with the spirit world through an individual recognized as spirit possessed and gifted in dealing with supernatural forces is shamanism.

5. C: The nature-worship theory of religion was developed by Max Müller; Sir James George Frazer studied religion as mythology.

6. C: According to Lewis Hopfe and Mark Woodward, there are three basic varieties of religious violence: those intended as punishment for people believed to be evil, acts of violence that are inherently religious, and violent clashes between religious communities.

7. B: Animism, found in many prehistoric and primal cultures, is the belief that the natural world—including trees, rocks, rivers, plants, and animals—is alive with souls and spirits. A—Creationism is the belief that God created the world and every form of life out of nothing. C—Traducianism is the belief that a child's soul is generated from his or her parents. D—Speciesism is discrimination against or exploitation of animals based on the belief that humans are superior to all other species.

8. D: North Native American religions have qualities of monotheism, the worship of one Supreme Being; polytheism, the worship of many gods; and monism, the metaphysical view that the universe is made up of only one kind of thing in the universe. Answer choice D, monastic, refers to life in a monastery.

9. C: The Incas of Peru and the Aztecs of Mexico routinely practiced human sacrifice, as if their cultures considered it to be of vast important in appeasing the gods.

10. A: The belief that there is a supreme High God who created the world and then withdrew from active participation in it is common in many African religions. For example, in the mythology of the Yoruba from Nigeria, orisha are lesser deities who carried out many tasks of creation and continue to help villages in times of trouble because Olorun, the High God, remains detached from the problems of the world. B—While people gave daily offerings, such as pouring out a little of their drink or tossing away a portion of food, the High God did not demand human sacrifices. C—The High God had little—if any—interaction with earth and its inhabitants, so he would not have cursed anyone's children. D—The High God was not believed to have been a human at any time.

11. C: The youngest major world religion is Islam, founded around 622 A.D.

12. C: The most rapidly growing religion in North America and Europe is Islam. In addition to the influx of Arabs, Iranians, Turks, and Pakistanis into these geographic areas, conversion within Muslim areas has contributed to the growth of Islam.

13. B: The Japanese government instituted State Shinto in 1889 to encourage patriotism and support for the nation's military, cultural, and business interactions with the rest of the world. A—The kami-dana is a household altar that almost every Japanese home has; State Shinto did not prohibit these altars. C—Sectarian Shinto emphasized the Shinto traditions that remained following State Shinto after shrines were taken over for political purposes by the rulers of Japan during the Meiji era. D—The Bushido warrior code was developed in the 1600s, two hundred years before State Shinto was introduced.

14. A: Zoroastrianism, one of the world's oldest living religions, was the religion of the ancient Persian Empire that once ruled most of the Middle East. It was founded by Aryans who did not migrate into India. Hinduism, Jainism, and Sikhism all were founded in India.

15. D: Of all the deities who emerged in Mesopotamia, Ishtar was the one who came closest to being worshipped universally. Ishtar was the universal queen of fertility, a woman warrior, and queen of heaven and the stars. A—Ceres was the Roman goddess of grain. B—Hera was the Greek goddess of marriage and queen of the gods. C—Itzama was the Mayan god of creation.

16. B: Ancient Greek and Roman civilizations looked to gods all around them to explain the forces of the natural world. Thunder and lightning, for example, were attributed to the anger of Zeus, king of the Greek gods. A—All classes in classical Greek and Roman society believed in the power of the gods; stories of the gods were told as moral instruction—or even as warnings—but were not used to oppress a class of people. C—Greeks and Romans celebrated polytheism in a pantheon, which is a set of the divine deities worshipped in a culture or region. D—Not all of the answer choices are correct.

17. B: Syncretism is the interweaving of ideas and rituals between religious groups.

18. D: The doctrine of the Trinity is distinctive to Christianity alone, holding that the Father, Son, and Holy Spirit are three distinct divine Persons sharing a single divine nature; this is opposed to Judaism and Islam, which deny any such divine distinctions. Judaism and Islam do not deny God's omnipresence. While Muslims revere Jesus as a prophet (but not as divine), Jews view him as a false teacher and blasphemer, believing that he is currently suffering severe punishment. And while Judaism is intended to be confined to one people-group, the Jews, Islam is intended to be universally propagated, the same as Christianity intends.

19. C: Hinduism, one of the world's oldest religions, traces the beginnings of some of its religious themes and forms to the third millennium B.C. A—The I Ching is an ancient Chinese book of divination. D—Stonehenge is a prehistoric monument with religious implications in England.

20. C: The Vedas are a collection of Indian sacred literature which includes hymns to the Aryan gods; the Brahmanas, which offer ritual instruction; and the Upanishads, which are philosophical works. The Avesta is a collection of the sacred literature of Zoroastrianism.

21. C: Bhakti is ardent devotion to a deity in grateful recognition of aid received or promised. A—Samsara is the cycle of rebirth and death that afflicts every living being until they reach moksha. B—Maya is the illusion-creating power of the cosmic mind. D—The system that sees the universe as a dualism of the forces of spirit and matter is known as Sankhya.

22. A: The Law of Manu is a piece of traditional Indian literature that outlines India's caste system. B—Although Hindus do carry out sacrificial rites, the Law of Manu does not contain guidelines for doing so. C—Soft secularism, the acceptance of a common religious basis for personal and social identity, is not part of the text. D—Hard secularism, which is the rejection of religion, is not mentioned in the Law of Manu.

23. B: Hinduism has been the source of three other religions: Jainism, Buddhism, and Sikhism.

24. C: Upanishads are philosophical writings from the classical teachers of Hinduism. A—Upanishads are not practices of self-denial for the attainment of spiritual enlightenment. B—The three major gods of modern Hinduism are Brahma, Vishnu, and Shiva. D—Upanishads are not evil spirits believed to cause sickness.

25. D: In Hindu sacred literature and stories, Vishnu is a major god who appeared in many forms known as avatars, or alternate forms or incarnations of a deity. A—Gopis are milkmaids or young wives who had love trysts with Krishna. B—A sati is a virtuous Hindu widow who is cremated in order to join her dead husband. C—Bhakti is devotion to the gods of Hinduism.

26. B: Dharma refers to duty and moral law incumbent on a person in traditional Hindu life, based on caste and situation in life.

27. C: Shiva, the most popular god in postclassical Hinduism, is the god of death, disease, and destruction. A—The Hindu god of creation is Brahma. B—Lakshmi is the goddess of good fortune and prosperity. D—The god of love, benevolence, and forgiveness is Vishnu.

28. D: India's caste system was inexorably linked with Hinduism. Statements I, II, and III best illustrate the belief that castes were morally and religiously justified. Statement IV contradicts the Hindu belief that any attempt to address the inequalities of society is impious and morally reprehensible.

29. C: Although it is true that Buddhism was founded by Siddhartha Gautama, Buddhism rejected the authority of the Hindu Vedas and the caste system. All of the other answer choices are true concerning Buddhism.

30. A: Before his enlightenment, Buddha lived as Siddhartha Gautama, a prince surrounded by beauty and luxury.

31. D: Tanah is desire, thirst, or craving, all of which keeps humanity bound to the endless cycle of birth and death. A—Upaya translates as "skill-in-means" and refers to compassion in action. B—In

Hinduism, tantric religion takes on the element of enlightenment through magical rituals. C—Karuna is pity or compassionate love.

32. B: Follow the Eightfold Path. A—The Kalpa Sutra is a part of scripture that recounts the lives of the Jinas. C—The Doctrine of the Mean is a Confucian text. D—The Chain of Causation, also known as Dependent Origination, is suffering that comes from a twelve-linked chain of causes and effects, both past, present, and future.

33. D: "Do nothing to satisfy one's own desires" and "Love everyone but not anyone" are among those principles essential to the elimination of anatta, or the ultimate unreality of the self, in one's daily life. Protecting one's family from the "Three Intoxications" goes against the teachings of Buddha that a person should avoid emotional attachments, even with family. The skandhas are five impermanent aggregates (form, feeling, conception, karmic dispositions, and consciousness) that give rise to the mistaken sense of self.

34. A: Theravada Buddhists follow the way or tradition of the elders. B—Mahayana Buddhism is known as the expansive way. C—Mysticism characterizes the Chen Yen, or True Word, a school of Buddhism found primarily in China. D—The sect of Buddhism that was established in Tibet and Mongolia was a form so different from Theravada that it is called by other names, including the Vehicle of Mantras.

35. C: Nichiren is a fourteenth-century monk who founded a Japanese national sect of Buddhism based on the Lotus Sutra. A—Siddhartha Gautama, better known as Buddha, is the founder of Buddhism. B—Bashō is a seventeenth-century Japanese Zen monk who is best known for his haiku poetry. D—Nanak is known as the first guru of Sikhism.

36. B: In Mahayana Buddhism, a bodhisattva postpones his attainment of nirvana so that he can help as many people as possible in the search for salvation and freedom from the sufferings of everyday life. A—A bodhisattva works among people instead of isolating himself in his religious quest. C—The Bodhisattva Doctrine says nothing about bearing witness to a miracle recognized by dharmic prophecy and transcribing the event as it pertains to the Eightfold Path. D—Reaching divine liberation, or nirvana, through strict moral and spiritual devotion to the original tenets of the elders the teachings is a practice of Theravada Buddhism, not Mahayana Buddhism.

37. D: A mandala is a sacred circle visualization chart that is used for meditative purposes in Tantric Buddhism. A—A lama is a monk in Tibetan Buddhism known as the "superior one." B—A stupa is a bell-shaped mound or circular tower that serves as a place for meditative walking. C—Mudra is a ritual hand movement.

38. B: Only by freeing one's mind from the emotional states of desire, craving, and delusion can a person achieve nirvana, or the unconditioned state of liberation. A—Although different schools of Buddhist thought have diverse teachings about whether nirvana can be attained before or after death, nirvana does not refer to life after death. C—Meditation at levels transcending ordinary consciousness is dhyana. D—The goal of Buddhist practice is to extinguish craving and desire, not to achieve a state of bliss in heaven.

39. C: The Warring States Period in China occurred from 475-221 B.C. Confucius died in 479 B.C., four years before the beginning of that period. During Confucius's lifetime, the feudal system had begun to decline, China's moral and social order was corrupt, and individual self-interest increasingly had begun to replace the concept of group responsibility.

40. A: Confucius taught that people should love one another and act with reciprocity toward each other, which is very similar to the Christian-taught Golden Rule that people should treat others as they themselves would want to be treated. B—"The Forty-Seven Ronin" is an old Japanese tale about samurais who become ronin, men who are bound by duty to avenge the death of their lord. C—The Kabbalah is a system of occult symbolism and mystical practice prevalent in Judaism. D—The "Five Pillars" of Islamic duty refers to the practices that Muslims are obligated to follow.

41. B: In Confucianism, jen is the fundamental virtue of goodness and benevolence. A—The term li is translated as propriety, courtesy, or ritual. C—The Analects is a collection of the sayings of Confucius and some of his disciples. D—Xiao means filial piety.

42. C: The rectification of names is the Confucian principle of moral and political reorganization which states that ideal human relationships must be clearly defined and then people should be shaped to fit those roles. A—The term li is translated as propriety, courtesy, or ritual. B—Jen refers to humaneness or the virtue of benevolence. D—The Doctrine of the Mean is a chapter in the Li Ji that deals particularly with the relation of human nature to the moral order of the universe.

43. C: The Confucian term Chun-tzu translates as the "Superior Man," or a gentleman. A—The Golden Mean, or chung yung, is a Confucian doctrine stating that moral virtue is attainable only by one who walks in the middle way and does nothing in excess. B—Filial piety refers to the love and respect a person shows parents and ancestors. D—Flowing vital energy is known as chi.

44. D: Fa-jia, or the Legalists, supported a rival view of Confucianism. A—Throughout the years following Confucius's death, the principles of Confucianism became an integral part of Chinese culture, religion, and government because of his disciples who trained and advised government leaders. B—The Book of Mencius, a work by Mencius, reinforced the teachings of Confucius. C—Hsün tzu expounded upon Confucius's ideas.

45. C: Most scholars agree that the Tao Te Ching was written as a manual for princes and the governing elite that advised nonintervention by the government in the lives of people. A—Expansionism directly contradicts the Tao Te Ching's picture of an ideal community: a small village-state that keeps within its boundaries. B—Taoism promotes pacifism because warfare is considered useless and wasteful. D—The Tao Te Ching does not mention polytheism in relation to politics.

46. D: All of the answer choices are correct, as the early teachings of Taoism focus on the following themes: the basic unity of the universe is a mysterious and indefinable force called the Tao; life is the most valuable possession anyone can have; life should be lived simply in accord with nature; fame, pride, and glory are undesirable and bring discord to society.

47. C: The decline of the feudal system in China from 722 to 221 B.C. was instrumental in the emergence of Taoism, which argued that government should have no presence in society. A—Confucianism was another school of thought born from the dissolution of feudalism; it did not contribute to the spread of Taoism. B—Yin and yang refer to the negative and positive forces in nature recognized in early Chinese religion. D—The White Cloud Abbey of Beijing was made the seat of the National Taoist Association in the 1980s, many years after Taoism had been established as a philosophy-religion.

48. A: Followers of Taoist magic believed they could attain immortality through daily breathing exercises, alchemy (finding an elixir for eternal life), and a diet free of meat and many grains. These Taoists remained sexually active. However, they practiced special techniques that were thought to prolong life.

49. B: Because Judaism is concerned with God's activity in history, it is considered a historical religion. Religious scholars describe Jewish beliefs and practices within a historical context, and the Hebrew Scriptures are regarded as a record of the nation's history. A—Although it does contain a mystical school of thought (Kabbalah), Judaism is not known as a mystical religion. C—Judaism is a monotheistic religion; Jews do not worship multiple gods, as is characteristic of polytheistic religions.

50. D: Moses was the key figure in the emancipation of the Hebrew people from slavery in Egypt. A—Abraham, known as the father of the Jews, was promised that his people would be given the land of Israel as their home if he and his descendants remained faithful to their covenant with God. B—Isaac was the son of Abraham. C—Jesus is known as the Christian Messiah.

51. C: Hebrew is the sacred language of Judaism and is often referred to as the language of the Bible. A—Israeli is not a single language; the official languages of Israel are Hebrew and Arabic. B—Urdu is an Indo-Aryan language spoken primarily in Pakistan and India. C—Arabic, one of Israel's official languages, is the Semitic language of Arabs.

52. D: Throughout the course of Judaism, all of the listed themes have remained constant. A—A single, righteous God is active in their history and their lives. B—The prophet Jeremiah revealed to the Jewish people that a new covenant would be made between God and redeemed individuals; people could no longer say that He dealt with them only through group relationships. C—Jews are God's chosen people and have a special mission to in history to spread God's word throughout the world.

53. D: Judaism recognizes many different names for God, including Elohim (from Hebrew scripture), El-Shaddai (the god of the covenant with Abraham), and Yahweh (the God who revealed himself to Moses). D—Asherah was a Canaanite goddess of fertility.

54. B: Elements of the occult in Judaism—from magical incantations, numerology, and dream interpretation to angels, demons, and charms—are grouped together under the term Kabbalah.

55. B: The scattering of the Jews from their homeland after waves of conquest, beginning with the Assyrian destruction of Israel in 721 B.C., is known as the Diaspora. A—The Talmud is the collection of ancient rabbinic oral tradition. C—Midrash is an explanation of scripture. D—Mishnah is the first section of the Talmud.

56. A: Orthodox Jews, who keep as close as possible to the Talmud, are the largest group within Judaism. B—Reformist Jews can be found primarily in the United States and Europe. C—The Conservative movement arose in the nineteenth century as a reaction against the extremes of the Reform movement. D—Reconstructionist Jews practice a sect of Judaism that was founded in the 1930s.

57. D: The Ark of the Covenant did not describe the rituals of Ramadan, which is a Muslim observance. The most sacred possession of the Israelites, the Ark of the Covenant contained the sacred relics of the Exodus and served as a portable shrine.

58. C: Basically, the Ten Commandments emphasize obedience to Yahweh, as well as decent behavior toward members of the community. A—The Talmud is an encyclopedic collection of ancient rabbinic oral tradition. B—The Qur'an is the holy scripture of Islam. D—The New Testament is a collection of books in the Christian Bible.

59. B: The holiest of all Jewish holidays is Yom Kippur, or the Day of Atonement, during which Jews spend the day in a synagogue praying for forgiveness of sins and reconciliation. A—Rosh Hashanah is the Jewish New Year. C—Passover commemorates the deliverance of the Israelites from slavery in Egypt. D—Hanukkah is a festival that celebrates the rededication of the Temple by Judas Maccabeus in 165 B.C.

60. A: Zionism, founded by Theodore Herzl in the late nineteenth century, is a movement dedicated to finding a national home for the Jews scattered all over the world. B—Established in the third century B.C., Hasidism was a sect of Judaism dedicated to promoting ritual purity and resisting Hellenistic influences. C—Gnosticism, a Christian heresy, is a dualistic view that completely separates God, goodness, and Spirit from the contaminated material world. D—Marcionism, an early Christian heresy named for Marcion of Rome, rejected the God of the Old Testament.

61. C: As a response to World War II and the Holocaust, the United Nations Assembly voted to found the state of Israel in what was once part of Palestine.

62. B: The Sabbath is the seventh day—Saturday—which is set aside as a day of rest and worship for Jews. B—The day of rest in Judaism is Saturday, not Sunday. C—Holi is the Hindu festival dedicated to the god Krishna. D—Shavout is a Jewish holiday celebrating the people's receipt of the Ten Commandments.

63. D: Orthodox Judaism seeks to preserve traditional Jewish culture and religion, emphasizing the view that the divine revelation in the Torah is complete and is simply awaiting its fulfillment. Kosher foods and food preparation are stressed, men and women are separated in the synagogue, and Hebrew is the language of Orthodox worship. Unlike Reform Judaism, Orthodox Judaism does not allow women to be ordained as rabbis.

64. D: Literally, "rabbi" means "my master." Rabbis are the teachers or leaders associated with the Jewish synagogue and are educated in Jewish law. Rabbis are charged with studying the Torah and other sacred writings and teaching them to the Jewish community. A—In Judaism, priests are those individuals responsible for performing religious rituals in the temple. B—Scribes were devoted to copying and circulating copies of the Torah in ancient times. C—Zealots were a group dedicated to rebellion and the overthrow of Roman rule in Palestine during the first century.

65. A: The earliest converts to Christianity were Jews; their teachings were presented in a Jewish context. B—Emperor Constantine legalized Christianity in Rome in 313 A.D. C—The Roman upper class was slow to adopt Christianity and supported the persecution of Christians, who refused to acknowledge the supremacy of the Roman gods. D—Jainists are followers of Jainism, an ancient religion of India.

66. D: Frequently called the "Second Founder of Christianity," Paul was among the most important of the early Christian missionaries and did much to establish Christianity as a distinct religion by spreading its message to non-Jews. A—Jesus is the Messiah to Christians. B—Simon Peter was a disciple of Jesus and an early leader in the Christian church of Jerusalem. C—James, the half-brother of Jesus, assumed leadership of the Jerusalem church when Simon Peter moved to other communities.

67. C: The original twelve followers of Jesus were the Apostles. A—Pharisees were a group within Judaism that, according to the Gospels, was responsible for the death of Jesus. B—Zealots were anti-Roman patriots who opposed the teachings of Jesus. D—The Sadducees were an aristocratic group whose leaders tried Jesus in Jerusalem.

68. D: Matthew and Luke are the only two of the four Gospels containing information about the birth and childhood of Jesus. A—The Gospels of Mark and John begin with the ministry of a mature Jesus. B—The Old Testament does not provide biographical information about the life of Jesus. C—The Epistle of Jude warns readers against false teachings and encourages them to lead moral lives.

69. D: From around 64 to 330 A.D., Christians were persecuted by the Roman Empire because they refused to accept the official Roman gods and would not pledge their allegiance to the emperor. Christians were also accused by the Romans of performing secret rituals involving cannibalism.

70. B: Two basic rituals of early Christianity described by the New Testament are baptism and the Eucharist. A—Animal sacrifice was not a ritual emphasized in the New Testament. C—The Eucharist is a communion meal. D—Yasht is a song of praise from the sacred literature of Zoroastrianism.

71. C: The expansion of the Christian canon during the second century reflects growing concerns about the lack of Christian unity. A—Although its creation allowed for liturgical literature to be widely circulated, the printing press was not invented until 1440; the Christian canon had been established many years before. B—Sapienza, Rome's first state-funded university, was founded in 1303, not during the second century. D—The division between Eastern and Western Christianity occurred after the second century.

72. D: Unlike other thinkers of his day, Augustine believed that because sacraments are instituted by God, not human beings, they communicate grace regardless of the character of whoever performs them. Answer choices A, B, and C can all be found in Augustine's religious doctrine.

73. C: In an attempt to preserve its integrity, the ancient Catholic Church sought to develop a system of doctrine that was clarified and purged of error. A—The policy of selling indulgences that allowed Christians to have their sins pardoned was a practice that brought great controversy and dishonor to the Church. B—Belief and ritual were not separate entities in the doctrine of the Catholic Church. D—The Catholic Church did not seek to develop a pragmatic policy of orthodoxy to preserve its integrity.

74. B: Liberalism is a religious movement born in the nineteenth century, believing doctrines like the virgin birth to be false. The Gospels provide a record of Jesus's ministry, including miracles, parables, and eschatology, but Jesus never denied his divinity or virgin birth, but instead affirmed the reality of the supernatural.

75. A: Under the reign of Constantine, Christianity became the official religion of the Roman Empire in the fourth century.

76. D: Emerging during the end of the nineteenth century, fundamentalists are conservatives who believe that the Bible should be interpreted as a scientific and historical text, as well as a moral and religious work. A—Liberation Theology is based on those portions of the Bible that mention social justice and economic equality. B—Mormonism was founded by Joseph Smith following a series of visions during which he received spiritual instruction. C—Evangelical groups use modern techniques of mass communication to reach thousands of members.

77. C: The primary issue dividing Eastern and Western Christians during the Middle Ages was the Papacy. A—The building of Catholic cathedrals did not cause a rift in the Christian church. B—The monastic movement began to develop in the third century. It was not a factor in the division of Eastern and Western Christians. D—Not all answer choices are correct.

78. B: Thomas Aquinas, a Dominican monk, studied the arguments of Aristotle in order to show that both reason and revelation were necessary for Christian belief. A—Aquinas never justified the Roman persecution of early Christians. C—The Protestant Reformation, which began around 1517, did not occur during the lifetime of Aquinas. D—Aquinas did not challenge the Eastern Orthodox Church's practice of conducting services in Greek.

79. D: Ignatius Loyola founded the Jesuit order during the Catholic Reformation. A—Martin Luther is traditionally regarded to be the founder of the Protestant Reformation. B—Ulrich Zwingli led the reform movement in Switzerland. C—Many scholars consider John Calvin the most influential mind of the Reformation.

80. C: The major factors leading to the Protestant Reformation include the decline of the papacy, the rise of European nationalism, and the new learning of the Renaissance.

81. A: The modern ecumenical movement in Christianity seeks a reunion between the Eastern and Western churches. The ecumenical movement does not involve answer choices B, C, and D.

82. B: In response to Christians leaving the Catholic Church for Protestant denominations, the Church convened the Council of Trent in 1545, which reaffirmed the traditional seven sacraments of the Catholic Church. A—A new set of dogmas was established during the Second Vatican Council in 1959. C—The Church did not issue a new version of the Bible. D—The Second Vatican Council was convened in 1959.

83. C: The oldest and most widely accepted Christian holiday is Easter. A—Observed fifty days after Passover; Pentecost is a Christian festival celebrating the coming of the Holy Spirit to the Church. B—Christmas, which marks the birth of Jesus, is celebrated on December 25 in Western Christianity and in January by Eastern Orthodox Christians.

84. B: The word "Muslim" means "one who submits." Muslims are expected to completely submit to the will of Allah.

85. C: The holiest city in Islam is Mecca, home of the Holy Mosque.

86. D: The religion of pre-Islamic Arabia was primarily polytheistic. A—Although Judaism had reached some regions, the majority of Arabs worshipped local gods and goddesses, as well as universal ones similar to those of Greek and Roman societies. B—Zoroastrianism was not prevalent in pre-Islamic Arabia. C—Because the majority of pre-Islamic Arabians worshipped many gods and goddesses, their religion cannot be categorized as monotheistic.

87. B: Islam originated with the Arabian desert people during the seventh century (622 A.D.)

88. D: The Ka'ba is a black stone structure that is the focal point of pilgrimage and prayer orientation in Mecca. A—The clear path, or right way of life, set forth for mankind in the Qur'an is known as Shari'a. B—Zakat is the alms-tax charitable obligation described in the "Five Pillars" of Islamic duty. C—The Ka'ba is not an incantation of worship for Allah.

89. A: The founding event of Islam—which marks the first year of the Muslim calendar—is the Hijrah, the migration of the Prophet Mohammad and his followers from Mecca to Medina. B—Sufism is a mystical sect of Islam that first emerged in the eighth century. C—Muhammad's first vision preceded the founding of Islam. D—Jews were assimilated into Muslim tribes for many years after the Hijrah.

90. C: Muslims believe that the Qur'an contains the exact words of Allah as revealed to the prophet Muhammad by the angel Gabriel. A—Muhammad was illiterate; he memorized the revelations and recited them to scribes who wrote them down. B—Iblis is a fallen angel who acts much like Satan in the Bible. D—Muhammad did not discover the Qur'an in Mecca; Allah sent the words of the Qur'an directly to Muhammad during prophetic transmissions.

91. B: An imam is a community leader who has been chosen to lead prayers because of his reputation as a pious and knowledgeable man.

92. D: Muhammad decreed Friday to be a special day of Muslim worship when Muslims are required to pray at a mosque with fellow Muslims. A—The Feast of Sacrifice is held on the tenth day of the month of the pilgrimage to observe the time when Abraham was commanded by God to sacrifice his son. B—Unlike the Christian and Jewish Sabbaths, which are days of rest, Friday is not a day of rest for Muslims. C—The Feast of Fast-Breaking, observed on the first day of the month after Ramadan, is a time of feasting after the prolonged fast.

93. D: The term "jihad" is translated as "holy war" and is associated with the Muslim duty to spread Islam by arms. It can also refer to war against other Muslims deemed to be too Westernized.

94. A: Shi'ite Muslims believe that the descendants of Ali-Zain should be the leaders of the Islamic faith. None of the other answer choices reflect the beliefs of Shi'ites.

95. B: The Five Pillars of Islam do not contain instruction about the afterlife. The Five Pillars are repetition of the Islamic creed, daily prayer, charity, the fast of Ramadan, and pilgrimage.

96. A: The most important declaration in the Muslim faith is, "There is no god but Allah." This is the creed repeated every day. B, C, and D—All are quotations are taken from the Qur'an but are not the central proclamation of Islam.

97. A: The Mutazilah school of Muslim thought taught that Allah granted humans free reason through which they are capable of both distinguishing good from evil and choosing between them. B—Mutazilites believed in free will; they did not believe that humans are subject only to the will of Allah. C—Mutazilites declared that the Qur'an could not be created by human hands. D—They did not believe in the anthropomorphism inherent in the literal interpretation of the Qur'an.

98. C: The Sufis are members of the mystical sect of Islam. A—A mojtahed is a scholar who is an expert in the application of reasoning in order to interpret Islamic law. B—Spirits capable of assuming human and animal shapes that can help or hinder humans are known as jinn. D—Awqaf refers to religious endowments for work that is pleasing to Allah.

99. D: The "Black Muslim" movement in the United States appealed primarily to poor African Americans in large cities. It has also been associated with anti-white, anti-Semitic, and anti-integrationist viewpoints. II—Unlike Malcolm X and Minister Louis Farrakhan, Martin Luther King, Jr. was not part of the Black Muslim movement.

100. B: The body of the tradition relating to the actions and sayings of the Prophet Muhammad is known as Hadith. A—The Qur'an is the scripture of Islam. C—Imam Mahdi is an imam appointed by a deity to a special messianic role. D—Pancasila consists of the five Principles of the Indonesian constitution

How to Overcome Test Anxiety

Just the thought of taking a test is enough to make most people a little nervous. A test is an important event that can have a long-term impact on your future, so it's important to take it seriously and it's natural to feel anxious about performing well. But just because anxiety is normal, that doesn't mean that it's helpful in test taking, or that you should simply accept it as part of your life. Anxiety can have a variety of effects. These effects can be mild, like making you feel slightly nervous, or severe, like blocking your ability to focus or remember even a simple detail.

If you experience test anxiety—whether severe or mild—it's important to know how to beat it. To discover this, first you need to understand what causes test anxiety.

Causes of Test Anxiety

While we often think of anxiety as an uncontrollable emotional state, it can actually be caused by simple, practical things. One of the most common causes of test anxiety is that a person does not feel adequately prepared for their test. This feeling can be the result of many different issues such as poor study habits or lack of organization, but the most common culprit is time management. Starting to study too late, failing to organize your study time to cover all of the material, or being distracted while you study will mean that you're not well prepared for the test. This may lead to cramming the night before, which will cause you to be physically and mentally exhausted for the test. Poor time management also contributes to feelings of stress, fear, and hopelessness as you realize you are not well prepared but don't know what to do about it.

Other times, test anxiety is not related to your preparation for the test but comes from unresolved fear. This may be a past failure on a test, or poor performance on tests in general. It may come from comparing yourself to others who seem to be performing better or from the stress of living up to expectations. Anxiety may be driven by fears of the future—how failure on this test would affect your educational and career goals. These fears are often completely irrational, but they can still negatively impact your test performance.

Elements of Test Anxiety

As mentioned earlier, test anxiety is considered to be an emotional state, but it has physical and mental components as well. Sometimes you may not even realize that you are suffering from test anxiety until you notice the physical symptoms. These can include trembling hands, rapid heartbeat, sweating, nausea, and tense muscles. Extreme anxiety may lead to fainting or vomiting. Obviously, any of these symptoms can have a negative impact on testing. It is important to recognize them as soon as they begin to occur so that you can address the problem before it damages your performance.

The mental components of test anxiety include trouble focusing and inability to remember learned information. During a test, your mind is on high alert, which can help you recall information and stay focused for an extended period of time. However, anxiety interferes with your mind's natural processes, causing you to blank out, even on the questions you know well. The strain of testing during anxiety makes it difficult to stay focused, especially on a test that may take several hours. Extreme anxiety can take a huge mental toll, making it difficult not only to recall test information but even to understand the test questions or pull your thoughts together.

Effects of Test Anxiety

Test anxiety is like a disease—if left untreated, it will get progressively worse. Anxiety leads to poor performance, and this reinforces the feelings of fear and failure, which in turn lead to poor performances on subsequent tests. It can grow from a mild nervousness to a crippling condition. If allowed to progress, test anxiety can have a big impact on your schooling, and consequently on your future.

Test anxiety can spread to other parts of your life. Anxiety on tests can become anxiety in any stressful situation, and blanking on a test can turn into panicking in a job situation. But fortunately, you don't have to let anxiety rule your testing and determine your grades. There are a number of relatively simple steps you can take to move past anxiety and function normally on a test and in the rest of life.

Physical Steps for Beating Test Anxiety

While test anxiety is a serious problem, the good news is that it can be overcome. It doesn't have to control your ability to think and remember information. While it may take time, you can begin taking steps today to beat anxiety.

Just as your first hint that you may be struggling with anxiety comes from the physical symptoms, the first step to treating it is also physical. Rest is crucial for having a clear, strong mind. If you are tired, it is much easier to give in to anxiety. But if you establish good sleep habits, your body and mind will be ready to perform optimally, without the strain of exhaustion. Additionally, sleeping well helps you to retain information better, so you're more likely to recall the answers when you see the test questions.

Getting good sleep means more than going to bed on time. It's important to allow your brain time to relax. Take study breaks from time to time so it doesn't get overworked, and don't study right before bed. Take time to rest your mind before trying to rest your body, or you may find it difficult to fall asleep.

Along with sleep, other aspects of physical health are important in preparing for a test. Good nutrition is vital for good brain function. Sugary foods and drinks may give a burst of energy but this burst is followed by a crash, both physically and emotionally. Instead, fuel your body with protein and vitamin-rich foods.

Also, drink plenty of water. Dehydration can lead to headaches and exhaustion, especially if your brain is already under stress from the rigors of the test. Particularly if your test is a long one, drink water during the breaks. And if possible, take an energy-boosting snack to eat between sections.

Along with sleep and diet, a third important part of physical health is exercise. Maintaining a steady workout schedule is helpful, but even taking 5-minute study breaks to walk can help get your blood pumping faster and clear your head. Exercise also releases endorphins, which contribute to a positive feeling and can help combat test anxiety.

When you nurture your physical health, you are also contributing to your mental health. If your body is healthy, your mind is much more likely to be healthy as well. So take time to rest, nourish your body with healthy food and water, and get moving as much as possible. Taking these physical steps will make you stronger and more able to take the mental steps necessary to overcome test anxiety.

Mental Steps for Beating Test Anxiety

Working on the mental side of test anxiety can be more challenging, but as with the physical side, there are clear steps you can take to overcome it. As mentioned earlier, test anxiety often stems from lack of preparation, so the obvious solution is to prepare for the test. Effective studying may be the most important weapon you have for beating test anxiety, but you can and should employ several other mental tools to combat fear.

First, boost your confidence by reminding yourself of past success—tests or projects that you aced. If you're putting as much effort into preparing for this test as you did for those, there's no reason you should expect to fail here. Work hard to prepare; then trust your preparation.

Second, surround yourself with encouraging people. It can be helpful to find a study group, but be sure that the people you're around will encourage a positive attitude. If you spend time with others who are anxious or cynical, this will only contribute to your own anxiety. Look for others who are motivated to study hard from a desire to succeed, not from a fear of failure.

Third, reward yourself. A test is physically and mentally tiring, even without anxiety, and it can be helpful to have something to look forward to. Plan an activity following the test, regardless of the outcome, such as going to a movie or getting ice cream.

When you are taking the test, if you find yourself beginning to feel anxious, remind yourself that you know the material. Visualize successfully completing the test. Then take a few deep, relaxing breaths and return to it. Work through the questions carefully but with confidence, knowing that you are capable of succeeding.

Developing a healthy mental approach to test taking will also aid in other areas of life. Test anxiety affects more than just the actual test—it can be damaging to your mental health and even contribute to depression. It's important to beat test anxiety before it becomes a problem for more than testing.

Study Strategy

Being prepared for the test is necessary to combat anxiety, but what does being prepared look like? You may study for hours on end and still not feel prepared. What you need is a strategy for test prep. The next few pages outline our recommended steps to help you plan out and conquer the challenge of preparation.

Step 1: Scope Out the Test

Learn everything you can about the format (multiple choice, essay, etc.) and what will be on the test. Gather any study materials, course outlines, or sample exams that may be available. Not only will this help you to prepare, but knowing what to expect can help to alleviate test anxiety.

Step 2: Map Out the Material

Look through the textbook or study guide and make note of how many chapters or sections it has. Then divide these over the time you have. For example, if a book has 15 chapters and you have five days to study, you need to cover three chapters each day. Even better, if you have the time, leave an extra day at the end for overall review after you have gone through the material in depth.

If time is limited, you may need to prioritize the material. Look through it and make note of which sections you think you already have a good grasp on, and which need review. While you are studying, skim quickly through the familiar sections and take more time on the challenging parts.

Write out your plan so you don't get lost as you go. Having a written plan also helps you feel more in control of the study, so anxiety is less likely to arise from feeling overwhelmed at the amount to cover.

Step 3: Gather Your Tools

Decide what study method works best for you. Do you prefer to highlight in the book as you study and then go back over the highlighted portions? Or do you type out notes of the important information? Or is it helpful to make flashcards that you can carry with you? Assemble the pens, index cards, highlighters, post-it notes, and any other materials you may need so you won't be distracted by getting up to find things while you study.

If you're having a hard time retaining the information or organizing your notes, experiment with different methods. For example, try color-coding by subject with colored pens, highlighters, or post-it notes. If you learn better by hearing, try recording yourself reading your notes so you can listen while in the car, working out, or simply sitting at your desk. Ask a friend to quiz you from your flashcards, or try teaching someone the material to solidify it in your mind.

Step 4: Create Your Environment

It's important to avoid distractions while you study. This includes both the obvious distractions like visitors and the subtle distractions like an uncomfortable chair (or a too-comfortable couch that makes you want to fall asleep). Set up the best study environment possible: good lighting and a comfortable work area. If background music helps you focus, you may want to turn it on, but otherwise keep the room quiet. If you are using a computer to take notes, be sure you don't have any other windows open, especially applications like social media, games, or anything else that could distract you. Silence your phone and turn off notifications. Be sure to keep water close by so you stay hydrated while you study (but avoid unhealthy drinks and snacks).

Also, take into account the best time of day to study. Are you freshest first thing in the morning? Try to set aside some time then to work through the material. Is your mind clearer in the afternoon or evening? Schedule your study session then. Another method is to study at the same time of day that you will take the test, so that your brain gets used to working on the material at that time and will be ready to focus at test time.

Step 5: Study!

Once you have done all the study preparation, it's time to settle into the actual studying. Sit down, take a few moments to settle your mind so you can focus, and begin to follow your study plan. Don't give in to distractions or let yourself procrastinate. This is your time to prepare so you'll be ready to fearlessly approach the test. Make the most of the time and stay focused.

Of course, you don't want to burn out. If you study too long you may find that you're not retaining the information very well. Take regular study breaks. For example, taking five minutes out of every hour to walk briskly, breathing deeply and swinging your arms, can help your mind stay fresh.

As you get to the end of each chapter or section, it's a good idea to do a quick review. Remind yourself of what you learned and work on any difficult parts. When you feel that you've mastered the material, move on to the next part. At the end of your study session, briefly skim through your notes again.

But while review is helpful, cramming last minute is NOT. If at all possible, work ahead so that you won't need to fit all your study into the last day. Cramming overloads your brain with more information than it can process and retain, and your tired mind may struggle to recall even previously learned information when it is overwhelmed with last-minute study. Also, the urgent nature of cramming and the stress placed on your brain contribute to anxiety. You'll be more likely to go to the test feeling unprepared and having trouble thinking clearly.

So don't cram, and don't stay up late before the test, even just to review your notes at a leisurely pace. Your brain needs rest more than it needs to go over the information again. In fact, plan to finish your studies by noon or early afternoon the day before the test. Give your brain the rest of the day to relax or focus on other things, and get a good night's sleep. Then you will be fresh for the test and better able to recall what you've studied.

Step 6: Take a Practice Test

Many courses offer sample tests, either online or in the study materials. This is an excellent resource to check whether you have mastered the material, as well as to prepare for the test format and environment.

Check the test format ahead of time: the number of questions, the type (multiple choice, free response, etc.), and the time limit. Then create a plan for working through them. For example, if you have 30 minutes to take a 60-question test, your limit is 30 seconds per question. Spend less time on the questions you know well so that you can take more time on the difficult ones.

If you have time to take several practice tests, take the first one open book, with no time limit. Work through the questions at your own pace and make sure you fully understand them. Gradually work up to taking a test under test conditions: sit at a desk with all study materials put away and set a timer. Pace yourself to make sure you finish the test with time to spare and go back to check your answers if you have time.

After each test, check your answers. On the questions you missed, be sure you understand why you missed them. Did you misread the question (tests can use tricky wording)? Did you forget the information? Or was it something you hadn't learned? Go back and study any shaky areas that the practice tests reveal.

Taking these tests not only helps with your grade, but also aids in combating test anxiety. If you're already used to the test conditions, you're less likely to worry about it, and working through tests until you're scoring well gives you a confidence boost. Go through the practice tests until you feel comfortable, and then you can go into the test knowing that you're ready for it.

Test Tips

On test day, you should be confident, knowing that you've prepared well and are ready to answer the questions. But aside from preparation, there are several test day strategies you can employ to maximize your performance.

First, as stated before, get a good night's sleep the night before the test (and for several nights before that, if possible). Go into the test with a fresh, alert mind rather than staying up late to study.

Try not to change too much about your normal routine on the day of the test. It's important to eat a nutritious breakfast, but if you normally don't eat breakfast at all, consider eating just a protein bar. If you're a coffee drinker, go ahead and have your normal coffee. Just make sure you time it so that the caffeine doesn't wear off right in the middle of your test. Avoid sugary beverages, and drink enough water to stay hydrated but not so much that you need a restroom break 10 minutes into the test. If your test isn't first thing in the morning, consider going for a walk or doing a light workout before the test to get your blood flowing.

Allow yourself enough time to get ready, and leave for the test with plenty of time to spare so you won't have the anxiety of scrambling to arrive in time. Another reason to be early is to select a good seat. It's helpful to sit away from doors and windows, which can be distracting. Find a good seat, get out your supplies, and settle your mind before the test begins.

When the test begins, start by going over the instructions carefully, even if you already know what to expect. Make sure you avoid any careless mistakes by following the directions.

Then begin working through the questions, pacing yourself as you've practiced. If you're not sure on an answer, don't spend too much time on it, and don't let it shake your confidence. Either skip it and come back later, or eliminate as many wrong answers as possible and guess among the remaining ones. Don't dwell on these questions as you continue—put them out of your mind and focus on what lies ahead.

Be sure to read all of the answer choices, even if you're sure the first one is the right answer. Sometimes you'll find a better one if you keep reading. But don't second-guess yourself if you do immediately know the answer. Your gut instinct is usually right. Don't let test anxiety rob you of the information you know.

If you have time at the end of the test (and if the test format allows), go back and review your answers. Be cautious about changing any, since your first instinct tends to be correct, but make sure you didn't misread any of the questions or accidentally mark the wrong answer choice. Look over any you skipped and make an educated guess.

At the end, leave the test feeling confident. You've done your best, so don't waste time worrying about your performance or wishing you could change anything. Instead, celebrate the successful completion of this test. And finally, use this test to learn how to deal with anxiety even better next time.

Review Video: Test Anxiety
Visit mometrix.com/academy and enter code: 100340

Important Qualification

Not all anxiety is created equal. If your test anxiety is causing major issues in your life beyond the classroom or testing center, or if you are experiencing troubling physical symptoms related to your anxiety, it may be a sign of a serious physiological or psychological condition. If this sounds like your situation, we strongly encourage you to seek professional help.

Online Resources

Due to our efforts to try to keep this book to a manageable length, we've created a link that will give you access to all of your online resources:

mometrix.com/resources719/dsstintrowr

It's Your Moment, Let's Celebrate It!

Share your story @mometrixtestpreparation